CHARITY LAW AND GOVERNANCE: A PRACTICAL GUIDE

CHARITY LAW AND GOVERNANCE: A PRACTICAL GUIDE

Cecile Gillard and Kirsty Semple

icsa
The Governance Institute

Published by
ICSA Publishing Limited
Saffron House
6–10 Kirby Street
London EC1N 8TS

First published as The ICSA Charity Law and Governance Handbook (2016)

Typeset by Paul Barrett Book Production, Cambridge
Printed in Great Britain by Lightning Source, Milton Keynes, Buckinghamshire

British Library Cataloguing in Publication Data
A catalogue record for this book is available from the British Library

ISBN 978-1-86072-695-8

Contents

List of Abbreviations

ACAS	Advisory, Conciliation and Arbitration Service
ACEVO	Association of Chief Executives of Voluntary Organisations
AGM	annual general meeting
BACS	Bankers Automated Clearing System
BIA	Border and Immigration System
BSI	British Standards Institution
CCNI	Charity Commission for Northern Ireland
CIC	community interest company
CIO	charitable incorporated organisation
CLG	company limited by guarantee
CLS	company limited by shares
EGM	extraordinary general meeting
FRSB	Fundraising Standards Board
FCA	Financial Conduct Authority
HMRC	Her Majesty's Revenue & Customs
HSE	health and safety executive
ICSA	Institute of Chartered Secretaries and Administrators
IHT	inheritance tax
IIA	Chartered Institute of Internal Auditors
NCVO	National Council for Voluntary Organisations
NHF	National Housing Federation
OSCR	Office of the Scottish Charity Regulator
PII	personal indemnity insurance
SAIL	Single Alternative Inspection Location
SORP	Statement of Recommended Practice
TII	trustee indemnity insurance
TUPE	Transfer of Undertakings and Protection of Employment
VAT	Value Added Tax
VBS	Vetting and Barring Scheme

1 Charity law

English law

Historical foundations

England has a legal system that traces its roots back to the Norman Conquest in 1066. The previous mix of localised rules, customs and practices changed into a more uniform and centralised approach as a new body of rules, based on local conditions in England, emerged. Other important gradual changes included the centralisation of government, the beginnings of public bureaucracy and the development of a centralised judiciary. The Curia Regis (King's Council) gradually developed into the Royal courts, presided over by professional judges. By 1250 the Royal judges oversaw a system of law common to the whole country (the English 'common law' had come into existence).

Modern English law framework

Modern English law is a mix of common law, statute law and law from the European Union.

Common law

Common law is that part of English law that is derived from custom and judicial precedent. 'Judicial precedent' enables binding precedents to be set that must be followed in subsequent similar cases in courts at the same or an inferior level. Flexibility is provided by the power of a higher court to overrule a lower court's decision on appeal (for example, if the decision was incorrect in law) and the power for judges in general to distinguish a case from a previous case in relation to a material point.

Statute law

Statute law is the body of English law rules and principles laid down in the written laws passed by the legislative body of the United Kingdom Parliament. Statute law is set out in Acts of Parliament (known as primary legislation) and in statutory instruments (known as secondary legislation or delegated or subordinate legislation).

An Act provides a broad framework. Statutory instruments provide the detail and bring the relevant Act into force (immediately or in stages). Texts of Acts of Parliament and statutory instruments are available at: www.legislation.gov.uk. An Act may apply to the entire UK or to parts of it. The practical implementation of an Act is the responsibility of the relevant government department. The Office for Civil Society, part of the Cabinet Office, is responsible for implementation of Acts that relate to English charity law.

English law is classified into criminal law, concerned with offences against society at large (crimes) and civil law, largely concerned with rights, relationships and disputes between individual parties. Charity law and the regulation of charities are civil law matters.

Legal jurisdictions in the UK

Legal systems and jurisdictions

For historic reasons, the United Kingdom does not have one unified legal system. Instead, there are three separate and different legal systems and legal jurisdictions.

Table 1.1: Legal jurisdictions in the UK

Country	Legal systems and jurisdictions
United Kingdom (UK)	England and Wales
	Scotland
	Northern Ireland

It is quite common for charities to be fundraising and operating 'cross border' in two or more of the UK's jurisdictions. Such charities may be accountable to more than one of the UK's charity regulators and may need to be registered as charities in more than one jurisdiction.

Courts, tribunals and the judiciary

The courts are the final arbiter between the citizen and the state and are therefore a fundamental pillar of the United Kingdom's constitution. That constitution is underpinned by the three-way balance between executive (government), Parliament and the courts, which are independent of both the executive and Parliament.

The hierarchy of the English civil courts is as follows:

Supreme Court for the United Kingdom
↑
Court of Appeal
↑
High Court
↑
County Court

Modern charity law matters are dealt with in the Chancery Division of the High Court of Justice. The Civil Division of the Court of Appeal hears all appeals from all Divisions of the High Court.

In civil matters, the Supreme Court for the United Kingdom, created by the Constitutional Reform Act 2005, is the court of final appeal for the entire United Kingdom (in civil matters) and the court of final appeal for criminal matters in cases from England, Wales and Northern Ireland. As an appeal court, it may only consider a case if a relevant order has been made in the lower court.

In addition, the Supreme Court can consider cases involving arguable points of law of general public importance. This gives it an important role in developing the common law, as the Supreme Courts Justices consider legal points of the greatest public or constitutional importance, affecting the whole population.

Devolution issues are within the Supreme Court's jurisdiction. So it can hear cases about whether the devolved executive and legislative authorities in Scotland, Wales and Northern Ireland have acted, or propose to act, within their powers or have failed to comply with any other duty imposed upon them.

The court's role is to interpret the law, including statute law made by Parliament. It does not determine public policy and it cannot 'strike down' law made by Parliament.

The impartiality of the courts and the independence of the judiciary in the administration of the law are fundamental features of the English legal system. This must be a demonstrable reality, so that justice is not only done, but is seen to be done. The core principle of separating the highest level of the judiciary from Parliament, to emphasise the independence of the courts, was a driving factor in the establishment of the Supreme Court.

The Tribunal system, now governed by the Tribunals, Courts and Enforcement Act 2007, provides a First-tier Tribunal and an Upper Tribunal. Both the First-tier Tribunal and the Upper Tribunal are divided into Chambers in which similar jurisdictions are dealt with by relevant experts. The Charity Tribunal is now part of the First-tier Tribunal's General Regulatory Chamber. In the Upper Tribunal, charity matters fall within the remit of the Tax and Chancery Chamber. The Upper Tribunal primarily deals with reviews and hears appeals arising from cases dealt with in the First-tier Tribunal. The Upper Tribunal is a superior court, so its decisions do generally create binding legal precedent.

United Kingdom Parliament

The principle of 'Parliamentary sovereignty' makes Parliament the supreme legal authority competent to create or alter law in the United Kingdom. It does so through the collective body of statute law and through individual pieces of legislation.

Making law is one of the principal roles of the UK Parliament. An Act of Parliament may alter existing law or introduce new law. Acts of Parliament are 'principal' legislation. In addition, under the authority of relevant provisions in an existing Act, Parliament can make detailed additional and supplementary law in regulations set out in statutory instruments. This is known as 'secondary legislation'.

Devolved legislative bodies in the United Kingdom

The Scottish Parliament, the National Assembly in Wales and the National Assembly in Northern Ireland are devolved legislative bodies within the UK. Charity law and regulation are devolved matters in all three areas of the UK (England and Wales, Scotland, Northern Ireland).

European Union and European law

The United Kingdom currently remains one of the member states of the European Union and is subject to European Union (EU) law as a result of being a signatory of European treaties. European law consists of the EU treaties, EU Regulations and EU Directives.

The EU treaties are the primary law of the EU and directly applicable to all member states. They define areas of policy for which the EU is responsible and set out general principles on particular areas. Secondary EU law is set out in Regulations, Directives and Decisions. The European Commission monitors the application of EU law. It can take action against a member state that fails to incorporate a Directive into that state's national law or breaches EU law. Ultimately, the Commission can instigate formal infringement proceedings leading to a referral of the member state to the European Court of Justice.

EU Regulations have direct binding effect throughout the member states of the EU, without the need for national legislation to be made in each member state. EU Directives set out goals that member states must achieve. Those are given effect by specific legislation adopted by each member state within that state's own law. Decisions of the European Court of Justice are directly applicable to and binding on those parties to whom the decisions are addressed, which can include EU member states.

A national referendum in 2016 resulted in a majority vote in favour of the UK leaving the EU – a decision that has come to be known as 'Brexit'.

During the 2017/2018 session of Parliament, the government intends to introduce a 'Great Repeal Bill' which will for the time being import UK law that emanates from EU law wholesale into UK law on a 'standalone' basis. The intention is that this will then allow a planned programme of legal reform to be addressed by Parliament to repeal or alter areas of law as appropriate to UK sovereign public policy and perceived reform need.

There are significant legal challenges involved in this. The law to be temporarily imported to sovereign UK law and then reviewed in this exercise is vast in scale and scope. In addition, that body of law is predicated on the basis that the UK is a member of the EU, so for example much of it refers to the powers of the

European Commission or the role of the European Courts or directly refers to particular EU regulations.

There is a two-year time limit for EU law to have any continued effect in a state leaving the EU. The period begins on the date the UK formally triggers the leaving process (by activating Article 50 of the Treaty of Rome, the founding document of the EU). At the end of the two years, EU law automatically ceases to apply in the UK. Some legal specialists consider it will be very difficult to complete the necessary programme of legislative change (in particular at primary legislation level) and policy change required to disentangle UK law within that two-year period. It has been suggested that part of the legal solution might be to introduce unusual additional measures, such as a so-called 'Henry VIII clause' to give ministers more power to create new wider regulatory regimes under statutory instrument.

Charity law foundations and framework

Charity law – foundations

Charitable activity in England and Wales has ancient origins, at least back to the sixth century. Those origins are particularly found in the early English church's initiatives to provide education for at least some children in the general population and to address some of the most chronic needs of the population arising from poverty, sickness and disease. By medieval and early Tudor times, the concept of philanthropic giving to charitable causes was deeply rooted in English culture, with appropriate mechanisms for giving to those in need available through gifts to monasteries, other religious institutions and some public institutions. The charitable activities of the aristocracy and the great trade guilds supplemented this work of relieving need.

The church's charitable work was effectively halted in 1538 when Henry VIII dissolved the monasteries and confiscated vast amounts of funds and a huge variety of other assets from the church. During Elizabeth I's reign, the continuing consequences of that, combined with growing urbanisation, population expansion and dispossession of land from England's peasants led to a poverty crisis. As part of the attempts to address that crisis, Parliament passed three statutes intended to rationalise and clarify the relative roles of the state and private charitable donations. One of those statutes, the Statute of Charitable Uses 1601 (often called 'the Statute of Elizabeth') set out in its preamble the first recorded description of a 'charity' in English law and the purposes or 'objects' for which a charity could be established. Although the 1601 Statute has long since been repealed, that definition provided the foundation on which modern English law's concept of 'charitable purposes' is built.

In the four centuries that followed the 1601 Statute the courts gradually developed the concept of charitable objects. The landmark House of Lords' decision in the case of *Inland Revenue Commissioners v Pemsel* in 1891 decided there were four broad 'heads' of charity:

- Relief of poverty
- Advancement of education
- Advancement of religion
- Other purposes beneficial to the community.

The fourth head enabled gradual legal change to reflect new social conditions and a changing world that could never have been envisaged by those responsible for the wording in the 1601 Statute.

Legal regulation of how charities operate has far more recent origins. In the nineteenth century, Parliament attempted to gather information more systematically on the assets and activities of English charities through the appointment of Commissioners. The emergence of the charity regulatory regime we have today can be traced back to the Charities Act 1960.

Charity law and regulation – modern framework

Modern English charity law is a mix of common law, developed largely out of trust law, and statute. The modern regulation of charities under the law of England and Wales is largely based on statute, supported by wider common law principles.

Charity law – principal statutes

The principal charity law statutes are:

- Charities Act 1992 (Part II) which deals with provisions relating to the regulation of fundraising in certain circumstances (see p. 142)
- Trustee Act 2000
- Charities Act 2011
- Charities (Protection and Social Investment) Act 2016.

The underlying aim of the Trustee Act 2000 is to provide trustees of unincorporated trusts (charitable trusts and other trusts) with the powers they require to make investments and to administer trusts in, especially in relation to trustees' duties and their default powers. Most of the Trustee Act provisions relevant to charitable trusts apply automatically to all unincorporated charitable trusts constituted under the law of England and Wales. However, those rules do not automatically apply to charities that are incorporated bodies (for example charitable companies incorporated under the Companies Act).

The Charities Act 2011 is a consolidating Act that came into effect on 14 March 2012. It repealed and replaced the Recreational Charities Act 1958 and the Charities Act 1993 (as then amended) and most, but not all, of the provisions of the Charities Act 2006. Most of the Charities Act 2011 only applies to England and Wales.

The Charities (Protection and Social Investment) Act 2016 provides a range of intended protections for charities against those who might abuse them and their charitable funds and assets, including updated, wider and additional new powers for the Charity Commission. Those powers are largely aimed at equipping the Commission to tackle abuse of charities more effectively and efficiently. In addition, the Act:

(a) introduced a new statutory power for most (but not all) legal forms of charities to make social investments, that provide a financial return and also a social return;
(b) made some detailed changes to the existing regulatory regime for certain types of fundraising relationships and activities, particularly those involving professional fundraisers (i.e. businesses that exist to raise funds for charities on a commercial basis) or other commercial organisations (i.e. non-fundraising businesses that at times carry out commercial activities to raise funds for charities);
(c) introduced additional compulsory disclosure and reporting requirements relating to fundraising for the trustees of charities that are subject to compulsory charity law audit requirements; and
(d) extended the scope of the reserve powers of the relevant Minister to introduce additional regulations relating to charity fundraising.

Role of the courts and other tribunals

All charities are subject to the ultimate supervision of the courts and all charitable assets are under the ultimate protection of the courts, acting as guardian of the public interest on behalf of the Crown. Charity matters, alongside trust law matters, fall within the jurisdiction of the Chancery Division of the High Court.

The principal focus of the activities of the English courts, in relation to charities, is the protection and proper application of charitable assets, ensuring those assets remain both safe and in actual use for the intended charitable purpose for which they were given. By contrast, the day-to-day regulatory oversight of charities, especially in relation to public accountability, is largely a matter for the Charity Commission.

The First-Tier Tribunal (Charity), usually known as the Charity Tribunal, is intended to provide a low-cost and user-friendly means to challenge certain decisions of the Charity Commission and to assist the development of the law, through its published decisions. The Upper Tribunal may hear applications for judicial review transferred to it by the High Court (this is not within the Charity Tribunal's remit) as well as appeals from decisions of the Charity Tribunal.

Charity proceedings

Definition

Section 115 of the Charities Act defines 'charity proceedings' as proceedings in any court in England or Wales brought under:

(a) the court's jurisdiction with respect to charities; or
(b) the court's jurisdiction with respect to trusts in relation to the administration of a trust for charitable purposes.

The courts have accepted that this is intended to distinguish between internal disputes within a charity, which are charity proceedings, and disputes with outsiders which are not charity proceedings. So, for example, a claim by a charity for breach of contract would not be charity proceedings requiring advance authorisation by the Charity Commission or High Court.

Charity proceedings in a court may not be pursued by or against a charity unless authorisation to bring those proceedings has been obtained from either the Charity Commission or the High Court (the rule does not apply to exempt charities). The definition of charity proceedings does not extend to proceedings of the charity tribunal because that is a tribunal, not a court. This is a longstanding rule, now set out in section 115 of the Charities Act.

> **CASE LAW**
>
> The courts have stated that the rationale for the charity proceedings rule is 'to prevent charities from frittering away money subject to charitable trusts in pursuing litigation relating to internal disputes' (*Muman v Nagasnea [1999] 4 All ER 178 at 183, Mummery LJ*).

The Charity Tribunal

Overview

Three types of cases can be dealt with by the Charity Tribunal:

- Appeals against some Charity Commission decisions by certain parties (see Schedule 6 of the Charities Act).
- Reviews regarding Charity Commission decisions.
- References made to the Tribunal by the Attorney General (or by the Charity Commission in connection with the exercise by the Commission of its functions).

In an appeal, the Tribunal is able to make a fresh decision if it considers that to be appropriate, in reaching its decision it can consider for itself the evidence the Charity Commission considered and also other evidence.

In a review, the Tribunal considers the procedure followed by the Commission, taking into account matters such as the fitness to the charity concerned. The Tribunal may, in certain circumstances, remit the matter to the Commission to make a fresh decision, taking into account the Tribunal's findings.

The Charity Tribunal considers an average of three to six cases a year, mostly appeals and reviews (a number of other applications are withdrawn before they reach a full hearing). Prior to the introduction of this Charity Tribunal, even fewer cases seeking to challenge Charity Commission decisions reached a hearing in the High Court (Chancery Division) (2006 one case; 2007 none; 2008 three). However, difficulties that have been identified with the present system include the limited range of Charity Commission decisions that can be challenged by applying to the Tribunal and the limited categories of persons who can make applications in relation to those challenges. A further perceived problem is that an applicant cannot bring a challenge against a failure by the Charity Commission to exercise a particular power (effectively 'non-decisions' cannot be challenged) (See Chapter 3).

Appeals from decisions of the Tribunal can be made to the Upper Tribunal (Tax and Chancery Chamber).

The Charity Commission

Legal basis

The Charity Commission for England and Wales (the Charity Commission) is a body corporate, performing functions on behalf of the Crown (Charities Act 2011, s. 13). In the exercise of its functions it is not subject to the direction or control of any Minister of the Crown or any other government department. The Commission is accountable to Parliament through the Home Secretary and ultimately answerable to the courts. The Charities Act specifies statutory objectives, functions and general duties for the Charity Commission.

Statutory objectives

1. To increase public trust and confidence in charities.
2. To promote awareness and understanding of the public benefit requirement (i.e. the obligation for charities to provide public benefit).
3. To promote compliance by charity trustees with their legal obligations in exercising control and management of the administration of their charities.
4. To promote the effective use of charitable resources.
5. To enhance the accountability of charities to donors, beneficiaries and the general public.

Statutory functions

1. To determine whether or not institutions are charities.
2. To encourage and facilitate the better administration of charities.
3. To identify and investigate the apparent misconduct or mismanagement in the administration of charities, and take remedial or protective action in connection with misconduct or mismanagement.
4. To determine whether public collection certificates should be issued and remain in force.

5. To obtain, evaluate and disseminate information in connection with the performance of the Commission's functions or the meeting of its objectives.
6. To give information or advice, or make proposals, to Ministers, on matters relating to the Commission's functions or objectives.

Item 1 is why the Charity Commission has responsibility for keeping the public Register of Charities in England and Wales and dealing with new charity registrations. It is also why the Commission has a duty to issue guidance on the public benefit requirements and has the task of monitoring whether or not existing charities deliver suitable public benefit.

Statutory general duties

1. To act in a way compatible with its objectives and most appropriate to meeting them.
2. To act in a way compatible with the encouragement of charitable giving and voluntary participation in charity work.
3. To have regard to the need to use its resources in the most efficient, effective and economic way.
4. To have regard to the principles of best regulatory practice (including the principles under which regulatory activities should be proportionate, accountable, consistent, transparent and targeted only at cases in which action is needed).
5. To have regard to the desirability of facilitating innovation by or on behalf of charities.
6. To have regard to such generally accepted principles of good corporate governance as it is reasonable to regard as applicable to the Commission.

Charity law and regulation in Scotland

Overview

Scotland has its own distinct common law of charities and public trusts. Scottish public trusts are ultimately supervised by the Court of Session, a civil court with functions broadly similar to the High Court and the Court of Appeal in England and Wales. A statutory system for the registration and regulation of charities in Scotland is provided for by the Charities and Trustee Investment (Scotland) Act 2005 (as amended). That Act also provides the legal basis for the Office of the Scottish Charity Regulator (OSCR) which is responsible for registration of charities in Scotland and the maintenance of the Scottish Charity Register. The OSCR has broadly similar functions and powers to those of the Charity Commission for England and Wales, including intervention and investigation powers largely intended to safeguard charitable funds and assets.

The 2005 Act specifies the 'charity test' (s. 7) which determines whether or not an organisation is a charity under the law of Scotland. The test has two elements:

(a) that the body has one or more of the charitable purposes set out in the Act; and
(b) that the body provides public benefit in Scotland or elsewhere.

The OSCR issues guidance on the charity test which includes guidance on demonstrating that a charity meets the public benefit requirement. It monitors compliance by charities with both elements of the test on an ongoing basis. A body constituted under the law of Scotland that meets the charity test must be entered on the Scottish Charity Register and its charitable status under the law of Scotland depends on that registration. There are no exemptions or exceptions from the registration requirement.

A body may not call itself a charity in Scotland unless it is on the Register (this is subject to the special rules regarding bodies established under the law of other territories, including the law of England and Wales). The charity regulatory regime in Scotland includes:

(a) obligations to file annual data, accounts and a trustees' report with the OSCR;
(b) requirements to obtain the prior consent of the OSCR to certain changes to a charity's constitution (including changes to its charitable purposes);
(c) obligations to notify the OSCR of all changes to a charity's constitution (whether or not those changes required advance consent from the OSCR); and
(d) obligations to keep public information regarding the charity on the Scottish Charity Register up to date.

Different tax-related tests and rules affecting charities in Scotland may now develop, following devolution of some tax matters to the Scottish Parliament under the Scotland Act 2012.

Charitable purposes

The list of potentially charitable purposes under the law of Scotland is:

1. The prevention or relief of poverty.
2. The advancement of education.
3. The advancement of religion.
4. The advancement of health. This can include the prevention or relief of sickness, disease or human suffering.
5. The saving of lives.
6. The advancement of citizenship or community development. This can include rural or urban regeneration and the promotion of civic responsibility, volunteering, the voluntary sector or the effectiveness or efficiency of charities.
7. The advancement of the arts, heritage, culture or science.
8. The advancement of public participation in sport (involving physical skill and exertion).

9. The provision of recreational facilities, or organisation of recreational activities, with the object of improving the conditions of life for the persons for whom they are primarily intended. This applies only to recreational facilities or activities that are:
   - primarily intended for persons who have need of them because of their age, ill-health, disability, financial hardship or other disadvantage; or
   - are available to members of the public at large or to male or female members of the public at large.
10. The advancement of human rights, conflict resolution or reconciliation.
11. The promotion of religious or racial harmony.
12. The promotion of equality and diversity.
13. The advancement of environmental protection or improvement.
14. The relief of those in need by reason of age, ill-health, disability, financial hardship or other disadvantage. This can include relief given by the provision of accommodation or care.
15. The advancement of animal welfare.
16. Other purposes reasonably analogous to any of the purposes above.

The advancement of any philosophical belief (whether or not involving belief in a god) can be analogous to the purpose set out at point 3 above.

Registration of foreign charities

A charitable organisation established under the law of another country (including the law of England and Wales) is also required to register on the Scottish Charity Register if it:

(a) is managed or controlled wholly or mainly in Scotland;
(b) occupies land or premises in Scotland; or
(c) carries out activities in an office, shop or similar premises in Scotland.

A charity in England and Wales would not have to register simply because it carries out fundraising across its UK supporter base; however, if that organisation fell within any of the above three conditions it would be subject to the foreign charity registration obligation under the 2005 Act.

The OSCR has issued guidance to assist charities constituted under the law of another territory in determining whether or not they are obliged to make a registration application. Foreign charities may need to amend their charitable purposes, to limit them to purposes wholly charitable under the law of Scotland, to meet the charity test and succeed in an application for registration on the Scottish Charity Register.

Foreign charities on the Scottish Charity Register are subject to annual public accountability obligations, involving making returns and filing annual accounts and trustees' reports with the OSCR.

Charity law and regulation in Northern Ireland

Overview

The Charities (Northern Ireland) Act 2008 introduces a new legal and regulatory regime for charities in Northern Ireland which is being implemented in stages over several years. The Act provides the legal basis for the Charity Commission for Northern Ireland (CCNI). CCNI has broadly similar functions and powers to those of the Charity Commission for England and Wales, including intervention and investigation powers. These are largely intended to safeguard charitable funds and assets. CCNI is a non-Departmental Public Body supported by the Department for Social Development in Northern Ireland.

To be a charity in Northern Ireland an organisation must be subject to the control of the High Court of Northern Ireland, in the exercise of its jurisdiction with respect to charities, and:

(a) have purposes that fall within one or more of the twelve descriptions of charitable purposes listed in the 2008 Act; and
(b) those purposes must be for the public benefit.

Trustees are obliged to have regard to the guidance issued by CCNI on this public benefit requirement.

The 2008 Act provides a system of charity registration in Northern Ireland which is being activated by CCNI carrying out tranches of registrations. There are no exemptions or exceptions from registration; the obligation applies regardless of income, size and the legal form of the organisation. It also applies regardless of whether or not an organisation is recognised by HMRC as a charity for tax purposes.

The legislation also provides a public accountability regime which includes obligations for charities to provide annual data, annual accounts and a trustees' report to CCNI. During the phased completion of charity registrations onto the new register, interim arrangements are in place to ensure that organisations that have been registered provide the required information and documents.

Charitable purposes

The list of potentially charitable purposes under the law of Northern Ireland is:

1. The prevention or relief of poverty.
2. The advancement of education.
3. The advancement of religion. 'Religion' includes:
   (a) a religion which involves belief in one god or more than one god; and
   (b) any analogous philosophical belief (whether or not involving belief in a god).
4. The advancement of health or the saving of lives. The advancement of health includes the prevention or relief of sickness, disease or human suffering.

5. The advancement of citizenship or community development. This includes rural or urban regeneration; the promotion of civic responsibility; volunteering; the voluntary section; or the effectiveness or efficiency of charities.
6. The advancement of the arts, culture, heritage or science.
7. The advancement of amateur sport (i.e. sports or games which promote health by involving physical or mental skill or exertion).
8. The advancement of human rights, conflict resolution or reconciliation or the promotion of religious or racial harmony or equality and diversity (this includes the advancement of peace and good community relations).
9. The advancement of environmental protection or improvement.
10. The relief of those in need by reason of youth, age, ill-health, disability, financial hardship or other disadvantage (this includes relief given by the provision of accommodation or care to the persons mentioned).
11. The advancement of animal welfare.
12. Any other existing purposes and analogous purposes.

Registration of foreign charities

Organisations that are established under the law of another territory are not within the jurisdiction of the High Court of Northern Ireland so do not fall within the legal definition of charities under section 1 of the Charities (Northern Ireland) Act 2008. However, foreign organisations that operate for charitable purposes in or from Northern Ireland are required to provide CCNI with financial and activity statements on their Northern Ireland activities (s. 167 of the 2008 Act). This requirement has not yet been brought into force.

The legislation also provides power for the Department of Social Development to seek the approval of the Northern Ireland Assembly to regulations that would require CCNI to keep a separate register of such organisations. It also has power to seek approval of regulations to apply or disapply particular provisions of the 2008 Act to these organisations. It is expected that such a 'parallel register' will be established in due course, with *no de minimis threshold and no other exceptions or exemptions*.

The full implications of these legal and regulatory provisions for foreign charities, including those registered in England and Wales, will only emerge once the relevant regulations have been made and implemented.

'Charity' in England

Legal definition

In English law, to be a 'charity' an organisation must be subject to the supervision of the High Court and:

(a) have one or more purposes that fall within the list of 'descriptions of charitable purposes' set out in the Charities Act 2011; and
(b) its purposes must be 'for the public benefit'.

The organisation's purposes must be exclusively charitable, not merely partly charitable (i.e. no non-charitable element of purpose is permissible). The older term 'objects' is often used in charity constitutions for what the Charities Act 2011 now calls 'purposes'. A charitable trust is, therefore, a trust for purposes (rather than a trust for individuals).

There is an important distinction between a charitable organisation's purposes and the activities it undertakes in pursuit of those purposes. The purposes are the organisation's fundamental aims – the reasons it exists.

> **Examples**
>
> Charitable purpose – advancing public education about wildlife.
> Activity – delivering educational courses about wildlife.

Descriptions of charitable purposes (Charities Act 2011)

The list of descriptions of charitable purposes under the law of England and Wales is set out in the Charities Act. These are potentially charitable purposes – not every organisation that has a purpose within this list will be capable of being a charity in law.

The list is:

1. The prevention or relief of poverty.
2. The advancement of education.
3. The advancement of religion. Religion can include:
   - a religion which involves belief in more than one god; and
   - a religion which does not involve belief in a god.
4. The advancement of health or the saving of lives. This includes the prevention or relief of sickness, disease or human suffering.
5. The advancement of citizenship or community development. This can include rural or urban regeneration and the promotion of civic responsibility, volunteering, the voluntary sector or the effectiveness or efficiency of charities.
6. The advancement of the arts, culture, heritage or science.
7. The advancement of amateur sport. This can include sport or games which promote health by involving physical or mental skill or exertion.
8. The advancement of human rights, conflict resolution or reconciliation or the promotion of religious or racial harmony or equality and diversity.
9. The advancement of environmental protection or improvement.
10. The relief of those in need by reason of youth, age, ill-health, disability, financial hardship or other disadvantage. This can include relief given by the provision of accommodation or care to the relevant persons.
11. The advancement of animal welfare.

12. The promotion of the efficiency of the armed forces of the Crown, or of the efficiency of the police, fire and rescue services or ambulance services.

13. Any other purposes:
   (a) not within 1–12 above but are recognised as charitable under section 5 of the Charities Act 2011 (recreational and similar trusts) or under the old law (i.e. the law relating to charities in England and Wales in force immediately before 1 April 2008);
   (b) that are analogous to, or within the spirit of, points 1–12 above;
   (c) that may reasonably be regarded as analogous to, or within the spirit of, any purposes which have been recognised, under the law relating to charities in England and Wales, as falling within (b) above or this sub-paragraph (c).

This 'sweeper' category (point 13 above) is important in carrying forward all existing charitable purposes, under previous charity law, that are not explicitly set out in the list. It also retains the traditional flexibility of charity law, so that it can change and develop over time as social conditions change. The purposes of the particular organisation must be for the public benefit in order for it to qualify as a charity.

Recreational and similar trusts

Provision of facilities for recreation or leisure-time occupation, in the interests of social welfare, can be charitable under English law, provided that these conditions are met:

(a) the facilities are provided with the object improving the conditions of life for persons for whom the facilities are primarily intended;
(b) those persons have need of the facilities by reason of their youth, age, infirmity or disability, poverty or social and economic circumstances; or
(c) the facilities are to be available to the public at large or to male or female members of the public.

The Charities Act specifies that this applies in particular to village halls, community centres and women's institutes, as well as the provision and maintenance of grounds and buildings for recreation or leisure-time occupation, always subject to the requirement that the facilities are provided in the interests of social welfare. The provisions of general charity law and of the Charities Act 2011 apply to recreational charities; there is no longer a separate Recreational Charities Act.

Public benefit requirement

Each purpose that a charity has must be 'for the public benefit' (as defined in s. 4(1)), a principle that is long established in common law but is now explicit in statute. Some purposes that fall within the 'descriptions of purposes' in the

Charities Act fail to be charitable because they are not also 'for the public benefit'. Section 4(2) states 'it is not to be presumed that a purpose of a particular description is for the public benefit'.

'Public benefit' in this context is a charitable public benefit, appropriate to the particular charitable purposes of each individual charity. A charity's activities must be appropriate to its stated purposes and the beneficiaries must also be appropriate to those purposes. A purpose cannot be charitable where any detriment or harm resulting from it outweighs the benefit. The Charity Commission takes an evidential, rather than an opinion-based, approach to considering any issues of detriment or harm.

Underpinning law

The statutory provisions relating to public benefit are underpinned by principles derived from case law. The Charities Act specifically provides for the continuity of court decisions that pre-date the current statutory provisions; in particular, it preserves the common law meaning of relevant terminology with regard to charitable purposes and public benefit (see s. 3(3)).

As with all common law, there is a gradual evolution of common law relating to public benefit, through the determination of individual cases by the courts on a case-by-case basis. Both the fact that there are principles relating to public benefit (rather than a fixed definition) and the fact that those are applied by the courts to help them make public benefit decisions on a case-by-case basis were recognised by the Charity Tribunal, in its judgment in *Attorney General v Charity Commission (The Poverty Reference) ([2012] WTLR 977 at [34]):*

> *The [legal] authorities do not provide a comprehensive statement of the public benefit requirement but provide rather a series of examples of when the public benefit requirement is or is not satisfied. There is no application of some overarching, coherent, principle by which the Courts have been guided.*

The Charity Commission has published its own analysis of the law that underpins public benefit: *Public benefit: Analysis of the law relating to public benefit.* This helps to clarify the Commission's approach on certain aspects and explains the reasons it takes that approach. The Commission's view is that, because it is inherent in every charitable purpose that the purpose is for the public benefit, the duties of charity trustees include:

- a duty to pursue their charity's purposes; and
- a duty to further that charity's purposes for the public benefit.

It also states that 'the concepts of the purposes of a charity and the activities undertaken to further its purposes, although closely related, are distinct'.

The Commission determines the recognition of new charitable purposes based on its understanding of the common law and its own previous decisions, not on whether or not the purpose it is considering enjoys 'fiscal privileges' (i.e. charity tax status). It states that 'fiscal (i.e. tax) privilege that flows from charitable status is a matter for legislation by Parliament and enforcement by HM Revenue and Customs'. That understanding, that charity tax status can only be considered after charitable status in charity law terms has been established, is reflected in the conditions applicable under tax law for an organisation seeking recognition from HMRC as a charity. One of those conditions is that the applicant organisation is established for charitable purposes only.

Meaning of 'public'

Purpose and beneficiary group are interdependent in the concept of public benefit. So the courts consider the sufficiency of the potential beneficiary group in the context of the nature of the relevant organisation's stated purpose.

'Public' means either the public in general or a sufficient section of the public. If the group of people who can potentially benefit is too restricted or is capricious, the purpose cannot be a charitable purpose.

Potential beneficiaries being linked by descent from one individual, or employment with one employer or by belonging to the same unincorporated association have been rejected by the courts as an insufficient beneficiary group. A purpose intended to provide benefit only to those who arc members of the organisation is unlikely to be charitable (unless the purpose is poverty relief of those members).

Example

A primary purpose of 'self-help' to members cannot normally provide a sufficient section of the public, even if there are a large number of members.

Those engaged in a particular occupation or profession can potentially be a sufficient section of the public, depending on the circumstances.

Example

A charity might have purposes to relieve sickness and disability amongst those engaged or formerly engaged in a particular occupation or profession, such as teaching, and their dependants.

Provided the potential beneficiary group is clear and sufficient, the inhabitants of a particular geographic area can constitute a sufficient section of the public, even if the area is very small. The area does not have to be within England and Wales.

Example

A particular parish.

As a matter of law, a purpose can be charitable when potential beneficiaries are outside England and Wales. The Charity Commission's approach is to consider whether the stated purpose would be charitable if confined to England and Wales. If so, the Commission will recognise that purpose as charitable unless it would be contrary to UK public policy to do so.

Political purposes are not charitable, including a purpose to further the interests of one political party or to procure changes in the laws of England and Wales or any other country. Reasons for this include that a court does not have the means to determine whether, say, a change in the law would be beneficial, also that changes to government policy or law are in essence matters for the government or for Parliament.

The poor and poverty

Definitions

The law recognises that 'the poor' and 'poverty' are relative terms, their precise meaning depending on the particular circumstances. The terms are not confined to the very poorest in society, in appropriate circumstances the courts have recognised they can extend to people of modest means.

> **CASE LAW**
>
> In *Attorney General v Charity Commission (The Poverty Reference)* [2-12] WTLR 977) the Charity Tribunal accepted that special legal treatment applies to a purpose for the relief of poverty. However, it also clarified that the purpose does have to be for the public benefit and agreed with previous judicial comment that there must be a discernible class of people who can benefit (not merely individuals).

It is not permissible to create a charitable purpose that excludes the poor as potential beneficiaries. The Charity Commission's approach is to consider this point in the context of the general rule that the purpose must be for the benefit of the general public or a sufficient section of the public.

Beneficiary group: recreational charities

Defining the beneficiary group by reference to 'protected characteristics'

Special conditions apply to the beneficiary group of a recreational charity (see 'Recreational and similar trusts' at p. 16).Charities are permitted by law to have purposes that define who can benefit by reference to 'protected characteristics', provided that to do so is justified in relation to the relevant purposes. The Charity Commission describes this as 'the charities exception' in the Equality Act 2010 which enables charities to limit provision of benefits to people who share a protected characteristic if:

(a) the charity's governing document *only allows people who share that characteristic to benefit;* and
(b) the restriction can be justified using one of the two specified tests:
   - tackling disadvantage (the charity's purpose is to tackle disadvantage amongst people who share the protected characteristic); or
   - achievement of a legitimate aim (although not tackling a particular disadvantage the charity's purpose seeks to achieve some other legitimate aim in a fair, balanced and reasonable (i.e. proportionate) way).

'Protected characteristics' are:

- Age
- Disability
- Sex
- Sexual orientation
- Gender reassignment
- Marriage and civil partnership
- Pregnancy and maternity
- Race or nationality
- Religion or belief.

Other exceptions in the Equality Act enable charities to target or restrict benefits or services to particular groups and, in some cases, to undertake fundraising or promotional activities for the charity through particular groups (e.g. a fundraising race for women to support cancer research). An overriding requirement is always that the restriction/limitation must be justified. The main exceptions relevant to charities are:

1. Restricted membership of associations (with 25 or more members and rules controlling admission to membership).
2. Men-only or women-only fundraising.
3. Membership based on acceptance of a religion or belief.
4. Positive action in service (i.e. proportionate action intended to help those disadvantaged or under represented to have access to the same chances as others do).
5. Restriction of membership/participation in activities/access to services provided/use of premises to those of particular religions or beliefs or sexual orientation.
6. Restricting admission to education (to single sex institutions or, for schools or higher/further education institutions of a religious character, giving admission preference to those of the particular religion).

7. Sporting organisations can, in certain circumstances, limit access on the basis of gender or gender reassignment.

Various additional conditions must be met for these exceptions to apply, especially for exceptions 4 and 5.

The Charity Commission has issued guidance on the Equality Act for charities (this is not statutory guidance) and the Equality and Human Rights Commission issues a range of general guidance on the equality legislation. Trustees of relevant charities should familiarise themselves with such guidance.

Meaning of 'benefit'

The 'benefit' aspect of the legal rule that a charitable purpose must be 'for the public benefit' means that the purpose must be beneficial. The Charity Tribunal has said:

> The requirement that the purpose of a trust ... should be, of its nature and without regard to the section of the community to be benefited, beneficial to the community ... is intrinsic to what was meant when it was said that a purpose was for the public benefit.
>
> *(Attorney General v Charity Commission (The Poverty Reference) ([2012] WTLR 977 at [32])*

The benefit must be identifiable and in principle capable of being proved by evidence. When considering the question of benefit, a court will take account of (a) relevant statute law and (b) notice of obvious facts. If need be a court will receive expert evidence to assist it in determining whether a particular purpose is for the public benefit. However, in appropriate circumstances the court can regard the benefits of a particular purpose in a trust as being so obvious that formal evidence of that fact need not be required and considered.

In general, the benefit should be tangible and objective. An intangible benefit may suffice in some circumstances. The subjective beliefs of donors about what is or is not beneficial are not relevant. Although a court is obliged to balance the benefit against any detriment, the Charity Tribunal has indicated that alleged detriment must be evidenced and that such alleged disadvantages must be clearly demonstrated before they can be given much weight. If a court regards a purpose as incapable of proof one way or the other on the matter of benefit, it will not recognise that purpose as charitable.

Fee charging

Case law has established that, in principle, there is no objection to charities charging fees for charitable services that they provide. However, when deciding whether to charge fees for any charitable services or when setting and reviewing fee levels, trustees need to be mindful of their duties and of the background law in relation to public benefit and access to benefits for potential beneficiaries. The Upper Tribunal's decision in *R (ISC) v Charity Commission ([2002] Ch 214)* suggests that factors for trustees to weigh, considering the issue of fee charging, include:

- that beneficiaries who can afford to pay fees and those who cannot do so must both be taken into account;
- if it is legitimate to consider whether the charity needs to charge fees to cover its expenditure;
- where the charges made are more than the poor can afford, the trustees should seek to provide benefits to the potential poor beneficiaries that are more than merely minimal or tokenistic;
- when considering whether a particular beneficiary is poor, the overall circumstances relating to that beneficiary may need to be taken into account;
- trustees are able to exercise their discretion in relation to making provision for beneficiaries who cannot afford the full charges; and
- having a primary focus on the direct benefits the charity provides, whilst also taking into account all benefits provided in furtherance of the charitable purposes (benefits unrelated to those purposes cannot be taken into account).

Although this case was decided in its particular context (charitable schools that charge fees) these factors may be useful when considering the complex issues around fee charging.

Private benefits

The main benefits conferred by a charitable purpose on individuals must be charitable benefits, conferred on them because of their charitable need. Any private benefit (i.e. personal or commercial benefit, rather than charitable benefit) which arises from a charity's activities to individuals, or to organisations and legal entities, must be necessarily incidental to those activities and to the delivery of charitable public benefit through those activities. For example the charitable activities of a charity that needs to employ specialist staff in order to deliver the charitable services (say medical staff in a charitable hospice who care for the patients) give rise to necessary incidental private benefits to the paid staff (their remuneration and rewards package).

Charity Commission statutory guidance

The Charities Act requires the Commission to issue guidance in pursuance of its statutory objective to promote awareness and understanding of the operation of the public benefit requirement (i.e. public benefit guidance). It is the Commission's view that this objective extends to promoting awareness and understanding of the duty of charity trustees to further their charity's purposes for the public benefit (see *Public benefit: Analysis of the law relating to public benefit*, Charity

Commission September 2013). It therefore includes in its statutory guidance material relating to the activities of charities, as well as their purposes.

The public benefit guidance is issued in three parts:

- *PB1 Public benefit:* the public benefit requirement (mainly focused on potential new charities, charity registration applicants and charities whose trustees wish to alter their charity's purposes).
- *PB2 Public benefit:* running a charity (this comments on the public benefit requirement in the context of running a charity).
- *PB3 Public benefit:* reporting (this explains trustees' duty to report on how they have carried out the charity's purposes for the public benefit).

The guidance states that there are two principal aspects to the public benefit requirement, for a purpose to be charitable:

1. The purpose must be beneficial, and any detriment or harm that results from the purpose must not outweigh the benefit (the Commission calls this the 'benefit aspect').
2. The purpose must benefit the public in general, or a sufficient section of the public (the Commission calls this the 'public aspect').

Both the 'public' and the 'benefit' elements must be satisfied for a purpose to be charitable (with an exception for the special rules on poverty purposes). Each purpose a charity has must satisfy this twin requirement; the public benefit of one purpose cannot be offset against a lack of public benefit in another. The 'public' element is about whom the purpose benefits. The 'benefit' aspect is about whether the purpose is beneficial (in a charitable way).

To be charitable, the purpose must be beneficial in a way that is identifiable, capable of being proved by evidence (where necessary) and not based on personal views. The guidance states that it should always be possible to identify and describe how a charity's purpose is beneficial, whether or not the benefit can be quantified or measured.

The guidance makes it clear that the Charity Commission makes decisions about public benefit in individual cases based on the law as it believes that law applies to the facts of the particular case. The Commission specifically points out that its guidance is not the law. Rather, it offers high-level general guidance for charity trustees, explains what the Commission understands to be the law and how it interprets and applies that law. It also points out that its general guidance cannot cover all the complexities of the law relating to public benefit.

Trustees and public benefit

Duties of trustees

Trustees have a duty to further their charity's purposes. Inherent in that is a duty to do so for the public benefit appropriate to those purposes. In order to fulfil this duty, trustees must understand the purposes and plan the charity's activities with a clear focus on those purposes and the relevant beneficiary group to which those purposes relate. They must also ensure that the charity operates within and not beyond its purposes.

In addition, the trustees have a specific statutory obligation to 'have regard' to guidance on public benefit issued by the Charity Commission when 'exercising any powers or duties to which the guidance is relevant' (see Charities Act s. 17(1) and 17(5)).

The Commission expects trustees to be able to show they are aware of the guidance and have taken it into account when making any decision to which it is relevant. In addition, if trustees decide to depart from the guidance, the Commission expects them to have good reasons for doing so (and be able to demonstrate those reasons).

Reporting

Charity reporting and accounting regulations require trustees to include a statement in their trustees' annual report as to whether they have complied with their legal duty to 'have regard' to the Charity Commission's public benefit guidance.

Trustees of registered charities also have a legal obligation to report each year, in their trustees' annual report, on how they have carried out the charity's purposes for the public benefit.

The trustees of smaller charities, below the compulsory audit threshold, must report by including:

(a) a brief summary setting out the main activities undertaken by the charity to carry out its charitable purposes for the public benefit; and
(b) the required statement as to whether they have complied with their duty to have regard to the Commission's public benefit guidance.

The trustees of larger charities, above the compulsory audit threshold, must report by providing:

(a) a review of the significant activities undertaken by the charity to carry out its charitable purposes for the public benefit;
(b) details of the charity's purposes and its strategic objectives;
(c) details of the strategies adopted and activities undertaken to achieve those purposes and objectives;
(d) details of the achievements of the charity by reference to the purposes and the objectives that the trustees have set; and
(e) the required statement as to whether they have complied with their duty to have regard to the Commission's public benefit guidance.

Other than the above requirements, there are no specific rules on how the reporting is to be done. Trustees are free to decide the best approach and the level of detail they wish to include.

The Charity Commission's guidance on public benefit clarifies that it is not necessary to include a separate section on public benefit in the trustees' annual report. Instead it can be dealt with throughout the body of the report. The guidance also reminds trustees that public benefit reporting is an opportunity to explain what has been done and achieved, demonstrate the value of the charity's work and also demonstrate transparency and accountability.

Trustees' annual reports, alongside the accounts to which they relate, are made publicly available on the Charity Commission website. The regulator checks random samples of trustees' annual reports for the quality of reporting, including the reporting on public benefit. It may consider a failure to report as a possible indication of problems that it may need to explore with the trustees of the charity in question. Persistent non-reporting of public benefit will be treated as a regulatory issue by the Charity Commission, with appropriate action taken.

Scotland

Under the law of Scotland, public benefit is part of the charity test which determines charitable status. A charity must have charitable purposes under the law of Scotland and provide public benefit, whether in Scotland or elsewhere. An organisation that cannot meet this requirement cannot be a charity under the law of Scotland and cannot be entered on the Scottish Charity Register by OSCR. This is an activities-based requirement for public benefit (whereas the English law public benefit requirement is purposes based). In determining whether an organisation's activities provide public benefit, the law requires a comparison to be made between the benefit provided to the public and:

(a) benefits to the organisation's members or third parties (other than as members of the public) (i.e. private benefits); and
(b) any 'disbenefit' incurred, or likely to be incurred, by the public.

Where benefit is only provided to a section of the public and any conditions apply to obtaining that benefit, the Charities and Trustee Investment (Scotland) Act 2005 requires consideration of whether those conditions are unduly restrictive. In this context, conditions include any charge or fee. OSCR issues guidance on the charity test, which includes guidance on the public benefit requirement.

Northern Ireland

The law of Northern Ireland requires any organisation seeking to be a charity in Northern Ireland:

(a) to have purposes that fall within the descriptions of charitable purposes set out in the Charities Act (Northern Ireland) 2008; and
(b) that those purposes are for the public benefit.

Charity trustees are required to 'have regard' to the statutory public benefit guidance issued by the CCNI.

Consequences of charitable status

Being a charity in law has key consequences for the organisation, its funds and assets and for the people involved in the organisation (members, if it is a membership structure charity, and trustees). Charitable status gives significant responsibilities to the charity trustees. A charity is subject to charity law and the charity regulatory regime. Some cross-border charities are subject to charity law and regulation in two or more of the UK's jurisdictions. Unless exempt or excepted from registration, a charity in England and Wales must be registered with the Charity Commission.

A charity is inherently outwardly focused, existing for public benefit rather than private gain. It is bound by law to pursue its charitable purposes (and act within them at all times). The trustees have a legal duty to ensure this is done.

Charitable funds and assets must be protected and used correctly, towards the charitable purposes of the organisation and in accordance with all applicable charity law restrictions and requirements. Any restricted funds must only be applied within the limitations of the relevant restrictions. No significant private or commercial benefits must arise from a charity's activities. Any private benefits can only be those that are necessary and incidental to the activities being undertaken in pursuit of the charitable purposes.

A charity is publicly accountable and must prepare and, subject to small charity exemptions, file annual accounts and a trustees' annual report with the Charity Commission. The accounts and report are available to the general public on the Charity Commission's website.

Members of a charity have no commercial interests in or ownership of the charity, unlike the members of a commercial company.

The charity trustees are stewards and custodians of their charity, with a range of general and specific legal duties. The members of a charitable incorporated organisation (CIO or, in Scotland, SCIO) have some legal duties. There are no comparable legal duties for the members of other types of charity.

Legal basis and features of other non-charitable civil society organisations

Community interest companies

Community interest companies (CICs) are a particular type of company, intended to be used for social and community enterprise activities. This provision of benefit to the community must be their primary focus, rather than private profit. Returns to investors are permitted but as the CIC Regulator's guidance points out, they must be balanced and reasonable because 'true community benefit is always at the heart of every CIC'. The CIC Regulator expects each CIC's annual community benefit report to set out publicly exactly how the CIC has met its obligation to deliver community benefit.

Useful guidance is published by the CIC Regulator in relation to CICs and their particular legal obligations and the CIC specific restrictions that apply to them. This is intended to help those wishing to set up CICs and those involved in owning, governing and operating them, as well as those who give professional advice relating to CICs and other stakeholders. The guidance (which is not of itself legally binding) can be accessed on the CIC Regulator's website.

CICs are subject to company law and to CIC-specific requirements and regulations. The main applicable statutory provisions are set out in:

- The Companies Act 2006
- Related company legislation, for example the Insolvency Act 1986
- The Companies (Audit, Investigations and Community Enterprise) Act 2004 (especially Part 2 and Schedules 3 to 7)
- The Community Interest Company Regulations 2005.

A CIC has independent legal identity and its own legal capacity, separate from that of its members and its directors. It is capable of holding assets, entering into contracts and other legally binding agreements and arrangements, having and enforcing legal rights and employing staff.

Like all companies, CICs have both members and directors. The usual legal eligibility rules for company directorship apply to CICs (e.g. directors must be aged at least 16 and not legally disqualified from acting as company directors). CIC directors have the usual company law duties and responsibilities and an additional range of CIC-specific duties and responsibilities (e.g. in relation to the wider public accountability of CICs). The usual legal capacity issues that apply to membership of any company member also apply to membership of a CIC.

The members of a CIC are protected by limited liability from personal liability for the CIC's debts and other liabilities. This operates through the legal mechanism of shares, if the CIC is limited by shares, or the members' guarantee, if it is limited by guarantee and has no share capital. Share CICs can be public or private companies; however public CICs limited by shares are very rare in practice.

A CIC is entirely responsible for its own debts and liabilities and can become insolvent if its assets are insufficient to meet its debts as they fall due. Other legal entities and individuals can enforce any lawful rights and claims they have against the CIC. They are subject to the usual taxation regime for corporate bodies and to the general VAT regime (there are no CIC-specific taxes or VAT exemptions). CIC status is normally permanent, as a CIC cannot convert into a normal limited company.

A CIC cannot be recognised as charitable under the law of England and Wales or Scotland or Northern Ireland (see s. 26(3) of the Companies (Audit, Investigations and Community Enterprise) Act 2004). However, conversion of a

CIC to a charity is possible, provided the necessary legal conditions for charitable status can be met.

The community interest test

CICs are required by law to meet the 'community interest test' by carrying out activities which a reasonable person might consider to be of benefit to the community. So the articles of a CIC must include specific (restricted) objects that help demonstrate that it meets this test. The benefits may flow either from the activities themselves or from how the profits generated by the activities are then used in the community or there may be both elements of benefit.

The community can be the public as whole or a definable sector or group, sharing a common characteristic, which a reasonable person might regard as a section of the community. Where the benefit is only for a sector or group, it is advisable that the CIC's articles include a clear definition. The group should normally be wider than simply the members of the CIC. It can only be registered by Companies House if the CIC Regulator is satisfied that the community interest test and all other applicable legal conditions for CICs are met.

Compliance with the community interest test is monitored on an ongoing basis by the CIC Regulator, in particular through monitoring of the annual accounts and community interest report that every CIC must file on an annual basis. A copy of the community interest report is passed to the CIC Regulator by Companies House when the accounts and report are filed by the CIC.

Companies that carry out activities that a reasonable person might consider only benefit the members of one organisation or the employees of one employer cannot meet the community interest test and register as CICs. In addition, political parties and organisations pursuing political purposes or lobbying for changes to the law (or against such changes) cannot be registered as CICs.

Applicable law

CICs are companies so they are subject to company law. In addition they are subject to the CIC-specific law (set out in the Companies (Audit, Investigations and Community Enterprise) Act 2004 as amended and the Community Interest Company Regulations 2005 as amended). CICs are also subject to the general law.

Regulation and accountability

CICs are dual regulated by Companies House and by the Community Interest Company Regulator. The CIC Regulator oversees CICs in relation to the CIC-specific legal requirements, in particular the community interest test, the asset lock and its supporting requirements and the additional public accountability of CICs.

Companies House has the usual oversight of compliance with company filing requirements and applicable deadlines and maintains the public record of CICs, on the register of companies. The public have the same access to public data on CICs as they do to data on other companies, via the Companies House website. CICs must file company annual returns and their annual accounts, with the community interest report, to meet the usual company law requirements and deadlines. They and their directors are subject to the usual penalty regimes for non-compliance.

The directors have a specific obligation to prepare and annual community interest report on the company's activities in the relevant year and file it with the annual accounts. The underlying purposes of the report are to demonstrate that the CIC continues to meet the community interest test, to show that it is engaging appropriately with its stakeholders and that the activities did benefit the community in an appropriate way. Although the precise format and contents are a partly a matter of choice, some matters must be included, such as information about the remuneration of the directors and disclosure of asset transfers to community purposes.

The CIC Regulator encourages CICs to provide the fullest possible information in their community interest reports, rather than following a 'minimal compliance' approach.

The asset lock

CICs are subject to a permanent asset lock, designed to ensure they retain their assets and continue to apply them to their community benefit purposes or, if they dispose of any assets, the full value is realised and kept in the CIC for those purposes. This reinforces the fundamental community benefit purpose of CICs. It operates through restrictions on the use of funds and assets and restrictions on the disposal of activities and assets. A CIC cannot return its assets to its members unless they are themselves asset-locked bodies. The limited exceptions, which are only of relevance to CICs limited by shares, are dividend payments to members (within the CIC dividend cap) and return of paid-up capital on winding up.

An asset-locked body is defined in the relevant regulations as:

- A charity
- Another CIC
- A permitted industrial and provident society
- An equivalent organisation set up outside the UK.

Restrictions on the use of funds and assets

A CIC must principally apply its funds and assets towards its objects (which are its community benefit purposes). There are restrictions on the level of remuneration a CIC can pay to its directors, on the disposal of a CIC's funds and activities and on the transfer of its final funds in the event of winding up. In addition there are some limits on performance-related loan interest levels that a CIC can pay (a maximum of 20%) and a cap on dividends that can be paid on shares, by share CICs (a maximum aggregate of 35% of distributable profits). The dividend cap means that 65% of a CIC's profits must either be retained to develop its activities or be used to benefit the community the particular CIC was set up to serve.

Subject to these restrictions, the particular CIC's specific objects and to any additional restrictions in its articles, a CIC can carry on normal trading and business activities and third parties can invest in CICs. Guidance from the CIC Regulator points out that the CIC's cash funds need to be spent wisely (e.g. expenditure on staff remuneration must be proportionate and services purchased must represent value for money).

Restrictions on the disposal of activities and assets

There are a number of legal restrictions on the disposal of a CIC's activities and assets. In general, any sale of assets or the transfer of any of the CIC's activities must be made at market price and in a genuine arm's-length transaction, to ensure the CIC realises the proper value of the assets or activities. Sale or transfer at a lower price is only permitted if the articles specifically permit that to a specified asset-locked body or the CIC Regulator gives formal prior consent to the proposed sale or transfer.

Guidance issued by the CIC Regulator points out that disposal of assets should be interpreted widely and that for this purpose 'assets' includes the CIC's cash resources. Transfers of assets to community benefit purposes are permitted; however, they must be within thc terms of the overall asset lock on CICs and must not be in contravention of the particular CIC's articles. Potentially, such a transfer might be to an asset-locked body or to an organisation that is not an asset-locked body. A transfer for community benefit purposes would not necessarily have to be made at full market value. Such transfers must be disclosed in the CIC's annual community interest report.

In a solvent winding up, if the CIC is limited by shares and subject to the terms of its articles, paid up share capital may be returned to the CIC's members. Otherwise on winding up the final surplus funds of a CIC can only be given to another CIC with similar objects or another asset-locked body specified in the CIC's articles or to an asset-locked body approved by the CIC Regulator as the intended recipient of those funds.

'Mutual' organisations and co-operatives

The term 'mutual' is an umbrella term for a kind of ownership of various legal types of organisation. The principal distinguishing characteristic is that mutual organisations are owned by and run for the benefit of their members, who are actively involved in the business or other activities of the organisation. A truly 'mutual' organisation is not a charity as it operates for the benefit of its members, not for charitable public benefit.

Mutual ownership organisations are increasingly important in the running of public services and the custodianship of public-use assets (such as sports centres). As a matter of public policy this is encouraged, as there are perceived benefits including empowerment of staff and improved public service delivery. Whilst some companies are structured on a full mutual basis and do operate as 'mutuals', it is more common for a company to be either employee-owned (50% or more employee ownership) or employee co-owned (a lower level of employee ownership).

A 'co-operative' is 'an autonomous association of persons united voluntarily to meet their common economic, social and cultural needs and aspirations through jointly owned and democratically controlled enterprise'. To be accepted as a co-operative by the International Co-operative Alliance, an organisation must reflect the co-operative values – self-help, self-responsibility, democracy, equality, equity and solidarity. It must also reflect four ethical values (honesty, openness, social responsibility and caring for others) and subscribe to the co-operative principles:

- Voluntary and open membership
- Democratic member control
- Member economic participation
- Autonomy and independence
- Provision of education, training and information
- Co-operation among co-operatives
- Concern for community.

Co-operatives are sometimes worker co-operatives (100% employee owned), consumer co-operatives (with the members as the customers of the business), producer co-operatives (with the producer members using the organisation as a consortium for activities such as marketing or distribution) or community co-operatives (with member from a local area or members who share a common interest). Co-operatives are not charities as they operate for the benefit of their members, not for charitable public benefit.

Friendly societies

Friendly societies are mutual assurance associations of individuals, in which the members contribute to a fund to be used for the welfare of the members or for their assistance when they are in particular need (e.g. poverty or ill health). Historically, friendly societies have operated in a number of different legal structures. Under modern law, a new friendly society can only be established as a corporate body, with its own legal capacity, registered as a friendly society with the Financial Conduct Authority on the Mutuals Register. Existing unincorporated societies can (but do not have to) convert into incorporated societies.

Registered friendly societies can only provide certain kinds of provident benefits to their members and their dependants. Although restricted, the range is potentially wide, including most forms of life insurance, annuity, unemployment and health insurance. Some friendly societies are charitable, they have exempt charity status and do not have to register with the Charity Commission (their 'alternative principal regulator' under charity law is the Financial Conduct Authority).

Registered societies – community benefit societies and co-operative societies (formerly industrial and provident societies)

Registered societies, once called industrial and provident societies, are incorporated bodies registered under the relevant legislation (Co-operative and Community Benefit Societies Act 2014). Registration is either with the Financial Conduct Authority or the Prudential Regulation Authority, depending on the particular society's activities. Registered societies have legal capacity in their own right and their members are protected by limited liability.

The governing document of a registered society is its rules, which are binding on its members. The rules must comply with relevant legal requirements (see s. 14 of the Co-operative and Community Benefit Societies Act 2014). All registered societies must meet the relevant legal conditions to be either community benefit societies or co-operative societies:

- *Community benefit societies* are formed primarily for the benefit of people who are not members of the society and this must be in the interests of the community at large.
- *Co-operative societies* are formed primarily to benefit their own members, who will participate in the primary business of the society.

Older organisations (i.e. old industrial and provident societies registered before 1 August 2014) whilst they must comply with the conditions for one or other of the two types of society, cannot actually use the terms 'community benefit society' or 'co-operative society'. Rather the legislation requires them to describe themselves simply as 'registered societies'. Conditions apply to each society category and all registered societies, including former industrial and provident societies, must meet the conditions for one of the two categories.

The legal conditions that apply to a co-operative society in part reflect the International Co-operative Alliance's Statement on the Co-operative Identity (in relation to community of interest of the member, the conduct of business for the mutual benefit of the members, member control, and a requirement that any profit distribution to members must reflect the participation of the recipients in trading with the company or taking part in its business). Membership must normally be open. For a community benefit society, the legal conditions are:

- the business must be run primarily for the benefit of non-members;
- if more than nominal share capital has been issued to members (i.e. more than one £1 share) or members make loans to the society, only reasonable interest rates necessary to fund the business capital can be paid;

- profits must be used to further the society's objects, neither profits or assets may be distributed to the members (the rules must reflect this);
- if the rules permit asset sales, the funds realised must be used to further the society's activities; and
- on dissolution, the rules must not allow assets to be distributed to the members, instead they must be transferred to a body with similar objects.

Charitable registered societies

A charitable registered society, including an old industrial and provident society that is a charity, must meet the community benefit society conditions (a co-operative society cannot be a charity because it exists for the benefit of its members). It must also meet the relevant legal conditions for charitable status, including having objects that are exclusively charitable and are for the public benefit.

Charitable societies are subject to charity law. However they are 'exempt charities', exempt from registration with the Charity Commission under regulations made under charity legislation. A charitable society that has its registered office in Scotland is subject to registration with OSCR on the Scottish Charity Register. Charitable registered societies are relatively common in the social housing sector and certain other fields of charitable activity. However, numbers are proportionately small compared with the overall number of charities.

Other non-charitable civil society organisations/'not-for-profits'

There are many other non-charitable civil society organisations (or 'voluntary sector' or 'third sector') and 'not-for-profit' organisations, from private social and sports clubs to professional bodies and trade organisations. They take a variety of different legal forms. Further information can be found in Chapter 2.

Charity trustees

Legal definition of 'charity trustee'

Under section 177 of the Charities Act 2011, the legal definition of a charity trustee is 'the persons having the general control and management of the administration of a charity'. The same definition is used under the law of Scotland (see s. 106 of the Charities and Trustee Investment (Scotland) Act 2005). In this definition, the word 'administration' is potentially misleading. The board of trustees is the governing body of the charity; its trustees are operating at the most senior leadership level within the charity. The trustees have ultimate legal responsibility for the direction and strategic leadership of the charity. In that capacity they have significant legal duties and if they fail to discharge those duties, they have potential legal liabilities.

The legal background of trustee's duties

Charity law imposes duties on trustees because they hold a position of utmost trust, which must be discharged with honesty and integrity. The more general duties, such as the overriding duty to act in the best interests of the charity, are largely common law duties. These general duties relate to the core fiduciary obligation of a charity trustee, which is the obligation of undivided loyalty to the charity that trustee serves. Specific statutory trustees' duties also exist, usually imposed by particular provisions in charity legislation, especially the Charities Act or the Trustee Act 2000 (and related regulations). Most of the specific statutory duties relate to:

- public accountability and reporting and disclosures;
- the protection and correct application of charitable funds and assets; and
- particular transactions or specific situations.

Some of the specific statutory duties vary in detail for different legal forms of charity or according to the circumstances of particular situations and activities. For example, particular statutory duties of trustees apply when they exercise the statutory powers of a charity to make social investments (under the Charities (Protection and Social Investment) Act 2016).

The trustees of CIOs and of unincorporated charitable trusts have some specific duties because of the legal forms of their charities. For example, many of the specific statutory duties in the Trustee Act 2000 are only compulsory for the trustees of an unincorporated charity.

General duties

Trustees' general duties have been developed by the courts over many centuries. Unlike company directors' duties they have not been codified (set out in statute). These general duties are matters of principle, effectively behavioural standards to which trustees are required by law to adhere. The general duties set the context in which trustees must govern and manage their charities. Trustees are subject to the overriding general legal duty to act in what they honestly believe to be the best interests of their charity. In effect, this is shorthand for the best interests of that charity's charitable purposes for the public benefit.

Trustees' general duties are summarised in the Charity Commission's core guidance for trustees (*The Essential Trustee: What you need to know, what you need to do* [CC3] July 2015) as:

1. Ensure the charity carries out its purposes for the public benefit (and does not go beyond its purposes).
2. Ensure the charity complies with its governing document and with the law.
3. Act in what the trustees believe to be the charity's best interests.

4. Manage the charity's resources responsibly.
5. Act with reasonable care and skill.
6. Ensure the charity is accountable.

The Commission expects that trustees will take reasonable steps to find out about legal requirements and will take appropriate professional advice when they need to do so (point 2).

The courts expect trustees to act on the basis of honest belief in relation to point 3. In the guidance, the Charity Commission states that a trustee 'must avoid putting yourself in a position where your duty to your charity conflicts with your personal interests or loyalty to any other person or body'. The guidance clearly links point 3 to point 1.

Point 4 is the duty of prudence, which requires trustees to act responsibly, reasonably and honestly in managing the charity on behalf of others (in particular on behalf of the charity's beneficiaries and the general public). To discharge this duty properly, the trustees need to exercise sound judgement. It is also essential that the trustees ensure the charity remains solvent and is able to meet its financial obligations and commitments as they fall due.

The Charity Commission guidance highlights the importance of ensuring that individuals are eligible to serve as charity trustees. This needs to be verified before an appointment is made. In order to properly discharge their general duties as charity trustees the existing trustees should pay due attention to this before any candidacy proceeds and any appointment is made. In addition, they should take appropriate steps to verify that a potential new trustee is a 'fit and proper person' to be involved in managing a charity (as required by tax law with regard to the legal conditions for an organisation being recognised by HMRC as a charity for tax purposes).

Charitable companies

The trustees of charities that are companies have the duties of company directors as well as the duties of charity trustees. There is significant overlap between the two.

CIOs

The trustees of CIOs have all the general duties of trustees. In addition, the trustee of a CIO also has CIO-specific trustee duties:

1. A duty to exercise the trustees' powers and perform the trustees' functions in a way the trustee decides, in good faith, will be most likely to further the CIO's charitable purposes.
2. In the performance of the trustee's functions, a duty to exercise such care as is reasonable in the circumstances, having regard in particular to:

(a) any special knowledge or experience the trustee has, or purports to have;
(b) if the trustee acts in the course of a business of profession, any special knowledge or experience it is reasonable to expect of a person acting in the course of that kind of business or profession.

(See Charities Act, s. 221(2))

Scotland

Charity law in Scotland imposes both specific duties on charity trustees (e.g. in relation to investments and in relation to public accountability) and general duties. The general duties set the context in which trustees must govern and manage their charities (see Charities and Trustee Investment (Scotland) Act 2005 s. 66(1)). Under these specified general duties, a charity trustee is required to act in the interests of the charity and, in particular, to:

(a) seek, in good faith, to ensure the charity acts in a manner which is consistent with its charitable purposes; and
(b) act with the care and diligence that it is reasonable to expect of a person who is managing the affairs of another person.

The legislation specifically provides that any breach of the general statutory duties is to be treated as misconduct in the administration of the charity (Charities and Trustee Investment (Scotland) Act 2005, s. 66(4)). This means that OSCR can potentially take regulatory action for misconduct against charity trustees who are in breach of their general duties. The legislation also specifies that trustees must:

1. Ensure the charity complies with any direction, requirement, notice or duty imposed in it by the Charities and Trustee Investment (Scotland) Act 2005.
2. If there has been any breach of the statutory duties of trustees, to take such steps as are reasonably practicable for the purposes of ensuring:
   (a) that any breach of the two principal statutory duties (see above) is corrected by the trustee concerned and not repeated; and
   (b) that any trustee who has been in serous and persistent breach of either or both of those duties is removed as a trustee.

In relation to a charity trustee who is appointed by any other person, that trustee has particular statutory duties in relation to conflicts of interest. In circumstances capable of giving rise to a conflict between the interests of the charity and the interests of that other person (i.e. the appointor) the relevant trustee must:

(a) put the interests of the charity before the interests of the appointor; and
(b) where any other duty prevents the trustee from doing that, the trustee must disclose the conflicting interest to the charity and refrain from participating in any deliberation or decision of the trustees with respect to the matter in question.

The trustees of any charity on the Scottish Charity Register must comply with these duties.

Potential liabilities – breach of trust

Trustees can potentially incur personal liability for breach of trust, for example operating the charity outside its stated charitable purposes, using charitable funds for non-charitable purposes or using those funds to make unauthorised payments to one or more trustees. This is a liability risk for all trustees, which the limited liability legal form of a charity cannot protect them against. It is essential to ensure the charity operates within the terms of its own charitable purposes and its own constitution at all times, as well as ensuring the charity's funds and assets are used correctly, to safeguard against the risk.

Potential liabilities – dishonesty

If trustees are deliberately dishonest (e.g. commit fraud or theft) they can be liable to relevant criminal penalties and be required to make good the charity's losses.

Other criminal penalties

There are various criminal penalties that can be imposed against trustees who default in meeting certain legal obligations, in particular obligations relating to the public accountability of charities and charity trustees.

Potential liablities – insolvency

If a charity becomes insolvent, having insufficient funds and assets to pay its debts and meet its liabilities, the trustee can be at risk of personal liability (in particular where they bear some legal responsibility for the financial failure). This is a liability risk for all trustees, which the limited liability legal form of a charity cannot protect them against. It is essential the trustees are aware of, understand and manage the charity's financial position to ensure it remains solvent and to safeguard against this risk.

Managing trustee liability risks

Incorporated legal structure of the charity provides limited liability protection to the trustees, subject to the issues regarding risk for breaches of trust or insolvency discussed above. Limited insurance protection may be available through trustee indemnity insurance (TII), which some unincorporated charities consider worth putting in place (perhaps mainly as a reassurance to prospective trustees). However, there are strict legal limits on the scope of such insurance. Those, together with the relevant restrictions, terms and conditions of the relevant policy render the likelihood of a successful claim on a TII policy quite low in most circumstances.

Trustees' risks are best managed by trustees ensuring they are aware of their legal duties and responsibilities and acting honestly and diligently in seeking to fulfil them. In addition, trustees should ensure that they:

- know and follow the charity's constitution;
- identify and deal appropriately with conflicts of interest;
- follow appropriate procedures to make reasonable decisions;
- take independent professional advice, when they need to do so;
- receive, consider and act on regular and accurate financial information; and
- monitor the charity's affairs properly (including its finances).

If trustees delegate to others, including staff or committees of the board, they should ensure that they give clear, documented authority and that they monitor and oversee the correct use of that authority.

Management of the trustees' personal risks should be carefully distinguished from management of the charity's own risks. The proper identification and effective management of the charity's own risks is part of the core function of the trustees and also helps them to discharge their duties correctly.

Other sanctions against charity trustees

A number of other sanctions can be imposed on charity trustees who fall short of the standards demanded of them or who are considered by the law to be unfit to serve as charity trustees on other specific legal grounds, in particular disqualification.

There are automatic legal disqualifications when individuals are adjudicated bankrupt or disqualified as company directors or when they are convicted of various specified criminal offences of dishonesty.

The courts have powers to disqualify individuals from acting as charity trustees on particular legal grounds. In addition, in certain circumstances where relevant legal conditions are met, the Charity Commission can disqualify people it considers to be unfit to act as charity trustees or as senior managers in charities.

Trusts and special trusts

Foundations of trust law

The law of trusts in England and Wales is a legal mechanism for protecting and administering funds or other assets, such as property, on behalf of others. Trust law has common law foundations; however, certain areas are subject to statutory provisions, including trust law as it applies to charities.

A trust separates the 'legal' ownership that is held by the trustees of the trust from the beneficial ownership (the legal interests of the beneficiaries of the trust). Trustees have legal duties to safeguard the assets that are subject to the trust and to apply them in accordance with the terms of the trust. Under the law of England and Wales, a trust has no independent identity or legal capacity in its own right. Therefore, the trustees must hold the trust assets in their own names or in the name of a nominee acting on their behalf. In addition, the trustees must enter into contracts and other legal agreements that relate to the trust in their personal capacities. This makes them open to personal liability.

A trust is not inherently a membership organisation so it usually only has trustees (no members). The trustees are subject to trustees' duties and can be liable to compensate the trust fund for breaches of their duties that lead to losses. Many trusts are private, rather than charitable in nature because only some trusts meet the legal requirements for charitable status.

Charitable trusts

Charitable trusts are usually established under a deed of trust or by a will but can be established by other documents (such as a conveyance or a transfer of assets). They can (provided there is no land involved) even be established orally, if there is adequate evidence of certainty on the three key matters described below. There must be certainty over three matters for any charitable trust to be established:

1. The charitable purposes.
2. The assets that are subject to the trust.
3. An intention to create a charitable trust.

The law specifically requires a trust over land, or interests in land, to be in writing.

A charitable trust is subject to the general principles of trust law but, in particular, it is subject to charity law. The law regards the beneficiaries of a charitable trust as being charitable purposes, so power to enforce the trustees' duties is given to the Attorney General and the Charity Commission, with a fundamental role of acting in the public interest to protect the charitable assets for the relevant charitable purposes.

The person establishing a charitable trust can, subject to meeting the fundamental charity law requirements, specify the terms on which the assets are to be held. The terms of trusts and also the powers and obligations of their trustees vary from one charitable trust to another. The detailed provisions of the relevant trust documents and how those interact with particular charity law rules and requirements must be considered with care.

Relationship of trust law to charity law

Charity law is, in essence, a specialist branch of trust law and its common law foundations are rooted in trust law. The fundamentals of trust law apply to unincorporated charitable trusts, so for example the trust assets are inherently held on trust for the charitable purposes.

Trusts in Scotland

Scotland has its own law of trusts, relating to private, public and charitable trusts. It is this law, together with relevant statutory provisions of the law of Scotland (in particular the Charities and Trustee Investment (Scotland) Act 2005) that would form the legal basis for a charity established as a charitable trust under the law of Scotland.

Special trusts in charities

Special trusts are additional trust restrictions over particular assets held by a charity that restrict the use of those assets to particular limited charitable purposes within the wider charitable purposes of that charity (e.g. a fund to pay for music scholarships to a charitable school that has charitable purposes to advance education in general, not simply musical education). The restrictions will usually have been imposed by the donor of the assets of their own volition or have arisen because the charity made a public appeal for funds for a particular purpose. A non-binding expression of preference by the donor, as to how the funds might potentially be used, will not create a special trust.

Income funds given by a donor with restrictions and which create a special trust must be spent or applied within a reasonable period of their receipt. In rare circumstances, trustees may have specific power to declare special trusts themselves over the charity's unrestricted funds. If they choose to exercise such a power, the funds affected will become restricted to the relevant special trust that has been declared.

The definition of 'special trust' is property which:

(a) is held by or on behalf of a charity for any special purposes of the charity, and
(b) is so held and administered on separate trusts relating only to that property.

(Charities Act s. 287)

A special trust does not constitute a separate charity for the purposes of charity accounting and reporting (i.e. it is accounted for and reported on within the charity's own annual accounts and annual trustees' report).

Assets held on 'special trust' are restricted funds (restricted to be used only with the purposes of the special trust, which are inevitably narrower than the charitable purposes as a whole) and should be reported as such in the annual accounts. Funds given on special trusts can only lawfully be spent on those restricted purposes.

Permanent endowment and functional permanent endowment

The Charities Act defines permanent endowment as:

> Property held subject to a restriction on its being expended for the purposes of the charity.

The concept of holding assets permanently on trust in this way is a unique charity law concept (not found in general trust law).

Permanent endowment may consist of investment property that produces an income to be spent on the charitable purposes of the charity. The Charity Commission refers to this as 'investment' permanent endowment or 'non-functional' permanent endowment. Permanent endowment may instead be property that is used by the charity directly to further its charitable purposes (e.g. property given by the donor in trust to be used as an almshouse). The Charity Commission refers to this as 'functional' permanent endowment.

The assets that represent a permanent endowment fund can be changed from time to time (e.g. the investments or property representing the fund can be changed). Permanent endowment is a complex legal concept; whether or not it exists as a matter of law in a particular charity must be determined by careful construction of the relevant legal documents (e.g. the documents by which property was originally gifted to the charity by a donor). It is more likely that older unincorporated charities will have permanent endowment.

If a fund is entirely expendable by the charity, for anything within its overall charitable purposes and powers, it is not a 'permanent endowment' fund in the strict sense of the Charities Act and charity law.

Release of permanent endowment restrictions

Subject to meeting applicable conditions, trustees may now sometimes use a general statutory power in the Charities Act to release permanent endowment spending restrictions where this would enable the charity to more effectively carry out the purposes for which the endowment itself is held. Charity Commission approval of the relevant trustees' resolution may be necessary. The legal conditions and safeguards are complex. Specialist legal advice should be taken before seeking to relax or remove any permanent endowment restrictions.

Non-endowed (unrestricted) funds and assets

Non-endowed funds and the assets that represent such funds are generally referred to in charity law terms as income funds (i.e. fully expendable funds) and in charity reporting and accounting terms as unrestricted funds (funds available to spend on anything within the charity's charitable purposes and powers).

The non-endowed funds are the overall financial resources of the charity that its trustees are free to apply towards any aspect of the charity's overall charitable purposes, without restriction. Trustees are broadly required to apply such funds to the charitable purposes within a reasonable period from the date of receipt.

Corporate property

The trust law concepts of permanent endowment and expendable endowment are only applicable to the administration of charitable trusts, not the administration of corporate charities. No such distinctions apply to the funds and assets of a charitable company, which is instead the outright owner of its property. Permanent endowment is always held on trust so it cannot be held directly by a charitable company. A charitable company can be the corporate trustee of the relevant trusts that apply to the permanent endowment. Subject to the terms of its articles and to the rules of charity law and company law, a charitable company is free to apply any of its corporate property in pursuit of its charitable purposes. However, a charitable company can hold restricted funds, which may only be used for the relevant restricted purposes.

Structures and legal forms

Different legal forms

Charitable status is conferred on an organisation because of the reasons why it is set up; it is not a description of a type of legal form or structure. Charities can adopt one of a number of different types of legal form and structure, and we will look at some of the forms most commonly used.

The most common legal forms for charities are:

- trusts;
- unincorporated members' associations;
- registered societies;
- chartered bodies;
- statutory corporations;
- companies limited by guarantee (CLG); and
- charitable incorporated organisations (CIO).

In addition, many charities will have subsidiaries, often for trading. These will usually take the form of either:

- a company limited by shares (CLS);
- a company limited by guarantee (CLG); or
- a community interest company (CIC).

It is sometimes difficult to identify what legal form a charity takes. In many cases it is specified on a charity's letterhead and website. This is a requirement for some legal forms, but does not always happen. If you want to determine a charity's legal form and it is not shown on its letterhead or website, some alternative ways of looking are:

- Read the annual report and accounts for the charity. These should make it clear what type of legal form it is.
- Consider the charity's name. If it has 'Ltd' in the title this implies that it is either a registered society or a company. However, note that charitable companies can be exempt from using 'ltd' or 'limited' in their name.

- Look on the Charity Commission's Register of Charities to see the title of the charity's constitution. Different legal forms have different titles for their constitution (see below) and so the title used can indicate its legal form.
- Search for it on the Register of Companies held by Companies House.

Table 2.1: Legal forms for charities

	Incorporated?	Members as well as board members	Regulator	Limited Liability
Trust	No	No	Charity Commission	No
Unincorporated members' association	No	Yes	Charity Commission	No
Company limited by guarantee	Yes	Yes	Charity Commission Companies House	Yes
Registered society	Yes	Yes	FCA	Yes
Chartered body	Yes	Yes or no	Charity Commission Privy Council	Yes
Charitable incorporated organisation	Yes	Yes	Charity Commission	Yes
Statutory body	Depends on statute	Depends on statute	Charity Commission	Depends on statute

Incorporation

A key issue with the types of legal form set out above is that some are incorporated, and some are unincorporated. Trusts and unincorporated members' associations are unincorporated organisations. Companies limited by guarantee; registered societies; CIOs, and chartered bodies are corporate organisations.

Incorporation means that an organisation is a corporate entity. This means that it has legal personality (i.e. the law recognises the organisation as a person). An incorporated organisation is seen as existing in its own right and being distinct from the people who control it. This means that an incorporated organisation can enter into contracts; own assets and land; and sue and be sued, all in its own right.

An unincorporated organisation has no separate legal identity or personality. So, the assets of an unincorporated charity are vested in the charity trustees or (in the case of some unincorporated members' associations) the members of the charity. This means that the charity trustees (and in some cases, the members) are personally liable for the debts and liabilities of their charity. If the charity has debts it must pay them. It someone wants to sue the charity, it cannot be sued in its own right as it is not a legal entity; the trustees or the members will be sued. What is more, the trustees of an unincorporated charity are jointly and severally liable. This means that the liability does not need to be shared equally between them all. If an unincorporated charity has 10 trustees, and somebody has a claim against them of £100,000, that person does not need to sue all 10 trustees for £10,000 each. They can sue a smaller number, or even just one trustee, for the full amount.

This liability exists in an unincorporated organisation whether or not the board has acted appropriately. Board members need not have breached their legal duties to be liable. However, if they have acted within their duties they can sometimes be indemnified out of the assets of the charity. Of course, this indemnity will only apply if the charity has the assets available to it. Trustees also have the right to be insured against liabilities, again only if they have sought to act in the interests of the charity (Charities Act 2011, s.189).

Incorporation provides *limited* liability. So trustees and members of incorporated charities still carry some liabilities, although these are greatly reduced. In a company limited by guarantee, as an incorporated organisation, a member's liability is limited to the amount of that guarantee – usually £1. Trustees' liability is limited to occasions when they have breached their duties; it is for the organisation itself to take action against trustees if these have been breached.

Having legal personality not only impacts on the issue of limited liability, it also has an effect with regard to the ownership of assets, and the question of contracts etc. As an unincorporated organisation cannot hold property, it needs to be held by individuals, on the organisation's behalf. These individuals will usually be the trustees, but it can be held by separate people, sometimes called 'holding' or 'custodian' trustees (Public Trustee Act 1906, s. 4). If the trustees themselves hold the property, every time the trustees changes, the title in the property will need to change. Also, the organisation itself will not be able to enter into contracts; these will need to be entered into by the trustees themselves, as individuals. It is much simpler if the property and contracts can be held in the name of the organisation itself; as they can be in an incorporated organisation (note that the Charities Act 2011 does provide some means of simplification here for unincorporated charities. It states that, for an unincorporated charity, the trustees can pass a resolution allowing two of them to act as signatories for the full trustee body (Charities Act 2011, s. 333)).

History of incorporation

The word 'corporate' derives from the Latin 'corpus', meaning body. The first grants of corporate status came from the crown, which granted the status either by a Royal Charter, or later, by an Act of Parliament. Corporate status was first developed for organisations that we would now describe as not for profit. So the first corporate entities in England and Wales were hospitals, universities and monasteries. A key feature from the start was that the Charter would specify the objects, or purposes, of the body, and it was not allowed to act beyond these. Such acts were deemed 'ultra vires' (i.e. beyond the power) and any ultra vires acts would be void.

By the sixteenth century, Royal Charters began to be granted to trade associations, and it was out of these that the first commercial corporations, which would later lead on to become companies, began to develop.

The development of companies

With the development of the Industrial Revolution, there was a growing desire for a simple means of establishing corporate entities, as it was felt that this would facilitate business activity. In 1844, the Joint Stock Companies Act was passed. This meant that companies could be created without a Royal Charter. Instead, there was a simple registration procedure to incorporate. Potential shareholders could now register a company themselves and were allowed to carry out any activity, as long as it was stated in their constitution, and the registration was approved by the Registrar of Companies. So, for the first time, the use of companies similar to their current form was developed. However, although the company was a separate legal entity, there was no limited liability. This was not available until 1855, when the Limited Liability Act allowed shareholders to limit their liability to the amount that they invested in the company. The Companies Act 1862 was the first Act to be given the title 'Companies Act', the title that has been used since then. This Act also permitted the registration of companies limited by guarantee. Companies limited by guarantee are the form which is used by charities.

Since 1862 there have been a number of Companies Acts, but they have essentially developed along the same themes, with the most recent being the Companies Act 2006.

During the twentieth century, one of the most significant developments was the erosion of the concept of ultra vires for commercial companies. Originally, all companies had to restrict their activities to the purposes, or objects, as set out in their constitution. This principle was gradually eroded over time. However, it is important to note that this erosion and removal of the ultra vires principle does not apply to charitable companies. A charitable company must still act within its objects and it is ultra vires (i.e. beyond its powers) for it to exceed them.

The second key development was the distinction between public and private companies. The Companies Act 1907 recognised that not all companies either wanted, or needed, publicly traded shares. It introduced the distinction between public and private companies. A private company does not offer its shares for sale to the public and its shares are not traded.

The final development was the principle of public disclosure. It is the principle that for the benefit of the veil of incorporation to be conferred there needs to be some transparency in the operations of a company. So, a company needs to make public the names of its board, its shareholders (in a share company) and its performance, via its annual report and accounts. A private company did not have a requirement to disclose its annual accounts until 1967.

Companies are now the most common type of incorporated body within the UK. Chartered bodes still exist and charters are still granted, but this is restricted to professional bodies and, in some rare instances, charities.

Veil of incorporation

The distinction between a company and its members and the fact that they are two different legal persons was established by the House of Lords in 1896.

CASE LAW

The case was *Salomon v Salomon Ltd*, in 1896. This concerned a company which had been set up by Mr Salomon. He had sold his existing business to it for a price of £39,000. At that time, it was a legal requirement that a company had at least seven members. Salomon held a share and his wife, daughter and four sons held the other shares, in trust for Salomon. The price was also paid for the issue of a debenture, secured by a charge, which gave Mr Salomon a priority claim against the company's assets. When the company went into liquidation, the other creditors claimed that 'the company was Mr Salomon in another form' and therefore a claim could be made against him as an individual. They also claimed that the company did not have seven members 'independent and unconnected' with each other. The House of Lords overruled the previous decisions of the High Court and the Court of Appeal and stated 'the company has a legal existence ... and it is impossible to deny the validity of the transaction (the purchase of the business and the issue of the debenture) into which it has entered' (per Lord Halsbury LC).

This was a key case, as the highest court recognised the distinction between a company and its members as separate persons. On the face of it, Salomon's sale of the business to the company, which was effectively owned by him alone made no change to the commercial position. Effectively, it was still his business. Yet by separating its legal ownership from himself, he could even become a creditor with priority rights over the assets (against other creditors of the business).

This principle is called 'the veil of incorporation' and it applies to all incorporated bodies. It essentially means that body is separate from the people who set it up, or its members. There are some exceptions and there are some rare times when the courts look behind the veil but essentially the core principle has held to this day.

Limited liability

Limited liability is not complete freedom from liability, it is a limitation of the liability to the amount the shareholder or member has invested or guaranteed. So, with a share company, if a shareholder purchases £100 of shares in the company, and the company goes into liquidation, his liability is limited to that £100. It is part of the assets of the company; these will go towards paying off creditors before being returned to him. But he will never be liable for any more. If a company has debts, limited liability means that those shareholders are not responsible for those debts. They can walk away from them. It is the same with a company limited by guarantee. The member's liability is limited to his guarantee, usually £1.

Share companies are principally about investment – shareholders put their money into a company in the form of shares, hoping that the value of the company will grow, and their share of the company will be worth more. They can also take advantage of the profits of a share company, taking dividends on those profits. Guarantee companies do not pay dividends, and the value of the guarantee does not increase. This type of company is more suitable for groups of people coming together to achieve a particular aim, rather than seeking to profit themselves.

People often think that the term limited liability refers primarily to the directors of a company, but actually it concerns the members in the first instance because it concerns the separation of the company from its owners. The reason why the term is also used for directors (also the trustees in a charitable company) is because it also refers to the fact the company is a separate legal entity, different from those who own it or manage it; it is the company that has action taken against it. So the trustees of an incorporated body are no longer personally liable. However, it is important to understand that, regardless of the legal form that a charity takes, charity trustees can still be liable if they breach their duties. If they do this, action can be taken against them by the charity itself; their fellow trustees; the Charity Commission or the Attorney General acting on behalf of the charity. Such actions are very rare, but trustees do need to remember that limited liability does not relieve them of their duties as trustees and directors.

CASE EXAMPLE

Stampton Arts Association and Stampton Sports are both small registered charities, located in Stampton village in Essex. They both have an income of £7,500 per year. Both of them have charitable objects that restrict them to Stampton. Stampton Arts Association is an unincorporated members association. Stampton Sports is a charitable company limited by guarantee. Neither charity holds any insurance. They both share the ownership of a small hall. The Arts Association uses it for putting on events; Stampton Sports uses it for sports. The hall is very well maintained and both charities take its security very seriously. It is kept securely locked and has a caretaker. However on one occasion, due to illness, the caretaker left the hall unlocked for a short while. A child trespassed into the hall and was injured by falling down its stairs. The child's parents now want to sue both charities. Neither set of trustees has breached their duties in regard to this incident, but there will be a difference in their liabilities. As it is incorporated, the legal action is taken against Stampton Sports itself and its trustees have no liabilities. As it is unincorporated, legal action in regard to Stampton Arts Association is taken against its trustees as individuals. One of its trustees is known locally to be quite wealthy, so the parents choose to sue that trustee, and that trustee alone, for the full damages.

Trustees in an incorporated charity can also be personally liable in the following limited circumstances:

Wrongful or fraudulent trading

Both of these types of liability arise under insolvency law, and therefore apply to charitable companies. They only apply when the company has gone into insolvent liquidation. Wrongful trading occurs when a director knew or ought to have known that there was no reasonable prospect that the company would avoid going into insolvent liquidation, yet allowed the company to continue to trade. Declarations of wrongful trading are quite rare and will not be made if the director took every step they could to minimise the potential loss to the creditors.

Fraudulent trading is similar, but occurs when a director allows the company to carry on, with the intention of defrauding creditors or for any fraudulent purpose. It is much stronger than wrongful trading, therefore it carries stronger penalties. It requires 'actual dishonesty involving ... real moral blame'.

In both situations the trustee/director could be held liable for the debts of the company. Directors who are liable for wrongful trading or fraudulent trading can be ordered to contribute to the assets of the insolvent company and are potentially disqualified from acting as a director.

Criminal acts or breaches of statutory duty

In a charitable company it is the company and not individual trustees that is generally responsible and liable for criminal acts or breaches of statutory duty. However, there are some limited situations where the individual trustees could be held personally liable:

- failure to operate PAYE;
- failure to comply with some statutory requirements in relation to legislation such as the Health and Safety, Trade Descriptions and Pensions Acts. These liabilities will usually only arise if the offence has been committed with their 'consent or connivance (or is attributable to their) neglect';
- corporate manslaughter;
- failure to comply with most Companies Acts requirements (i.e. submission of accounts); and
- failure to comply with some Charities Act requirements.

It is possible to apply to the court for relief from personal liability in these situations.

Acting whilst disqualified

A person who serves as a trustee whilst disqualified from doing so may be held liable for all the charity's debts incurred whilst they were a trustee. Acting as a company director or charity trustee whilst disqualified is also a criminal offence and, in the case of acting as a charity trustee, can carry a sentence of up to two years' imprisonment.

Other ways of dealing with liabilities

If an organisation is unincorporated, the trustees will not have limited liability. However there are other ways that their liabilities can be dealt with.

Trustee indemnity insurance

Section 189 of the Charities Act 2011 permits the purchase of trustee indemnity insurance (TII) without explicit authorisation being required in the constitution. Many charities now make use of such insurance. However, the Act does state that such insurance must exclude:

(a) any liability to pay a criminal fine, or a penalty for non-compliance with a regulatory requirement;
(b) any liability for defending criminal proceedings in which the trustee is convicted of an offence arising out of any fraud or dishonesty, or wilful or reckless misconduct; or
(c) any liability that arises out of any conduct which the trustee knew (or must reasonably be assumed to have known) was not in the interests of the charity, or did not care whether or not it was in the best interests of the charity.

These are wide exclusions and they potentially make TII not very worthwhile, particularly for trustees of incorporated charities.

Charity Commission relief

Section 191 of the Charities Act 2011 currently states that if a trustee is, or may be, personally liable for a breach of trust or breach of duty but 'has acted honestly and reasonably and ought fairly to be excused for the breach of trust or duty' the Commission may make an order relieving the trustee wholly or partly from any such liability.

Incorporation of trustees

Under section 251 of the Charities Act 2006, the Charity Commissioner also has the power to grant incorporation for trustees. It can grant a certificate of incorporation to the trustees of a charity. The trustees then become a body corporate. However, this form of incorporation only applies to the trustees of the organisation, not the organisation itself. It also does not confer limited liability.

Types of legal forms

Charitable trusts

A charitable trust is a very simple form of organisation. It is formed when someone gives money or property to another person, trusting them to use it for a specified charitable purpose. (You can also have non-charitable trusts, set up in a similar way, but for a non-charitable purpose such as providing income for your own children.) Trusts are usually established by a trust deed; however, as they are so simple, they can even be set up verbally.

Trusts are one of the more traditional ways in which charities were set up, although they are less commonly used today. However, they are still used by some as their form is so simple and they are often considered ideal for grant giving charities or small charities where the trustees will not face significant potential personal liability. The difficulty is that these charities often grow. As a trust is unincorporated, it is a much less suitable form if a charity wants to own assets, employ staff or enter into contracts. If a charity has been set up as a trust and it later wants to incorporate, it will need to change its legal form.

Advantages

- Quick and easy to set up.
- Less regulated than many incorporated bodies (as only regulated by the Charity Commission).
- No need for a two-tier structure (i.e. no need for both members and trustees).
- Appears to many to be the traditional form for a charity, and therefore suited to a charity (although there is no reason why the other legal forms are not just as suitable).

Disadvantages

- It is an unincorporated form, therefore it has no legal personality and the trustees are jointly and severally personally liable for the debts and other liabilities of the trust. If the charitable trust suffers a loss or faces debts, the trustees' personal assets are at risk. Any legal action will be taken against the trustees, not the trust.
- There is less of a body of law to support their operation. Legal forms such as companies have extensive legislation, such as the Companies Act 2006, that can be relied upon for clarity on how the charity operates.
- VAT grouping is not available for unincorporated organisations.

Unincorporated members' association

This is another type of unincorporated body. It is created when a group of people come together with a shared aim, without a profit motive. Like a trust, it is a simple form. Typically, a group will come together with a common purpose (e.g. to start a local theatre group). It may operate for a while with no written constitution and then one will be adopted. Sometimes this will be because it wants something written down (e.g. who the core management committee will be, or how they are appointed). However, often a constitution is adopted because the organisation is seeking a grant. Having a constitution will often be a requirement of that grant application.

There is no legislation supporting unincorporated members' associations. The closest thing to a legal framework is that the constitution can sometimes be regarded as a contract between the members. Typically, an unincorporated members' association will have a broader membership and then a management committee, who are the trustees if it is a charity. So, an unincorporated members association (e.g. the friends group for a primary school) could have all of the parents as its members; they then elect a management committee each year.

Advantages

- Quick and easy to set up.
- Less regulated than many incorporated bodies (as only regulated by the Charity Commission if they are a charity).
- Allows a new organisation to grow and develop itself organically. They can operate fairly informally. For this reason, unincorporated members' associations are one of the most common forms of small charity. Many charities begin to operate in this way, and then seek to incorporate at a later stage.
- They provide a form that enables there to be a wider membership, thereby allowing a wider stakeholder group to be involved in the charity.

Disadvantages

- They are unincorporated therefore they have no legal personality. The trustees are jointly and severally personally liable for the debts and other liabilities. If the unincorporated members' association suffers a loss or faces debts the trustees' personal assets are at risk. In addition, legal actions will be taken against the trustees and not the unincorporated members' association.
- There is less of a body of law to support their operation. Legal forms such as companies have extensive legislation, such as the Companies Act 2006, that can be relied upon for clarity on how the charity operates.
- VAT grouping is not available.

Chartered body

As set out above, chartered status is the oldest way of conferring incorporation on an organisation in England and Wales. It was the form of incorporation available before registered companies and it pre-dates that form. Although they can technically be described as companies, chartered bodies are not governed by the Companies Act. At one time this was the only way of gaining incorporation, but it has now been overtaken by the registration of companies. Chartered status is conferred on an organisation by the Privy Council. It is less common for chartered status to be granted now, and the right to become a chartered body is generally restricted to professional bodies (which may or may not be charities) or (in rarer cases) some charities. There are quite strict criteria for becoming a chartered body. A professional body will need to show that it is of sufficient size; financially sound; and that it represents a unique field of activity. It will also need to demonstrate how the regulation of its profession will be in the public benefit. Chartered bodies are generally professional bodies; but there are also some chartered charities, such as the British Red Cross.

Advantages

- Incorporated status, without the need for full dual regulation. Chartered bodies are regulated by Privy Council (as well as the Charity Commission if they are charities) but that regulation is effectively restricted to the requirement for Privy Council approval for changes to the charter and byelaws.
- Status. A Royal Charter can be seen to confer authority and respectability onto an organisation.

Disadvantages

- It is very difficult to obtain chartered status. Whilst it is granted to charities in rare circumstances, it is usually only available to professional bodies that meet the criteria.

- Privy Council approval is also required for any changes to the charter and any byelaws, and this can add to the administration and time for changes to be made.
- There is less clarity regarding the law supporting chartered bodies. Whilst the duties of board members are equivalent to the duties of company directors, this is only supported by common law rather than legislation.

Statutory charities

There are a small number of charities which are established by Acts of Parliament, known as statutory charities. Whilst these are established by the government they must still fulfil all of the requirements of independence for a charity. Charities established in this way include NHS charities (i.e. bodies that hold charitable funds associated with NHS hospitals and services) and a range of other bodies, such as the National Trust. The governance arrangements for such charities and whether or not they are incorporated will depend on the individual circumstances and the Acts of Parliament or orders that govern them. Being established by an Act of Parliament is rare; this is not an option for an organisation seeking to establish itself as a charity. In addition, charities set up in this way are usually very limited in their options re legal form; they will not necessarily have the option of changing legal form. For this reason, we have not chosen to list the advantages and disadvantages of being such a charity. However one key disadvantage is that it is often very difficult to amend the constitution of these charities as it requires a new Act of Parliament. Sometimes, the constitution can be added to via a Charity Commission Scheme, and this process can also be used to amend the constitution. So, in the case of the National Trust, a Charity Commission Scheme setting out the details of this constitution became enshrined in an Order, the Charities (National Trust) Order 2005. However, it is also quite common for statutory charities to have quite short constitutions, containing only the most basic requirements. Statutory charities can be either incorporated or unincorporated, depending on the statute that establishes them. For example, NHS charities are unincorporated.

Registered societies

These types of society were previously referred to as Industrial and Provident Societies (IPSs). This legal form provides incorporated status, and has been available for nearly as long as companies. They were first created in the nineteenth century, and the primary legislation was the Industrial and Provident Societies Partnership Act 1852 and Industrial and Provident Societies Act 1893. Before 2014, the primary piece of modern legislation was the Co-operative and Community Benefit Societies and Credit Unions Act 1965. (To add to the confusion with regard to these societies, key pieces of legislation have been renamed: the Co-operative and Community Benefit Societies and Credit Unions Act 1965 was originally the Industrial and Provident Societies Act 1965; it was renamed in 2010.)

Following the Co-operative and Community Benefit Societies Act 2014, there are two types of registered society – community benefit societies and co-operative societies. Community benefit societies are set up to benefit the community as a whole; co-operative societies are set up to benefit their members. As co-operatives are established for the benefit of their members rather than for the public benefit, they are not usually charitable so they shall not be considered here.

Just like companies, registered societies are incorporated bodies and the personal liability of their members and board members is limited. Like a company, they have a two-tier structure, with shareholders and a board of directors. Registered societies have shareholders rather than guarantee members; shareholders each purchase a share in the society as they would in a shareholding company. However, unlike a share company, those shares are not traded and shareholders are not entitled to a dividend.

Although they provide a means of obtaining incorporated status, registered societies are not commonly found outside the social housing sector. They can be more expensive and complex to set up than a company and are not as well understood.

Registered societies are registered with the Financial Conduct Services Authority (FCA), which regulates them, rather than the Registrar of Companies.

For many years these societies operated under quite archaic laws. The Co-operative and Community Benefit Societies and Credit Unions Act 2010 (the 2010 Act) was enacted following a review of Industrial and Provident Societies by HM Treasury. The intention was to update the governance of the societies, and bring them more in line with other corporate forms. A key feature of the 2010 Act was to give HM Treasury the power to make regulations which apply company law to IPSs.

The Cooperative and Community Benefit Societies Act 2014:

- replaced the 'industrial and provident society' legal form with two new legal forms – community benefit society and co-operative society; and
- consolidated previous industrial and provident society legislation.

Before the Act came into force, all societies registered in this way were legally referred to as 'Industrial and Provident Societies'. Now, pre-existing societies are referred to as 'registered societies'. Any new societies are referred to as co-operative societies or community benefit societies. A community benefit society can, but need not be, charitable. For ease we have used the term 'registered societies' throughout this chapter.

Advantages

- They provide a means of incorporation that is specifically designed for non-commercial entities.
- They provide a form that enables there to be a wider membership (via shareholding) thereby allowing a wider stakeholder group to be involved in the charity.

- Registered societies were previously exempt from registration with the Charity Commission, so this provided a means of incorporation that did not require dual registration. However, the legal position in regard to exempt charities is changing and many registered societies may now need to register with the Charity Commission in future.

Disadvantages

- Registration as a registered society is more complex than registration as a company.
- This is a legal form that is less well understood. When entering into agreements and contracts this can have an impact, as the bodies that you are working with will have a less clear idea of how you are established, and whether you are incorporated.
- Some of the regulatory requirements for registered societies are a bit more involved than for companies, and quite arcane. So, for example, if the rules are amended, they need to be signed by three shareholders and the application to register the change must then be signed as a statutory declaration by an officer, before a solicitor or notary public.
- Registered societies are still exempt from registration with the Charity Commission. Whilst this may seem like an advantage, it is also arguably a disadvantage. It means that charitable registered societies do not have a Charity Commission registration number which indicates that they are charitable. Also, they need to establish their charitable nature via applications to HMRC rather than the Charity Commission. This can make it more difficult to indicate to third parties, including potential funders, that you are a charity.
- Unlike charitable companies, registered societies are not exempt from using 'Limited' or 'Ltd' in their name.

Company limited by guarantee

We have discussed companies above, in the context of the development of incorporation. Companies are the form of incorporation that people are most familiar with; whilst they tend to be associated with commercial organisations, they can also be charitable.

Registered companies are established under the Companies Act 2006. When a company is created, the legal form essentially creates a separation between the owners of the company (shareholders or members), and those who run the company, its board. A company has a separate legal personality, distinct from those who set it up. If it fails, they can then walk away from it, and do not have any liabilities (with certain exceptions). As a balance to this benefit, companies have certain requirements regarding transparency and reporting. They must prepare accounts and make them available to members; they have to be open about who their board members are; and they must file this and other information at Companies House.

There are two types of company: a company limited by shares; and a company limited by guarantee. The latter form is the more usual one within the voluntary sector; it is not possible to register a charitable company limited by shares with the Charity Commission, with very rare exceptions.

Any company has to have at least one member (the shareholders or guarantors) and at least one director. These are two separate roles. The same people may carry out both roles; it is quite common for directors to also act as members, but they are still separate and distinct roles.

Under company law, members have distinct rights. They amend the Articles (Companies Act 2006, s. 21) and have the statutory right to remove directors (Companies Act 2006, s.168) and to require the directors to call a general meeting (s. 303). It is also common for the Articles to provide that members have a right to appoint directors.

Companies are regulated by Companies House and are required to submit annual confirmation statements; annual accounts; and to file certain information. They are governed by the Companies Act 2006 and also have legal requirements regarding the records and registers that they keep.

CASE EXAMPLE

Stampton Sports is a charitable company limited by guarantee. It has a board of 12 trustees, who are therefore also its company directors. When it was first established, the trustees were the only members of the company but it has recently decided to widen its membership. Now any member of the local community who applies for membership and guarantees £1 can become a member of the company. The Articles provide that the members elect trustees onto the board.

Advantages

- A company is incorporated and so it provides the protection of an incorporated form. As an incorporated body, it is a legal entity in its own right; it is the company that enters into contracts, owns property; sues and is sued and not the trustees (who are its directors). The trustees and the members have limited liability.
- Companies are very quick and easy to set up. A company can be set up in one day, if necessary. Once set up, if the charitable company has an income of more than £5,000 it will then need to register with the Charity Commission and this will take time. However, the charitable company will exist from the date it was set up as a company, and will be charitable from that date, if the Articles have been drafted correctly.

- Although it carries additional regulation by Companies House, this is fairly minimal.
- It is a legal form that is very familiar to many people. This means that in entering into contracts and agreements, the other parties will be familiar with the legal form of your charity.
- There is a detailed body of company law, both statutes and common law, that sets out how you operate, and that provides a good reference.

Disadvantages

- Charitable companies are subject to dual regulation – they are registered with both the Charity Commission and Companies House.
- For some people, the fact of being a company, which is more usually a commercial form, does not sit easily with being a charity.

Companies are governed by the Companies Act 2006. This is a very detailed piece of legislation, which draws together much of the previous legislation and common law on companies. It sets out how companies should be formed and constituted; the regulatory requirements; how they are wound up and the role and duties of company directors.

The trustees of a charitable company will also be its company directors. Whilst their duties as charity trustees are established in common law their duties as company directors are set out in the Companies Act 2006. Actually, the two sets of duties are, in many ways, very similar. In practice, trustees of a charitable company who are meeting their duties will also be meeting their duties as company directors.

Duties of a company director

The duties are set out in sections 171–177 of the Act

- To act within the powers. This duty means that a director must comply with company law and the company's Articles. They can exercise the powers only for the reasons for which they were given.
- To promote the success of the company. This is one of the few occasions when the Companies Act makes a difference for charitable companies. For commercial companies the Act says that promoting the success of the company is acting 'for the benefit of its members as a whole. It then goes on to say that if the 'purposes of the company consist of or include purposes other than the benefit of its members ... promoting the success of the company [is] achieving those purposes' (s. 172). So in a commercial company, the directors must work for the benefit of the members; in a charitable company, they must work to achieve the charitable objects.

- To exercise independent judgment.
- To exercise reasonable care, skill and diligence. As with the common law charity trustee duties, this means applying the level of care, skill and expertise that the director as an individual would be expected to have. If they have specific skills (e.g. as an accountant) they are expected to apply them.
- To avoid conflicts of interest.
- Not to accept benefits from third parties.
- To declare interests in proposed transactions or arrangements.

Charitable incorporated organisation

The charitable incorporated organisation (CIO) is a new type of legal form, specifically designed for charities, so if your organisation is a CIO, it must be a charity. CIOs were created by the Charities Act 2006, but did not come into existence for some time after that. In Scotland, CIOs started in 2011. England and Wales had to wait a bit longer – the first CIOs were registered in 2013. The purpose of the CIO was to give charities an incorporated legal form, without the need for dual regulation. As you can see from Table 2.1 on page 44, for nearly all the incorporated legal forms other than a CIO, there is another regulator as well as the Charity Commission. For CIOs, the Charity Commission is the sole regulator.

A CIO is incorporated, like a company, so the trustees have limited liability. As an incorporated body it can hold assets, employ staff, enter into contracts, sue and be sued, in its own right. Like a company, it has to have members as well as a board (the trustees), although it can have just one member. CIOs take two different forms – an association CIO, which has a body of members who are distinct from the trustees; or a foundation CIO, where the members and the trustees are one and the same people.

Being a CIO can seem like a simpler way of being incorporated without having to become a company. However, it should be remembered that there are a number of advantages in being a charitable company. It is actually simpler and quicker to set up a company; what then takes more time is registration with the Charity Commission. In addition, it is arguable that being a company is a more widely recognised legal form. This can give a number of advantages in contracting and working with third parties. It also means that there is an established body of law behind the legal form.

One of the real advantages of a CIO as a form is for smaller charities. At the present time, charity registration is not an option for charities with an income below £5,000 each year unless they are a CIO. The Charity Commission just does not have the resources to offer registration to smaller charities. Although registration with the Charity Commission carries obligations regarding annual returns and filing of accounts these are not onerous and there are a number of real advantages with being a registered charity. It clearly shows that an organisation is a charity and gives security to funders and donors. Charities with a registration number can find that it helps them to fundraise. If a small charity wants to be registered with the Charity Commission, becoming a CIO is a way of becoming registered without having to meet the income requirements.

Advantages

- Charitable incorporated organisations are incorporated, so it provides the protection of an incorporated form. As an incorporated body, it is a legal entity in its own right; it is the company that enters into contracts, owns property; sues and is sued and not the trustees (who are its directors). The trustees and the members have limited liability.
- Charitable incorporated organisations are regulated only by the Charity Commission.
- They give a means by which smaller charities with income below £5,000 can be registered with the Charity Commission.
- It is a form designed specifically for charities.

Disadvantages

- It is a legal form that is not familiar to many people. When entering into agreements and contracts this can have an impact, as the bodies that you are working with will have a less clear idea of how you are established, and whether you are incorporated.
- It is a new form of legal entity and the body of law to support its operation is not as established as other forms (e.g. companies).
- It is slower and more complex to set up than a company. Establishing it as a body is tied in with registering it with the Charity Commission. This means that much needs to be resolved at an early stage (e.g. setting up a bank account) and this can be difficult.

Group structures

Some charities are very simple and all of their activities are carried out by one legal entity, the charity itself. However it is also common for charities to have some form of group structure. Many charities will have a trading subsidiary, and some will have a number of different subsidiaries, for a number of different reasons and purposes.

There are a number of reasons why group structures emerge:

- The restrictions on trading for charities means that many charities will have a trading subsidiary.
- Subsidiaries are sometimes created due to tax or VAT considerations.

- Sometimes there is a need or desire to separate out governance of particular activities (e.g. a housing association which also provides care homes may want to have a separate board with particular expertise running that part of its work).
- Having a subsidiary is sometimes seen as a way of managing risk. As the subsidiary is a separate legal entity the parent charity will not be liable for any losses. Although it will 'own' the subsidiary, usually as the sole shareholder, limited liability will apply. However, this risk management has its limitations. The subsidiary will usually share the same branding as the charity, and so its insolvency could be a significant reputational risk for the charity.
- A need for separate identities. For example, charities that have merged will sometimes still operate as separate legal entities within the same group, keeping their previous names and identities but sharing resources.

The definition of a group is set out in section 474 of the Companies Act 2006 as 'a parent undertaking and its subsidiary undertakings'. Whilst this definition comes from the Companies Act, note that neither the parent, nor the subsidiaries need to be companies, they just need to be undertakings. The significant feature of a parent/subsidiary relationship is one of control. Section 1162 of the same Act gives a more complete explanation:

> An undertaking is a parent undertaking in relation to another undertaking, a subsidiary undertaking, if—
> (a) it holds a majority of the voting rights in the undertaking, or
> (b) it is a member of the undertaking and has the right to appoint or remove a majority of its board of directors, or
> (c) it has the right to exercise a dominant influence over the undertaking—
> (i) by virtue of provisions contained in the undertaking's Articles, or
> (ii) by virtue of a control contract, or
> (d) it is a member of the undertaking and controls alone, pursuant to an agreement with other shareholders or members, a majority of the voting rights in the undertaking.

Trading subsidiaries are the most common type of subsidiary. A charity should usually only carry on trading activities which are either directly in pursuance of its objects or which are ancillary to their objects (together known as primary-purpose trading). The amount of other non-primary-purpose trading they can carry on is strictly limited. Charities who want to carry out non-primary-purpose trading, beyond these limits will probably need to do this via a trading subsidiary established as a separate company.

A trading subsidiary is usually a company limited by shares; with the charity as the sole shareholder. This then gives the charity complete control over appointments to the subsidiary board. The trading subsidiary will usually Gift Aid its taxable profits to the charity. Any profits transferred in this way will therefore be free from corporation tax. It is important for the subsidiary to remember that it should not necessarily transfer all of its profits in this way. It will usually need to retain some of its profits for working capital and investment in future work, and these profits will therefore still be liable to corporation tax. The donation to the parent charity needs to be paid over to the charity within nine months of the trading company's year end, in order to obtain tax relief for the financial year in question.

A charity's assets can only be used for charitable purposes; they cannot be used to support a non-charitable subsidiary. A charity can invest in its trading subsidiary, but only if:

- it can show evidence that the investment by way of loan funding was made to benefit the charity;
- there are terms and conditions for repayment (including interest);
- the charity gets a fair return that is paid to it; and
- the charity and its trustees comply with applicable charity investment rules and requirements.

The need to protect the charitable assets of the charity also means that the trading subsidiary must be kept separate from the charity; the relationship between the two must be kept at arm's length. A key feature of this is that whilst it is common for charity trustees also to be directors of its trading subsidiary, there can be conflicts of interest. In the interests of good governance, it is recommended that there should be at least one person who is a charity trustee, but not a director or employee of the trading subsidiary; and at least one person who is a director of the trading subsidiary, but not a charity trustee or employee of the charity.

A charity with a trading subsidiary should also ensure that:

(a) the charity and its trading subsidiary should have separate bank accounts – there should be no mixing of funds;
(b) there is no subsidy in the form of income, staff time or the use of shared facilities, interest-free loans, or the guaranteeing of loans – the charity should make a management charge for the use of any shared resources; and
(c) it is advisable to have an intra-company agreement between the two companies and/or some form of service level agreement.

We have talked above about the simplest type of group structure, a charitable parent organisation with one subsidiary, usually a trading subsidiary. However, group structures can be much more complex than this. Some key things to remember are:

- a parent organisation can have a number of subsidiaries. Not all will be non-charitable – it may have some charitable subsidiaries and some non-charitable subsidiaries;
- a subsidiary can itself have a subsidiary. There can be more than one tier in a group structure;

- the subsidiaries do not need to be wholly owned. The parent may have control over it (e.g. a right of appointment of the board) but it may not own all of the shares. Sometimes the ownership of a subsidiary may be shared with others;
- when we think of charities in a group structure, the charity itself does not need to be the parent. In some cases, a non-charitable organisation sets up a charity as a subsidiary, then it is the parent who gift aids profits to the subsidiary. In these instances the charity needs to take care that it clearly acts in the interests of its beneficiaries and for the promotion of its objects; and that it does not act in the interests of the parent. It is vital in these scenarios that the board of the charitable subsidiary is independent.

CASE EXAMPLE

The Those in Need group is a group of registered societies and companies, operating in the field of social housing. The parent is Those in Need Ltd, a registered society and a registered social landlord. It is charitable, but exempt from Charity Commission registration. It has three subsidiaries. The first is Those in Need Care. This is charitable company limited by guarantee, registered with the Charity Commission. It is a wholly owned subsidiary. It provides care homes for the elderly. This company was set up as Those in Need felt that this work required a board with specialist expertise in care. The second subsidiary is Those in Need Developments Ltd. This is a non-charitable share company, wholly owned by Those in Need Ltd. It is used to undertake housing developments that are non-charitable. It gift aids its profits to Those in Need Ltd or Those in Need Care. The third subsidiary is Haste Housing Ltd. This is a registered society and a registered social landlord. It is charitable, but exempt from Charity Commission registration. Its rules give Those in Need Ltd control over appointments to the board, so it is classed as a subsidiary. However, its board members are also shareholders, along with Those In Need Ltd. Haste Housing Ltd came into the Those in Need group as the result of a merger five years ago. However, it has to be maintained as a separate organisation due to potential liabilities with regard to its pension scheme that Those in Need Ltd cannot take on.

Charity constitutions

Definition

The definition of a constitution, as set out in the *Oxford English Dictionary* is 'a body of fundamental principles or established precedents according to which a state or other organisation is acknowledged to be governed'.

A charity needs a constitution; there are only some very rare examples of charities which do not have one. It is possible to establish a trust, or an unincorporated members' association by verbal agreement, without having any documents. However even if a charity is initially established in this way, over time there will need to be some reference to these principles, so some form of constitution will be written down.

The fundamental principles that are contained within a charity's constitution are essentially its purposes, powers and the rules on its governance. The constitution of a charity will take a different form, depending on the type of legal form the charity takes – but all types of constitution will cover the same types of content, no matter what the type of organisation. Different legal forms have different titles for their constitutions; the key ones relevant for charities are set out below.

Table 2.2: Key titles

Trust	Trust Deed/Declaration of Trust/ Charity Commission Scheme
Unincorporated members' association	Rules or Constitution
Company limited by guarantee	Memorandum and Articles of Association
Statutory charity	Act of Parliament; Order or Charity Commission Scheme
Registered society	Rules
Chartered body	Charter (and byelaws)
Charitable incorporated organisation	Constitution

The constitution is the most important document for an organisation. It is very important that the board and those advising it have both read and understood it. Trustees have a legal duty to operate within the constitution of the organisation.

The constitution of a company can be called the Memorandum and Articles of Association (or just Articles of Association). Traditionally, the constitution was split between the Memorandum and the Articles. The Memorandum included the objects, the powers and any clauses that should be unalterable. Following the Companies Act 2006, the Memorandum now just includes the name of the company and the people setting it up (the subscribers). All other clauses are now contained in the Articles.

Content of constitution

The actual contents of a constitution will vary, but will typically include many of the following:

- Name.
- Location – for a company the Memorandum and Articles will state in which country the company is registered. For a registered society, the Rules will actually include the address of the registered office, so changing this address will require the amendment of the Rules.
- Objects.
- Powers – following on from the objects, it is typical for a charity to have a section that sets out the powers of the organisation (i.e. what it can do in pursuit of its objects). Companies will generally have powers listed, and many other types of constitutions replicate this form.
- Non-distribution clause (or asset lock) – there will be a clause in a charity's constitution that states that its assets and profits can only be used in pursuit of the objects, and cannot be distrusted to members.
- Benefits to members or trustees – linked to the non-distribution clause a charity will often have a section setting out whether benefits can be granted to trustees or members and if so, what benefits.
- Limited liability/and guarantee – there will be clauses relating to these issues in company Articles and in registered society rules.
- Dissolution clause – sometimes there will be a clause setting out how the charity can be dissolved or wound up and what should happen to its assets if this happens.
- Membership – a charity that has members (i.e. an unincorporated members' association or a company) will have a section setting out who the members are, or how they are admitted; the rights of the members, and any obligations on them; how and why membership can cease.
- Meetings of members – a charity which has members will usually have a section setting out the arrangements for meetings of members – usually called general meetings. This will typically cover the notice that must be given; and voting and proxy rights. If the charity is a company, many of the members' rights re general meetings are enshrined in the Companies Act 2006, and so these will need to be considered alongside the Articles.
- Board – this section will cover who the board members are, or how they are appointed, the role of the board and its powers, arrangements for how the board meets or takes decisions.
- Delegation – it is good practice to have an explanation of the board's power to delegate and arrangements for setting up committees.
- Conflicts of interest – there are legal requirements in regard to conflicts of interest, for both charity trustees and company directors. The constitution will often set out how conflicts of interest should be handled, and sometimes when they are allowable.

- Reporting and regulation – including the requirements on accounting and the records and registers to be kept.
- How the constitution can be amended.

There are a number of model constitutions that can be used, or adapted. The Charity Commission provides models, as does the Charity Law Association. A number of umbrella organisations also provide models that organisations associated with them can use.

If the charity is a company it is important to note that there are model articles, as prescribed under the Companies Act. The Companies (Model Articles) Regulations 2008 includes a range of model articles, including those for private companies limited by guarantee. Section 20 of the Companies Act 2006 states that:

> On the formation of a limited company—
> (a) if articles are not registered, or
> (b) if articles are registered, in so far as they do not exclude or modify the relevant model articles, the relevant model articles (so far as applicable) form part of the company's articles in the same manner and to the same extent as if articles in the form of those articles had been duly registered.

This means that, for a company, this model will apply unless it is expressly excluded from the articles. The model articles contained within the regulations are not specifically designed for charities, and so it is usually a good idea for the articles of a charitable company limited by guarantee to expressly say that the model articles are excluded. If there is not such a clause, and if the articles are then silent on something that is covered in the model articles, the relevant model article will apply.

CASE EXAMPLE

Stampton Sports is a charitable company limited by guarantee. It has adopted a set of articles. There is no clause in those articles saying that the model articles as set out in the Companies (Model Articles) Regulations 2008 are excluded. There is nothing in Stampton's own articles regarding membership applications and the board thinks that these should be considered by the existing members and not the trustees. However, as the articles are silent on this point, the model articles apply. These state:

> No person shall become a member of the company unless—
> (a) that person has completed an application for membership in a form approved by the directors; and
> (b) the directors have approved the application.

> If Stampton Sports wants this model article not to apply, it must amend its articles to agree different wording and/or to exclude the model articles.

Amendment

The amendment of constitutions can be provided for within the constitution itself, but there are also a number of statutory powers of amendment. The ways in which the constitutions can be amended and the statutory powers that will apply will differ according to what type of legal entity the charity is.

Charitable trusts

The trust deed may include an express power of amendment and this power will usually be granted to the trustees. The deed may require the consent of the Charity Commission before a particular amendment can be made. It is usually the case that a trust deed will specifically state that the objects clause cannot be amended without the Charity Commission's prior written approval. However, it is possible that the power to amend will be wide enough to enable amendments to be made to the charitable objects without the agreement of the Charity Commission.

It is also quite common for trusts to have no power of amendment within their constitution. In this instance, the trust will need to rely on statutory powers.

Section 280 of the 2011 Act gives the trustees of an unincorporated charity (i.e. a charitable trust or unincorporated association) power to modify any provisions in their charity's governing documents which are either an administrative power or an administrative procedure. This power cannot be used:

- to modify the objects clause;
- to provide any benefit to the trustees or connected persons;
- to spend capital held as permanent endowment; and
- to change provisions giving third parties rights to nominate trustees.

If the trustees want to exercise this power they will need to pass a resolution and then send a copy of the resolution to the Charity Commission. Whilst the Charity Commission's approval is not required, it should be notified of the changes. If the trust is a small charity, it has further statutory powers. Section 275 of the 2011 Act provides power for the trustees of an unincorporated charity with gross income in its last financial year of £10,000 or less to change their charity's objects. The trustees can do this without the consent of the Charity Commission, provided that:

- the amended objects are charitable;
- they are satisfied that it is in the best interests of their charity to make the changes; and

- the new purposes, so far as is reasonably practicable, are similar in character to those they replace.

If the trustees want to exercise this power they will need to pass a resolution by not less than a two-thirds majority and then send a copy of the resolution to the Charity Commission, together with a statement of their reasons for passing it. The Charity Commission can ask for additional information or explanation from the trustees or require them to give public notice of the resolution. If the Charity Commission does not object or seek further information or require public notice the resolution will automatically take effect 60 days after it has received a copy of it.

Unincorporated members' associations

The constitution of the charity will first need to be reviewed to see if it includes an express power to amend. If it does, it is usually the case that the approval of the membership will be required, sometimes with a higher majority (e.g. two-thirds or three-quarters). If there is no express power to amend, the association will need to rely on the same statutory powers as charitable trusts.

Section 280 of the 2011 Act also applies to unincorporated associations (see the comments above in relation to charitable trusts). The resolution must be approved by the members of the association in general meeting, either by a majority of two-thirds of those voting on the matter; or by a decision taken without a formal vote but without any expression of dissent when the matter is put to the meeting. The Charity Commission should be notified of the change.

Section 275 of the 2011 Act, which allows a small unincorporated charity to change its objects, is also available to charity trustees of unincorporated associations with an annual income of £10,000 or less and the same procedures apply as are set out above for charitable trusts.

Like charitable trusts, if the association is a larger charity, and it wants to make any of these changes, it will need to apply to the Charity Commission for a scheme to make the amendments.

Chartered bodies

A chartered body's Charter and/or byelaws can be altered only with the agreement of the Privy Council. In addition, if the body is a registered charity, the Charity Commission will need to be consulted about proposed amendments which have a bearing on the charity's objects or how it distributes its funds.

The internal process for approving the change within the body itself will be set out in the Charter and byelaws. If the body is a membership body it is usual for the members to have the power to approve changes, often following the same process that companies use. The consent of the Privy Council and Charity Commission should be obtained before the matter is put to the vote by members. The Privy Council has a detailed procedure for this. Once agreed, in principle, by the Privy Council the changes can be voted on by the members. Following this vote, the changes will need to be filed with the Privy Council and the Charity Commission and will not take effect until the Privy Council gives its full and final consent.

Because of this requirement for Privy Council approval it is now becoming more common for chartered bodies to also have regulations or statutes as a part of their governing documents. These sit one level down from the Charter and bylaws, and contain much more of the detail of how the body will be governed. When these are amended, they do not need to go to the Privy Council for approval, although in some chartered bodies they still need to be approved by members. So a chartered body may choose to have a statement in its Charter and byelaws that it will have a board, and perhaps the maximum size, and then the detail on how that board is comprised is included in its regulations. This gives it much more flexibility re adaptation.

Registered societies

The rules of a registered society will usually include a provision on amending them. All amendments will usually need to be made by the members and require at least a two-thirds majority vote.

Once the amendment has been passed, it must be filed with the Financial Conduct Authority (FCA) and it will not take effect until it has been filed. The society will need to provide the FCA with two printed copies of the amended rules signed by three members and the secretary of the society. The secretary will also need to complete and send an application form to the FCA, together with a statutory declaration by an officer and a copy of the amended rules.

Companies limited by guarantee

The amendment of the articles is a statutory right and is governed by the Companies Act 2006. The articles are amended by the members of the company (not the trustees) by passing a special resolution either at a members' meeting or by signing a written resolution. However, section 198 of the Charities Act 2011 provides that a charity which is a company must obtain the consent of the Charity Commission before it can make a 'regulated alteration' to the Memorandum or Articles of Association. Regulated alterations are:

- any alteration of the objects clause;
- any alteration of any provision directing the application of property of the charity on its dissolution; and
- any alteration which authorises a director or member (or persons connected to them) to obtain a benefit.

Also, under section 105 of the Charities Act 2011, any alteration which removes an express prohibition on paying directors will require prior authorisation by Charity Commission order if either all of the directors of the charitable company are also its members or where the company does not have a sufficient number of members who are not directors to form a quorum to vote on the resolution.

The consent of the Charity Commission must be prior consent (i.e. before the matter is put to a vote). Charitable companies should always check their articles to see if Charity Commission consent is required for any other changes. The articles of some charitable companies incorporated before 1982 include a requirement to obtain the Charity Commission's consent to all changes. If this is the case, and an amendment is proposed, it is good practice to also seek the Charity Commission's approval to the removal of this clause at the same time.

When the special resolution is put to the members the notice of the meeting must state that it is a special resolution; and contain the precise wording of the resolution. A special resolution requires a majority of at least 75% of the members who are present and/or voting (or of all members if being considered as a written resolution).

When the special resolution is passed, a copy of it, certified by a director or the company secretary, together with a copy of the amended Articles of Association must be filed with the Registrar of Companies within 15 days of the resolution being passed. An amendment to the objects will not take effect until filed with Companies House (Companies Act 2006, s. 31). A copy of the amended Articles of Association and the special resolution should also be filed with the Charity Commission.

Charitable incorporated organisation

The Charities Act 2011 contains a power for CIOs to amend their constitution (ss 224–227). This power is also included in the Charity Commission model constitution. A CIO's constitution can only be amended by:

- a resolution agreed in writing by all of the members; or
- a resolution passed by 75% majority of votes cast at a general meeting.

Any amendments to provisions in the CIO's constitution which relate to any of the following will, in addition, require the prior written consent of the Charity Commission:

- the CIO's purposes;
- any application of the CIO's property on winding up; or
- any authorisation of benefits to trustees, members or those connected to them.

The CIO must send the Charity Commission a copy of the resolution agreeing the changes, together with a copy of the amended constitution, within 15 working days from the date on which the resolution was passed. The amendment does not take effect until the Charity Commission has recorded it in the Register of Charities.

Regulation and compliance

Charity regulators

Charity Commission

Charities in England and Wales are regulated by the Charity Commission. Although there are some charities exempt from registration by the Charity Commission the Charity Commission still has a role in regard to the regulation of these charities.

The role of the Charity Commission is set out in the Charities Act 2011. Section 13 of the Act establishes the Charity Commission as a body corporate (i.e. an incorporated body) and then section 14 sets out the objectives of the Charity Commission. These are:

1 The public confidence objective
The public confidence objective is to increase public trust and confidence in charities.
2 The public benefit objective
The public benefit objective is to promote awareness and understanding of the operation of the public benefit requirement.
3 The compliance objective
The compliance objective is to promote compliance by charity trustees with their legal obligations in exercising control and management of the administration of their charities.
4 The charitable resources objective
The charitable resources objective is to promote the effective use of charitable resources.
5 The accountability objective
The accountability objective is to enhance the accountability of charities to donors, beneficiaries and the general public.

Section 15 of the Charities Act then sets out the general functions of the Charity Commission, which are:

- Determining whether institutions are or are not charities.
- Encouraging and facilitating the better administration of charities.

- Identifying and investigating apparent misconduct or mismanagement in the administration of charities and taking remedial or protective action in connection with misconduct or mismanagement in the administration of charities.
- Determining whether public collections certificates should be issued, and remain in force, in respect of public charitable collections.
- Obtaining, evaluating and disseminating information in connection with the performance of any of the Commission's functions or meeting any of its objectives (This function includes maintaining the register of charities).
- Giving information or advice, or making proposals, to any Minister of the Crown on matters relating to any of the Commission's functions or meeting any of its objectives.

OSCR

Charity law in Scotland is governed by the Charities and Trustee Investment (Scotland) Act 2005. The Office of the Scottish Charity Regulator (OSCR) is a department of the Scottish Government with responsibility for the regulation of charities in Scotland. OSCR is a non-ministerial department. It is directly answerable to the Scottish Parliament but not to either Ministers or the Scottish Government. It is the equivalent of the Charity Commission for England and Wales. Charity regulation was previous carried out by the Scottish Charities Office, a department in the Crown Office, but this function was transferred to the OSCR in December 2003.

OSCR is the regulator and registrar for more than 23,000 Scottish charities and charities that are based elsewhere (e.g. England and Wales) but which also operate in Scotland – cross-border charities. Its functions are:

- Determining whether bodies are charities.
- Keeping a public register of charities.
- Facilitating compliance by charities with the legislation.
- Investigating any apparent misconduct in the administration of charities.
- Giving information or advice to Scottish Ministers.

Under the Charities and Trustee Investment (Scotland) Act 2005, all organisations who represent themselves as charities in Scotland must register with OSCR. This includes bodies that are established and/or registered as charities in other legal jurisdictions, such as England and Wales. (There are some exceptions where a cross-border charity does not have substantive activity in Scotland.)

Charities with substantive activity in Scotland need to apply for charitable status in Scotland, even if they are established in England and Wales. Cross-border charities need to submit their annual report and accounts to OSCR (within nine months of the financial year end) and also need to complete an Information Return form at the same time. The regulatory requirements of OSCR are slightly different to those of the Charity Commission, so cross-border charities need to be aware of these. Charities regulated by OSCR must seek its prior consent, 42 days before making the change, for the following changes:

- changing the name of the charity;
- amending the objects or purposes of the charity;
- merging the charity with another body;
- changing the charity's legal form; and
- winding up the charity.

It is also a requirement that OSCR is notified, within three months, of the following changes:

- change of the principal contact for the charity, or their contact details;
- change of accounting year end;
- changes to the constitution unrelated to the objects; and
- when any change consented by OSCR is implemented.

Finally, cross-border charities need to be aware that the charitable purposes in Scotland, as set out in the Charities and Trustee Investment (Scotland) Act 2005, are slightly different from those listed in the Charities Act 2011. In addition, the interpretation of charitable purposes by both OCSR and the Scottish courts can be slightly different from that in England and Wales. This means that some activities may be charitable in England and Wales, but not Scotland, and vice versa. To give an example, the legal requirements regarding sport are slightly different. In Scotland, public participation in sport must be promoted; the sport must involve physical skill and physical exertion. In England and Wales, the advancement of amateur sport means the advancement of any sports or games which promote health by involving physical *or mental skill* or exertion and which are undertaken on an *amateur* basis.

Northern Ireland Charity Commission

The Charities Act (Northern Ireland) 2008 established a Charity Commission for Northern Ireland (CCNI). It also introduced a new definition of 'charity' and 'charitable purpose' for Northern Ireland. Like Scotland, the definition is slightly different to that in England in Wales, so an organisation can be charitable in one country, but not another.

The Charity Commission for Northern Ireland is currently setting up the register of charities. It has yet to decide on the specific regulatory requirements for cross-border charities.

Other regulators

Registered societies are regulated by the Financial Conduct Authority (FCA). The regulatory requirements are set out below. Charitable companies limited by guarantee are regulated by Companies House, in addition to the regulation by the Charity Commission. The regulatory requirements for a company are also set out below. Charitable chartered bodies are regulated by the Privy Council, in addition to regulation by the Charity Commission. However, the only form that this regulation takes is approval of changes to the charter and bylaws. A summary of regulators for different legal forms of charity is set out in Table 3.1.

Table 3.1: Regulators for different legal forms of charity

	Charity Commission	OSCR (if operating in Scotland)	CCNI (if operating in Northern Ireland)	FCA	Companies House	Privy Council
Trust	X	X	X			
Unincorporated members' association	X	X	X			
Company limited by guarantee	X	X	X		X	
Registered society		X	X	X		
Chartered body	X	X	X			X
Charitable incorporated organisation	X	X	X			
Statutory body	X	X	X			

Registration with the Charity Commission

In accordance with section 30(1) of the Charities Act 2006, a charity must register with the Charity Commission if:

(a) it is a charity in law (i.e. it must be established exclusively for purposes which are recognised as charitable in the law of England and Wales; and its purposes are for the benefit of the public (see Chapter 1));
(b) it has, or reasonably considers it will have, an annual income of at least £5,000; and
(c) it is not an exempt or excepted charity (see below).

There is no voluntary registration for charities with an annual income of less than £5,000, but a charity which is a CIO will be registered with the Charity

Commission regardless of its size. A charity applies for registration online, using the application form provided. Along with the application form the constitution of the charity must be provided, as well as a declaration signed by each trustee and evidence that the organisation either has or will have income of over £5,000. The application must demonstrate that the organisation's aims are charitable and for the public benefit.

A charity that wants to be a CIO will apply to take on this legal form and to be registered as a charity, as part of the same process. Other charities will need to establish their legal form first. So an organisation which wants to be a charitable company limited by guarantee will first need to be registered as a company, and then apply to be registered as a charity. In addition, the Charity Commission will want to know with which bank the applicant organisation intends to open its account.

The Charity Commission assesses the initial application; if it then requires further information it will request it. For example, it may require copies of key policies; a business plan or information about fundraising. The Charity Commission will aim to respond as quickly as it can, but it may take some time. In addition, its initial response will often be a request for more information. Further questions may be asked. Whilst there are limits on the amount of information that charities can provide with their initial online application, they should ensure that their application is as full as possible.

CASE EXAMPLE

Seats for Schools was set up in 2014. Denise was a mother who liked the 'buddy seat' that was used in her son's playground, for children to sit on when they wanted someone to play with. She set up Seats for Schools to raise money and buy these seats. To help her to get a grant, in early 2015 she registered the organisation as a company limited by guarantee. It has a board of two trustees: Denise and a friend. She intended it to be charitable and the objects were 'To be charitable and provide buddy seats for children'. Seats for Schools received a grant of £10,000 and it set up a bank account for the company. Denise realised that it was now a legal requirement that Seats for Schools is registered with the Charity Commission. She submitted an application. The Charity Commission responded raising two issues. First, it asked that the objects be amended to give greater clarity to the charitable purpose. Second, it asked that more trustees be appointed, as it considered that a charity should have at least three trustees. The objects were amended to read 'To advance the education of primary school children by supporting their play and friendships'. Two more trustees were appointed. Denise resubmitted the application and the charity was registered.

If all the criteria for registration are satisfied, the Charity Commission will register the charity and provide a registered charity number. Whilst charity status is ultimately for the courts to determine, if the Commission determines that an organisation should not be registered as a charity, it is clearly a major setback for an organisation that sees itself as being a charity. If an organisation has its application turned down, it can seek to challenge the decision of the Charity Commission, either through its decision review process or via the First-Tier Tribunal (Charity).

Exempt charities

Historically, there were a number of charities that were either exempt or excepted from registration with the Charity Commission. These charities were required to comply with the general law relating to charities but they were not subject to regulation by the Charity Commission in the same way as registered charities. In addition, until the Charities Act 2006, the Charity Commission could not investigate suspected wrongdoing in an exempt charity, although an exempt charity was able to ask the commission for help or advice.

The Charities Act 2006 was intended to change the way that exempt charities were regulated, and to improve their compliance with charity law. It was intended that a charity would only be exempt from registration with the Charity Commission if it had another 'principal regulator' to regulate it as a charity. In addition, the Charity Commission now has a role in regard to investigations and inquiries, with the agreement of the regulator.

This was potentially quite a radical change in regard to exemption. Charities that were previously exempt were now meant to fall into two categories:

- those that would have a principal regulator assigned which would remain as exempt charities; and
- those without a principal regulator, which would now be required to register with the Charity Commission.

However, the Charity Commission could not manage to take on the registration of so many of the previously exempt charities, so these changes are being made over a period of time. At the present time, only those charities in the second category which have an income exceeding £100,000 per annum are required to register with the Charity Commission. Also, not all of the charities that will be in the first category have yet been assigned a principal regulator.

Note that, although they do not need to register, exempt charities still have to comply with general principles of charity law, such as trustees' duties.

As well as exempt charities, there are also excepted charities. These are charities that historically have been excepted from registration either by regulation or by Charity Commission order. These include some religious charities, scout and guide groups and some armed forces charities. These will all be required to register with the Charity Commission at some stage, but at the present time, registration is only required for those with a gross income in excess of £100,000 per annum.

Changing legal form

The primary reason why a charity changes legal form is to convert an unincorporated charity into an incorporated charity. At present, unincorporated charities most commonly incorporate as companies limited by guarantee or become a Charitable Incorporated Organisation (CIO).

Incorporating an unincorporated charity as a charitable company means setting up a charitable company; having it registered as a charity; and then transferring all of the assets (and liabilities) of the unincorporated charity to it. The process of incorporating an unincorporated charity as a CIO involves setting up and registering a CIO and transferring all of the assets (and liabilities) of the unincorporated charity to it.

When changing legal form, the trustees need to consider the following:

- *Is there the power to transfer?* Does the constitution of the unincorporated charity include the power to transfer the charity's assets? If no express power is provided, the constitution may need to be amended before any transfer can take effect.
- *Are there employees?* If this is a transfer of business to a new organisation the Transfer of Undertakings (Protection of Employment) Regulations 2006 (TUPE) will apply and all employees must be consulted about the transfer of their employment.
- *Does the charity have existing contracts and grants?* All of these contracts will need to be assigned and the existing terms of the contracts may not provide for this to happen without the agreement of the other party.
- *Does the charity have property?* Title in all of the charity's leasehold and freehold properties will need to be transferred. A landlord's consent will almost certainly be required to assign any leases.
- *Does the charity have permanent endowment?* If so, it may be necessary to appoint the new organisation as a trustee or a Charity Commission scheme may be required. An alternative is to retain the original charity as an associated charity of the new one, holding on to the permanent endowment.
- *Does the charity have substantial assets?* Where the incorporation involves the transfer of substantial non-cash property assets from an unincorporated charity to a new charitable company it is necessary to obtain prior written Charity Commission consent to the transaction. Under section 190 of the Companies Act 2006, the transfer of a substantial non-cash asset from an unincorporated charity to a charitable company; when one or more of the directors of the company are trustees of the unincorporated charity requires the approval of the members of the company. Section 201 of the 2011 Act states that the section 190 resolution is ineffective without Charity Commission consent.

- *Are the trustees of both the existing and new organisations the same?* When they are, there is potentially a conflict of interest regarding the transfer of the assets – as they are agreeing to transfer the assets to a organisation that they are trustees/directors of. This means that the Charity Commission's authority is usually needed to make the decision. If an application has been made for consent to a substantial non-cash asset under section 201 of the 2011 Act above, the Charity Commission regard this as sufficient approval; it will also authorise the conflict of interests. Otherwise, the Charity Commission will need to give authority by an order under section 105 of the 2011 Act.

The new body will need to be registered with the Charity Commission. Whilst the application process should be simpler than for a new charity, as there is a mechanism available for indicating that the new registration is to enable an existing charity to incorporate, a new charity registration number will still need to be assigned.

Regulatory requirements

Charity Commission

As well as maintaining the register of charities, the Charity Commission regulates charities on an ongoing basis, in the following ways:

Annual returns to Charity Commission

All charities with an income above £10,000 that are registered with the Charity Commission must complete and submit an annual return to the Charity Commission. The annual return is made up of a number of parts. The parts that need to be completed will depend upon the charity's income in the financial period that is being reported on.

Whilst charities with an income of £10,000 or less in the reporting period are not required to complete an annual return, they are asked by the Charity Commission to complete an annual update of the information that forms part of the charity's entry on the Register. Charities with an income above £25,001 must also submit their annual report and accounts. It should be noted that although only charities with an income greater than £25,000 submit their trustees' annual report and accounts to the Commission, all charities, regardless of their level of income, must prepare accounts and make these available to the Commission on request.

Annual returns and the trustees' annual reports and accounts must be completed and submitted within 10 months of the end of the charity's financial year. The Charity Commission publishes the compliance history of all charities on the register of charities. Much of the information given in annual updates and annual returns is made available on the Register of Charities, which is open to public inspection at the Charity Commission's office and on its website. This does not include trustees' addresses or dates of birth, but the names of the trustees, and summary data on the income and expenditure and financial history of the charity is available. Charities should regularly review their register entry to ensure that it is correct, and should bear in mind the data that is published when they prepare their annual report and accounts and the annual return.

Prior to 2014, charities with income of above £1 million also had to complete a much more detailed summary information return. This practice has ceased, although previous year's returns are still available on the Charity Commission website. However, from 2015, all charities now have to answer more questions in the annual return and many of their answers will be published on the register. The new question areas included:

- In the reporting period, how much income did you receive from:
  - contracts from central or local government to deliver services?
  - grants from central or local government?
- Does your charity have a policy on paying its staff?
- Has your charity reviewed its financial controls during the reporting period?

Charities are also encouraged to use the free text box to provide further information.

The format for annual returns for 2016 onwards has also recently changed, but remains broadly similar to that for 2015. One core change is that charities now need to complete the return in two completely separate sections. They must firstly check and confirm that all of the details held by the Commission are up to date. They then must access a separate annual return. Also, the financial information required from charities with an income of £500,000 and over now reflects the changes needed as a result of the new SORP. In December 2016 the Charity Commission began a consultation on potential further changes to the annual return format from 2017.

Electronic filing with the Charity Commission

The filing of annual returns is now done electronically and the Charity Commission no longer provides paper forms. The Charity Commission now also provides a range of services online, and prefers charities to update their details online and to communicate in this way. The details which are held by the Charity Commission that can be updated online are:

- activities of the charity;
- where the charity operates;
- contact details;
- trustees – name; address and date of birth;
- classification – what the charity does; how and to whom;
- financial year;
- main bank or building society details; and
- internet details (e.g. e-mail and website addresses).

To access the online services you will require the charity registration number and a password.

In accordance with the Charitable Incorporated Organisations (General) Regulations 2012 (SI 2012/3012), the trustees of a CIO must notify the Charity Commission of any changes to information held on the central register within 28 days. Whilst it is good practice for other charities to update their entries as soon as possible after any changes, there is not a direct legal requirement for them to do so.

The annual report and accounts can be submitted either in hard copy or electronically. If submitted electronically, the annual report and accounts must be in a PDF format and if submitted in this format the signatures do not need to appear on the document (provided that they have been signed and that you retain a signed copy). The Charity Commission actually recommends that you file the accounts in this way, to keep signatures secure.

Registered societies

Many charities that are registered as registered societies are exempt from registration with the Charity Commission and therefore do not need to submit annual returns to it. However, those societies are regulated by the Financial Conduct Authority (FCA) and there is a requirement to submit an annual return to it. The annual return must be submitted within seven months of the year end; failure to submit your return by the due date is an offence which may result in prosecution. It is the duty of the society's secretary to submit the annual return.

The annual return for a society is made up of two parts. Part 1 is available from the FCA. Part 2 is normally the annual accounts. However, societies not producing accounts to the minimum standard required by the FCA must also complete a supplementary return as Part 2 of the annual return. Other than the completion of the annual return there is no requirement for a society to inform the FCA of any changes in its trustees during the year. However, changes to the rules, including a change of name and change of registered office, must be filed with the FCA.

Charitable companies

Filing requirements

Charitable companies will also need to meet the Companies House regulation requirements. There are two types of filing requirements: annual filing requirements, and event-driven filing requirements.

Event-driven filing

There is a range of information that a charity that is a company will need to lodge with Companies House as and when events occur. These are:

- *Change of accounting reference date (i.e. financial year end):* Note that there are limits on how much an accounting reference date can be extended by and how often this can be done.
- *Change of registered office*: The change only becomes legally effective when Companies House has registered the form.
- *SAIL:* All registers may be held at the registered office address or at a single alternative inspection location (SAIL). Companies House must be notified if a company has set up a SAIL address or if the SAIL address has moved. A company may only have one SAIL address at a time. Once the address is set up, a company can move some or all registers to the SAIL address by notifying Companies House. A SAIL address is useful if the company's registers are maintained by an external provider (e.g. an outsourced company secretary).
- *Change of directors and secretary and their details:* Any change of a company's directors or secretaries must be notified to Companies House within 14 days of the change. The company must also make a statement of truth that the person has consented to be a director/company secretary. The Registrar of Companies will write to directors following their appointment. Directors will be able to object to their names being on the public register if they assert that they are not, in fact, a director of the company. The letter from the registrar will also include details of directors' general statutory duties. Note that changes to existing directors' or secretary's' details must also be filed (e.g. if they change residential address).
- *Allotments of shares:* If your company has shares (e.g. if it is a trading subsidiary) Companies House must be notified of an allotment of shares within one month of the allotment of shares.
- *Change of articles:* You must send copies of the special resolution passed to change the articles, or adopt new ones, along with a copy of the revisions to Companies House within 15 days of them being passed by the company. If you do not comply with this requirement you will commit an offence and could be liable to a civil penalty of £200. This is in addition to any liability to criminal proceedings.
- *Mortgages and charges:* Details of every mortgage or charge created by the company and requiring registration must be sent to Companies House within 21 days of its creation.

Electronic filing with Companies House

Any submission of information to Companies House forms can be done by downloading and completing the relevant form in Adobe's PDF file format. (You will then need to print it and return it by post.) In addition, Companies House provides an electronic filing service (WebFiling) for the vast majority of its event-driven and annual forms. This enables you to file the information online.

To use WebFiling you must first register for a security code (which is e-mailed to you) and next register for an authentication code for the company (which is posted to the company's registered office address). If you are filing for more than one company – you will be issued with one personal security code and then a different authentication code for each company. You can change your personal security code if you wish.

Companies House usually accepts documents that are filed in this way very quickly. However, electronically filed documents are covered by the same five-day processing targets as paper documents. This should be taken account of when filing documents close to a deadline (e.g. confirmation statements). All electronically filed documents will be acknowledged by an acceptance or rejection message e-mailed by Companies House to the sender.

CASE EXAMPLE

Seats for Schools has appointed two new trustees. One of its existing trustees has changed occupation. The details of the new trustees, and the change of occupation, all need to be notified to Companies House within 14 days. Denise has set up the company for electronic filing, so she can log on using her personal security code and the company's authentication code. She also takes the opportunity to notify the Charity Commission of the new appointments, adding them to the list of trustees that is held on the Register of Charities. She also does this online.

Confirmation statement – companies

In addition to the requirement to submit an annual return to the Charity Commission, all charitable companies also need to submit a confirmation statement to Companies House. They need to submit such a statement, confirming that all of the information held by Companies House is correct, at least once each year. A fee of £13 applies. They can make the statement at any time during the year, or even more than once, e.g. every time they file a change with Companies House, but they will only be charged once each year.

The confirmation statement covers:

- the name of the company;
- its registered number;
- the type of company it is, for example, private or public;
- the registered office address of the company;
- the address where the company keeps certain company registers if not at the registered office;
- the principal business activities of the company (which must be stated in accordance with a prescribed classification system based on the Standard Industrial Classification). If the classification cannot be determined, a brief verbal description of the company's principal business activity or activities may instead be given;

- the name and address of the company secretary, where applicable;
- the name, usual residential address, service address; date of birth, nationality and business occupation of all the company's directors;

Unlike with the Charity Commission, the latest date that the confirmation statement is due is not governed by the accounting reference date, but by the date of the formation of the company. Whilst the last confirmation statement date can be changed, this must be done before the due date. A confirmation statement must be filed with the Registrar within 14 days of the date of the last due date.

Annual report and accounts

Companies are also required to file their annual report and accounts with Companies House within nine months of the accounting reference date. There is an automatic late filing penalty if the accounts are not filed on time, and Companies House also now moves quite quickly to strike off any company with overdue accounts.

Charity Commission investigations and inquiries

Statutory objectives and functions

The objectives and functions set out at the beginning of this chapter are the key to the Charity Commission's role in investigations and inquiries. Firstly, its statutory objectives 1 and 3 – to promote public trust and confidence in charities and to ensure that trustees comply with their legal obligations in managing charities. Secondly, its statutory function to identify and investigate apparent misconduct or mismanagement in the administration of charities and taking remedial or protective action in connection with misconduct or mismanagement in the administration of charities.

The Charities Act 2011 gives the Charity Commission a number of powers. Section 46 gives it the power to 'institute inquiries with regard to charities or a particular charity or class of charities, either generally or for particular purposes'. This power applies to all charities, but in the case of exempt charities, 'no such inquiry is to extend to any exempt charity except where this has been requested by its principal regulator'. A formal inquiry can involve one particular charity or a class of charities. The Charity Commission also has the choice of carrying out the inquiry itself or appointing any other person to conduct the inquiry on its behalf.

The Charity Commission has also now gained additional powers under the Charities (Protection and Social Investment) Act 2016.

When the Charity Commission has concerns about a charity, or receives allegations its first step is to consider the level of risk and whether it should take steps to intervene. It has a risk framework to which it refers to determine whether a statutory inquiry should be opened, and if not, whether some other type of intervention is required. The Charity Commission identifies three different types of investigation and inquiry. These are:

- *Operational compliance cases*: This is the most common type of action. These cases are not formal investigations, but the Charity Commission can still use certain powers (e.g. to require charities to provide information or documents). The cases are usually concluded by the Charity Commission providing regulatory advice to the trustees, or instructing the trustees to fulfil an action plan.
- *Pre-investigation assessment cases*: This is when the Charity Commission examines whether the issue meets the requirements for the opening of a formal investigation (statutory inquiry).
- *Statutory inquiries:* This is for the cases with the highest risk and where the concerns are most serious. When it opens a statutory inquiry the Charity Commission can use the full range of enforcement powers including appointing an interim manager or suspending a trustees.

The Charity Commission considers what action to take by reviewing its Risk Framework. It says within this that it aims to be 'proportionate, accountable, consistent, transparent' and to use its resources in the most effective way. Having said all this, the Charity Commission is placing more emphasis on taking action against charities, and the number of investigations and inquiries are increasing. In 2014–2015, 1,569 charities were subject to an investigation. During this period, the Charity Commission used its compliance powers 1,200 times compared to 212 times in 2012–2013. In 2014–2015, the Charity Commission placed 109 charities under inquiry, compared to 64 inquiries the previous year, and only 15 the year before that.

Charity Commission powers

The powers that the Charity Commission will use in regard to investigations and inquiries fall into three areas, as set out in its 2015 report 'Tackling abuse and mismanagement'. The Charities (Protection and Social Investment) Act 2016 has also given the Commission additional powers.

Information-gathering powers

The 2011 Act gives the Commission quite wide information-gathering powers, including the power to obtain search warrants (s. 48) and the power to call for documents (s. 52). The Charity Commission has the power to direct any person to give written accounts and statements on the matter under investigation; to return answers in writing to questions posed; and to verify any accounts, statement or answers by making a statutory declaration. It also has the power to enter premises; to seize documents, computer disks and other electronic storage devices; to take copies and to require any person on the premises to explain any such document or information or to state where they may be found. To exercise this power the Charity Commission must first obtain a magistrate's warrant.

Temporary protective powers

Once a statutory inquiry has been instigated, the Charity Commission has the following protective powers under section 76 of the 2011 Act:

- to suspend trustees, officers, employees or agents of the charity from their duties;
- to appoint additional trustees;
- to vest any of the charity's property in the Official Custodian for Charities;
- to freeze the charity's assets and bank accounts;
- to restrict any of the charity's transactions;
- to appoint an interim manager, who acts as receiver and manager of the property and the affairs of the charity (the Charity Commission maintains a panel of experts approved to carry out this role);
- to remove and replace trustees (ss 79 and 80); and
- to issue an order directing a trustee, officer or employee of the charity, or the charity itself to take any action which the Charity Commission considers to be expedient in the interests of the charity (s. 84). The Charity Commission cannot order any action which would be unlawful or inimical to the charity's trusts or purposes.

These powers enable the Charity Commission to take steps to protect charity property at risk for a temporary period while it continues investigating a matter. Before it exercises any of its powers under sections 76, 79 or 84 of the 2011 Act, the Charity Commission must be satisfied either:

- that there is or has been misconduct or mismanagement in the administration of the charity; or
- that it is necessary or desirable to act in order to protect the property of the charity or to ensure that any property the charity has or is due to receive is properly applied for its charitable purposes.

It is a criminal offence (punishable by a fine and/or imprisonment for up to two years) to knowingly or recklessly provide the Charity Commission with information which is false or misleading in a material particular or to wilfully alter, supress, conceal or destroy any document required to be produced to the Charity Commission.

The Charities (Protection and Social Investment) Act 2016 has now extended the Commission powers once it has opened a statutory inquiry into a charity. Now, when an inquiry has been opened the Charity Commission can:

- when considering what further action to take, it can now take into account not only misconduct or mismanagement but also failure to comply with an order or direction of the Commission and/or failure to remedy a breach specified in an official warning;

- take into account not only conduct in relation to the charity itself, but also wider conduct which does not necessarily relate to the charity concerned; and
- suspend a charity trustee, agent or employee for up to 24 months.

Remedial powers

These powers enable the Charity Commission to implement long-term solutions to any issues identified by an inquiry. These powers include:

- Suspending or terminating the membership of a trustee, officer, agent or employee of a charity and prohibiting resumption of membership without the Charity Commission's approval (although this power can only be exercised where the Charity Commission has suspended or removed that person from being a trustee, officer, agent or employee of the charity (Charities Act 2006, s. 83). (This power can only be used in the context of a formal inquiry.)
- Directing that a charity's property can be used or transferred in a particular way if those in control of it refuse to use or apply the charity's property for the purposes of the charity (Charities Act 2006, s. 85). (This power can be exercised by the Charity Commission irrespective of whether a formal inquiry has been instigated.)
- In addition to these powers, the Charities (Protection and Social Investment) Act 2016 has also now given the Charity Commission the power to remove a trustee following a statutory inquiry, even if the trustee resigns before the removal takes effect. The Act has also extended the Commission's existing powers to give directions to charities to take specific action once it has opened an inquiry so that the Commission will also be able to direct a charity not to take specified action. Finally, the Commission is now also able to wind up a charity following a statutory inquiry.

Although the number of investigations has increased, it is still the case that in the majority of cases, a matter will be dealt with by the Charity Commission providing advice to the charity. The Commission will usually only intervene in circumstances where it considers that:

- it needs to be involved;
- the nature and level of risk deem intervention necessary; and
- its intervention is the most effective response in the circumstances.

The types of matter that the Charity Commission will intervene in are:

- matters causing significant financial loss to the charity;
- matters causing serious harm to beneficiaries and, in particular, vulnerable beneficiaries;
- activities which threaten national security, particularly terrorism;
- criminality within or involving a charity;
- setting up of sham charities for an illegal or improper purpose;

- individuals deliberately using charities for significant private advantage;
- activities that seriously call a charity's independence into question;
- serious compliance breaches within a charity that could damage its reputation and/or the reputation of charities generally; and/or
- serious non-compliance in a charity which, left unchecked, could damage public trust and confidence in the Charity Commission as an effective regulator.

Once an inquiry has concluded, the Charity Commission may publish the results of its investigation in a report or make a statement. Reports are usually published on the Charity Commission's website. The organisation involved will usually be given an opportunity to review and make representations on the draft report before it is published.

Charities (Protection and Social Investment) Act 2016

In addition to the powers set out above, this Act also gives the Commission the following powers

- Power to disqualify trustees. The Charity Commission may only exercise this power if it is satisfied that the person is unfit to be a charity trustee; that disqualification is in the public interest in order to protect public trust and confidence in charities; and that at least one of a list of conditions has been satisfied. The conditions include:
  - the person having been cautioned for an offence which would trigger automatic disqualification if convicted;
  - the person having been convicted overseas for certain offences which would trigger automatic disqualification if convicted in the United Kingdom;
  - HMRC has decided that the person is not a 'fit and proper person' to be manager of a charity under tax legislation;
  - the person having been involved in misconduct or mismanagement of a charity; or
  - the person having displayed any other past or continuing conduct, whether in relation to a charity or not, which the Commission considers may be damaging to public trust and confidence in charities. (It is this last final condition that some have argued is potentially too wide.)

  Whilst the use of these powers may arise in connection with an investigation, or an inquiry, they are powers that can be used by the Commission at any time provided the conditions are met. The Commission is also able to suspend a trustee while it is considering whether to make an order. Disqualification can last for up to 15 years.
- Power to issue written warnings. The Commission is now able to issue an 'official warning' to charities or charity trustees where it believes there has been misconduct or mismanagement, or a breach of trust or duty. There is no need for an inquiry to have been opened. If the Commission intends to issue

a warning to a charity or its trustees it must give prior notice of its intention, and allow them to make representations. The notice must specify what the Commission considers should be done to rectify the position, although the power cannot be used to issue directions to a charity.

The significant feature of this power is that once a warning has been issued, the Commission is able to publicise it. Receiving a warning could mean significant reputational damage for a charity. While a warning can be amended or withdrawn there is no right of appeal to the Charity Tribunal. The Charity Commission intends to publish guidance on how it will use the new warning power.

Power to disclose information about charities

As well as the powers set out above, the Charity Commission also has the power:

- to share information about charities with other public bodies (such as local authorities, the police, HMRC or any other government department) and such public bodies have the power to disclose information to the Charity Commission to assist it in the discharge of its functions; and
- to disclose information to and receive information from the principal regulators of exempt charities.

(Charities Act 2011, ss 56–58.)

Other enabling powers

The Charity Commission's powers are not restricted to investigations and inquiries. The Charities Act 2011 gives the Charity Commission the following powers to assist charities:

- *Power to authorise dealings with charity property, etc. (s. 105)*: The Charity Commission has the power to issue an order to sanction any action proposed or contemplated by the charity which it considers is expedient in the interests of the charity. This means that the Charity Commission can authorise a particular transaction or give a more general authority. Under its new Risk Framework, the Charity Commission will usually only give permissions under section 105 where the matter is outside the trustees' powers.
- *Power to establish schemes: (s. 67)*: The Charity Commission can establish schemes for the application of a charity's property *cy-près*. This means 'as near as possible to the testator's or donor's intentions when these cannot be precisely followed'. Essentially, this power is intended to cover situations where a charity has objects that can no longer be followed, or a restricted fund that it can no longer use.

The Charity Commission will now only create *cy-près* schemes to amend a charity's objects where the trustees cannot amend their purposes under their own powers (with or without Charity Commission consent) or under section 275(2) of the 2011 Act.

Before establishing a scheme, the Charity Commission must give public notice of its proposal to make it and invite representations to be made within the period specified in the notice. (Although, in certain circumstances, the Charity Commission may determine that it is unnecessary to give public notice.) If a scheme is to remove a trustee, officer, agent or employee of a charity without his or her consent, the Charity Commission must, before sealing the scheme, give the individual concerned at least one month's notice of its proposals (unless that person cannot be found or has no known address in the UK).

- *Power to authorise* ex gratia *payments (s. 106)*: This is a payment made by a charity where the trustees believe that they are under a moral obligation to make the payment; but they are not under any legal obligation to make it; the trustees cannot justify the payment as being in the interests of the charity. In these circumstances, the Charity Commission has the power to authorise trustees to waive the charity's right to receive property or to enable the trustees to apply the charity's property in circumstances where they have no power to do so, but they consider they have a moral obligation to do so.
- *Power to give advice and guidance (s. 110)*: The Charity Commission can assist any trustee who applies in writing for its opinion or advice (e.g. on the performance of his or her duties as a trustee or about how his or her charity should be properly administered). A trustee who follows the Charity Commission's opinion or advice, acting in good faith, is protected from any breach of trust claim. However, although it has this power, in recent years the Charity Commission has been reluctant to give out such advice.
- *Power to determine membership of charities (s. 111)*: The Charity Commission has the power to determine who the members of a charity are.

The Charities (Protection and Social Investment) Act 2016 extends the powers of the Charity Commission.

Challenging Charity Commission decisions

Decision review procedure

The two main ways in which you can challenge a decision of the Charity Commission are either:

- through its decision review procedure; or
- through the First-tier Tribunal (Charity)(referred to in this chapter as 'the Tribunal').

In some instances you may also be able to challenge it through the courts, but these are the two primary routes. There is no requirement that you engage in the Commission's decision review procedure before appealing to the Tribunal. However, you still have the option of taking the matter to the Tribunal if you have already used the decision review procedure.

You can request that the Charity Commission reviews any decision which is subject to review by the First-tier Tribunal (Charity) (as set out in Schedule 6 to the Charities Act) and any decision either to exercise or not to exercise a legal power. However, this procedure cannot be used to review a decision to grant consent to a charity. Once consent is given, only the tribunal or court can overturn it. So, for example, these processes cannot be used to challenge a Charity Commission's decision to register a charity, but they could be used to challenge a decision not to register a charity.

The Charity Commission may also refuse to conduct a review for a number of reasons. If this happens, you may still be able to challenge the decision in the Tribunal or the courts.

The Charity Commission provides an online form to apply for a decision review. The time limit for applying for a decision review is usually within three months of the original decision, but it can be extended in exceptional circumstances.

The Charity Commission aims to complete the review within three months, but it says that in most cases it is able to complete its reviews more quickly. If you are dissatisfied with the Charity Commission's decision at the end of the review, you may be able to apply to the Tribunal. As with a referral of an original decision (see below) the application should be made to the Tribunal within 42 days of the date on which the notice of the commission's decision was sent to you or published. The Charity Commission may publish a summary of its decision review on its website.

The First-tier Tribunal (Charity)

Prior to the Charities Act 2006, the only way in which it was possible to challenge decisions of the Charity Commission (other than its internal complaints procedures) was to bring an appeal to the High Court. However, the Charities Act 2006 provided a new route for challenging a decision of the Charity Commission: The First-tier Tribunal (Charity). This is now contained in Part 17 of the 2011 Charities Act.

The Tribunal is an independent legal body. It has the power to review decisions made by the Charity Commission. It can revoke, change or amend the decisions and can also direct the Charity Commission to take further action. Schedule 6 of the 2011 Act includes a detailed table setting out which decisions, directions or orders of the Charity Commission are subject to appeal or review by the Tribunal.

The following can, in most instances, bring proceedings before the Tribunal:

- the charity trustees;
- the charity itself;

- any other person who is or may be affected by the decision; and
- the Attorney General, acting as the protector of charities on behalf of the Crown.

In addition, both the Charity Commission and the Attorney General may refer questions of law to the Tribunal. An application to the Tribunal must be received within 42 days of the date on which the notice of the Charity Commission's decision was given; or within 42 days of the date on which the decision was published. The Tribunal aims to complete all of its cases within 30 weeks.

It is free to make an application to the Tribunal. However, most charities take legal advice, and this can mean that high costs are involved. The Tribunal has a power to make a costs order if it concludes that a party has acted unreasonably in bringing, defending or conducting the proceedings or if it considers that the Charity Commission's decision, direction or order was unreasonable. However, aside from costs orders, the Tribunal has no power to award compensation to charities for losses caused by a decision of the Charity Commission which is subsequently overturned. Any party can appeal Charity Tribunal decisions to the High Court, with the consent of the Charity Tribunal or of the High Court itself.

CASE EXAMPLE

Competitive Hugging is an organisation that was set up in 2001. It arranges hugging competitions across England – with medals being given for length of hug; complexity of hold; and level of comfort. The organisation applied for registration with the Charity Commission, but was turned down. The Charity Commission did not consider that it was charitable, and gave quite a complex response regarding the definition of amateur sport. Competitive Hugging wanted to challenge the decision, but had too few resources to take on legal advice. It, therefore, took this matter back to the Charity Commission, via its decision-review procedure. The result of this was that the Charity Commission did not vary its decision. However, whilst the review was ongoing, the organisation made contact with Competitive Kissing. Its charity registration application had been turned down for similar reasons. The organisations decided to pool their resources, and refer the matter to the Tribunal. The outcome is still awaited.

Records and registers

Legal form of charity

Many charities keep registers of information such as a list of their members, their trustees; and records of meetings. There are various legal requirements regarding such registers depending on the type of legal form the charity takes. Charities that are CIOs, companies limited by guarantee or registered societies are required to keep registers (we shall not be dealing with this requirement for registered societies in this text). The requirements for other charities will be set out in their constitutions. For a charity that is established under a trust deed, it is quite common for no registers to be required. Even if this is the case, it may still be advisable to keep a register of trustees to assist the record keeping of the charity. For membership charities, the most common constitutional requirement is for a register of members to be maintained. The constitution may also require a register of trustees to be kept and sometimes a register of secretaries, mirroring company law. For charities that are not companies, there is no legal right of access to the registers by the members or by the general public unless this is specified in the constitution.

CIOs

Under Regulation 26 of the Charitable Incorporated Organisations (General) Regulations 2012 every association CIO must keep a register of members and a register of charity trustees. Every foundation CIO must keep a register of charity trustees (who are also the members of the CIO). Schedule 1 of the Regulations sets out the requirements for these registers. In addition, a CIO must keep proceedings at general meetings of the CIO; meetings of the charity trustees and committees of charity trustees; and a record of decisions made by the charity trustees otherwise than in meetings (regs 37–45). The records must be kept for a minimum of six years from the date of the meeting, resolution or appointment. They can be kept in electronic form, but must be able to be reproduced in hard copy form (reg. 46).

Schedule 1 of The Charitable Incorporated Organisations (General) Regulations 2012 states that anyone can inspect or ask for a copy of all or part of the register of trustees kept by a CIO, on payment of a reasonable fee to cover the costs of providing the information. A trustee or member of the CIO can inspect or ask for a copy of all or part of the register of trustees without payment if the request is made either:

- for the purposes of carrying out the requester's duties as a charity trustee or member of a CIO; or
- the request is to inspect or be provided with a copy of the requester's entry in the register.

A member or charity trustee of a CIO can inspect or request a copy of all or part of the register of members where:

- the request is for the purpose of carrying out the requester's duties as a member or trustee; or
- the requester wants to inspect or see a copy of their entry on the register.

Charitable companies

The Companies Act 2006 is very prescriptive about the registers that must be kept; what information they must contain; how they are kept and the rights of public access to the registers. This Act requires every company to keep the following:

- a register of members (s.113);
- a register of directors (i.e. trustees in a charitable company) (s.162);
- a register of directors' residential addresses (s. 163);
- a register of secretaries (s. 275); and
- a register of charges (s. 876)

Under the Small Business, Enterprise and Employment Act 2015 companies are also now required to keep a register of people who have significant control over the company (see below).

Registers

Location and format

If the charity is a company, there are legal requirements as to where the registers are kept: this is usually its registered office. For other charities, this may be a requirement of the constitution. For companies, if the registers are not to be kept at the registered office they may be kept at 'a single alternative inspection location' (or SAIL).

Private companies, which will include all charitable companies, now also have the option of keeping any of their registers at Companies House. This is a very recent change. When a company exercises this option it will be required to keep the information currently required to be in its company register up to date on the public register instead (i.e. at Companies House). All the information currently available for inspection on the company register would then be publicly available on the public register.

Whilst holding the registers at Companies House may seen like a simple solution, it needs to be remembered that to do so usually requires the consent of those affected. So, a company can, on incorporation, agree for its register of members to be kept in this way, by all of its subscribers agreeing. If the company is already incorporated, it can hold its register at Companies House, but only if all of its members agree.

Again, with a register of persons with significant control, its retention at Companies House can be agreed at incorporation. After that time a company can elect to hold it there but only if has given notice to the persons on the register at least 14 days before the date of the election and none of them have objected in that time.

For the registers of directors; directors' residential addresses; and the register of secretaries it is a little bit simpler. A company can elect at any time to have the registers held at Companies House and there is not the same need for complete consent. So, if the board voted by a majority to keep these registers in this way, it would be a valid decision.

The ability to hold registers at Companies House only came into effect in 2016, and it is not as readily available an option as it at first seemed. It seems likely that few charitable companies will make the change at this time. As well as the difficulties re obtaining consent is the fact that for a company limited by guarantee, deciding to hold the register of members at Companies House would mean a bigger change. Shareholding companies are required to provide the names of their shareholders to Companies House annually. This does not currently apply for guarantee company members, so it would mean beginning to provide this information for the first time.

When held by the charity, the statutory registers and books can be kept in either electronic or hard copy form. However, there are requirements that must be met for companies regarding the security of the registers and this may make hard copy form a better option for most charitable companies. Section 1138 of the Companies Act requires that where company records are kept otherwise than in bound books, adequate precautions must be taken to guard against falsification, and to facilitate the discovery of falsification. If a hard copy is kept, bound books (and loose-leaf registers) are available from most legal stationers. A bound book is the most secure format; where the register is not kept in a bound book, adequate precautions must be taken. As a basic measure, the registers should be kept in a secure cabinet to which access is restricted. It is also possible for statutory registers and books to be kept on computer or in other non-legible form provided, again, that adequate precautions are taken for guarding against falsification and facilitating their discovery and, in addition, that they are capable of being reproduced in legible hard copy form (s. 1135(2)).

If the charitable company has a large membership, it may be preferable for it to keep the register of members on a computer. However, any software used for this purpose must provide adequate security for such data. It is unlikely that a standard computer program will contain the security elements required and so whilst it may seem simpler to keep an electronic copy, this could cause difficulties in meeting the legal obligations regarding security and if the register needs to be relied upon as evidence. Charities with a smaller membership may find it easier to maintain the register by manual methods using standardised bound books. If an electronic copy is maintained it is advisable to print out and retain a hard copy record on each occasion that the register is added to.

Contents of registers – charitable companies

Register of members

Section 113 of the Companies Act 2006 states that the following information must be held on the register:

- the names and addresses of the members;
- the date on which each person was registered as a member; and
- the date at which any person ceased to be a member.

If the company has a share capital (e.g. this may apply to a trading subsidiary) there must be entered in the register a statement of the shares held by each member, distinguishing each share by its number (as long as the share has a number) and where the company has more than one class of issued shares, by its class, the amount paid or agreed to be considered as paid on the shares of each member. If the company does not have a share capital but has more than one class of members (as is the case in some companies limited by guarantee), there must be entered in the register, with the names and addresses of the members, a statement of the class to which each member belongs. If the register contains more than 50 names it must be accompanied by an index of the members. If there is only one member (as is commonly the case for subsidiary companies) the register of members must contain a statement to this effect.

Register of directors

Section 163 of the Companies Act 2006 requires that a company's register of directors (i.e. the trustees in a charitable company) must contain the following information (SI 2007/3495, Sch. 4, para. 2, as amended by SI 2008/674, Sch. 3, para. 6):

- name and any former name of the director;
- a service address (and this may be stated to be 'the company's registered office');
- the country or state (or part of the United Kingdom) in which he is usually resident;
- nationality;
- business occupation (if any); and
- date of birth.

Although it is not specified as a requirement, the register should also include for each director the date on which he or she became a director or the date on which they ceased to be a director.

Register of directors' residential addresses

Under the Companies Act 2006, a company must also keep a register of directors' residential addresses. The register must state the usual residential address of each of the company's directors. The requirement to keep such a register applies even when the register of directors only has the director's residential addresses as their service addresses. Section 165 of the Companies Act 2006 states that if a director's usual residential address is the same as his service address (as stated in the company's register of directors) the register of directors' residential addresses need only contain an entry to that effect. The register will still need to be kept.

Register of secretaries

If the charitable company has a secretary, it should maintain a register of secretaries that should include the name and address of the secretary. Unlike the register of directors the addresses of secretaries have never needed to be residential addresses and there is also no need for a separate register of residential addresses for secretaries. As with the register of directors, it should also include the date the person was appointed as the secretary and the date on which they ceased to be the secretary.

Register of charges

Every company, including every charitable company, is required to keep a register of charges (whether or not it has any entries made in it). For many charitable companies this may mean keeping an empty register. If there are any charges on the register, it is also a legal requirement for the company to keep at its registered office a copy of every instrument creating a charge requiring registration.

Persons of significant control (PSC) register

Under the Small Business, Enterprise and Employment Act 2015 companies are also now required to keep a register of people who have significant control over the company. This list will also need to be filed at Companies House annually. It needs to include individuals who directly or indirectly own or control 25% of voting rights or shares (for share companies) in the company; individuals who directly or indirectly have control over the appointment and removal of the majority of the company's board of directors; or who otherwise have significant influence over the company. So this requirement impacts on wholly owned trading subsidiaries; some companies where certain parties have rights to appoint board members; and companies with fewer than five members. The information that must be kept on the register is similar to the register of directors. It includes

- name;
- date of birth;
- nationality;
- country, state or part of the UK where the PSC usually lives;
- service address;
- usual residential address (which must not be disclosed when making your register available for inspection or providing copies of the PSC register);
- the date he or she became a PSC in relation to the company (for existing companies 6 April 2016 should be used); and
- which conditions for being a PSC are met (i.e. what makes them a person of significant control).

Inspection of the registers – companies

The registers of charitable companies are open to inspection by any member of the public as the Companies Act gives a right of inspection for all of them (with the exception of the register of director's residential addresses).

The register of the directors; secretaries and charges are available for inspection by any member of the company without a charge (and any creditor for the register of charges) and by any other person on payment of a prescribed fee.

Companies also need to make their PSC register available for inspection on request at the company's registered office or provide copies on request. When making the PSC register available for inspection or providing copies of it the PSC's usual residential address must not be included.

The register of members is also open to inspection by any member free of charge or by any other person on payment of such fee as may be prescribed. Under the Companies Act 2006, access to the register of members can be restricted to requests that are for 'a proper purpose' (s. 117). A person wishing to inspect or obtain copies of the register of members must give details about themselves and explain the purpose for which the information is to be used. A company cannot refuse to give access itself, but it can apply to the court for such a refusal. It must do this within five working days of receiving the request. If the court considers that the request has not been made 'for a proper purpose' it will direct the company not to comply with it. Also, if the court considers that further requests for a similar purpose are likely to be made (whether or not made by the same person) the court may give an overall direction that the company is not to comply with any such requests.

The 2006 Act gives no guidance on the meaning of the term 'proper purpose' – that is for the courts to determine. However, the ICSA has a Guidance Note *Access to the Register of Members: The proper purpose test*. This gives an analysis of matters that may in practice be reasonably considered to be proper or improper purposes, and is likely to be of assistance in such scenarios. In addition in 2014, in *Burry & Knight Limited & Another v Knight* the Court of Appeal considered, for the first time, the prevention of access to a company's register of members under section 117 of the Companies Act 2006. Some of the conclusions of that case were:

- Where a request is made for multiple purposes, and some are proper and some are not, the company does not have to provide access to the register.
- Where it is a member of the company, rather than a member of the public, who is requesting access to, a proper purpose ought generally to relate to the member's interest in that capacity.
- If a member is seeking access in order to communicate with other members, the court will exercise its discretion sparingly, as it requires a strong case to prevent access.

- Courts might have regard to guidance published by ICSA, although it is neither binding nor exhaustive.

Other registers and records

A charity will also be required to keep other statutory records. A charity that has employees will be required to keep records regarding PAYE, National Insurance, pensions and employment records. Charities also have to keep records regarding Health and Safety, insurance and VAT (if VAT registered).

Minutes

Charitable company

The keeping of minutes of the board, the general meetings and committees will often be a requirement of the constitution. It is also the clear recommendation of the Charity Commission that such records are kept for the lifetime of the charity.

If the charity is a company, there are also legal requirements set out in the Companies Act 2006:

- minutes must be kept of all general meetings for 10 years (s. 355);
- minutes must be kept of all board meetings and board committee meetings for 10 years (s. 248);
- records of all written resolutions of the board must also be kept for 10 years (s. 248) as must all records of written resolutions of the members, also for 10 years (s. 355).

CIO

If the charity is a CIO, the Charitable Incorporated Organisations (General) Regulations 2012 state that the CIO must keep the following records:

- appointments of officers made by the charity trustees;
- proceedings at general meetings of the CIO;
- meetings of the charity trustees and committees of charity trustees; and
- decisions made by the charity trustees otherwise than in meetings.

These records must all be kept for a minimum of six years from the date of the meeting, resolution or appointment.

Retention and inspection of minutes

Although the legal requirement is for minutes of companies to be kept for 10 years and for CIOs for six years, it is recommended practice to retain them for the life of the charity. In addition, it may be necessary to retain agenda papers if these are necessary to understand the minutes.

The Companies Act 2006 makes no provision for the inspection of minutes by anyone other than the auditors. However, under common law, a director has a right to inspect company minutes and a member of a company also has the right to inspect the minutes of general meetings. Members, or the general public, have no right to inspect board or committee minutes unless this is given to them by the constitution. For a CIO, a member has the right to inspect the record of members' decisions, free of charge, or to obtain a copy on the payment of a reasonable fee.

A minute book should to be used to keep a copy of all the original minutes as signed by the chair of the meeting (or the next meeting). Copies of minutes can be stored on a computer, but see the comments below regarding the issue of the minutes as evidence.

Minutes can be authenticated by the chairman of the meeting or by the chairman of the next meeting by their signature. For charitable companies or CIOs minutes signed by the chair of the meeting at which the business was transacted or by the chair of the next succeeding meeting (or by the secretary in the case of resolutions of members) are evidence of the proceedings. When minutes have been signed in this way, the meeting is deemed to have been duly convened and held, and the proceedings duly transacted unless the contrary is proved (Companies Act 2006, ss 249 and 356; Charitable Incorporated Organisations (General) Regulations 2012, reg. 38.2).

A charity may choose to keep its minute books in computerised form; however, this could reduce their value as evidence. If minutes are tendered in legal proceedings as evidence of the proceedings of a meeting, their evidential value could be undermined if there is any doubt as to whether they were signed by the chairman. The law is still rather unclear on this matter, and the wording of the Civil Evidence Act 1995 does imply that an original document is not the only admissible evidence in a civil court. Electronic copies of documents could be acceptable as long as their integrity can be shown. This means that, at the very least, the electronic copy should be a pdf, unalterable, copy of the signed minutes; including the signature. A word copy of the minutes as drafted will not be sufficient.

Signed minutes are *prima facie* evidence of the proceedings, but they can be set aside by the court if inaccuracies can subsequently be established.

Annual report and accounts

Accounting records

Charities have a legal obligation to maintain accounting records. The source of the legal duty to keep accounting records depends on whether or not the charity is a company. All charities that are not companies are governed by Part 8 of the Charities Act 2011. Charities registered under the Companies Acts are governed by section 386 of the Companies Act 2006. If the charity is registered for VAT it must also keep VAT records.

Transparency regarding annual report and accounts

There are also a number of legal requirements regarding charities' obligations to make their report and accounts available to the public, and to circulate them to members.

Format and content of annual report and accounts

All charities (including exempt charities) must prepare annual accounts and make them available on request. In addition, all registered charities must prepare a trustees' annual report and also make this available on request.

The format for a charity's accounts depends on the size and type of charity. They can be prepared on either the receipts and payments basis or the accruals basis, depending on the income level of the charity and whether or not it is a company.

The format and content of the Annual Report and Accounts is also governed by the Statement of Recommended Practice (SORP). For financial years beginning on or after 1 January 2015 charities have a choice of which SORP to apply. They can use either SORP FRS 102 if they are preparing their accounts in accordance with the Financial Reporting Standard applicable in the UK and Republic of Ireland (FRS 102), or SORP (FRSSE): the Statement of Recommended Practice applicable to charities preparing their accounts in accordance with the Financial Reporting Standard for Smaller Entities (the FRSSE).

Regardless of size, or the SORP used, there are some basic contents of the annual report which are mandatory for all registered charities. This includes administrative details about the charity (e.g. registration number/s; registered address; trustee names); information about the structure, governance and management of the charity; and a financial review, including the policy on reserves. Annual reports should also provide details of the objectives and activities; achievements and performance, although the level of detail will depend on the size of the charity.

All registered charities have to report on public benefit, including a statement confirming whether the charity trustees have complied with their duty to have due regard to the guidance on public benefit published by the commission in exercising their powers or duties.

Larger charities have to provide information about the organisational structure of the charity and how decisions are made; the charity's plans for the future and information on the charity's main risks and risk management.

Filing of annual report and accounts

Charities must make their report and accounts available to regulators, who will, in turn, make them available to the public.

- Charities with an income above £25,001 must submit their annual report and accounts to the Charity Commission within 10 months of their year end.

It should be noted that although only charities with an income greater than £25,000 must do this, all charities regardless of their level of income must prepare accounts and make these available to the Commission on request.

- Companies are also required to file their annual report and accounts with Companies House within nine months of the accounting reference date. There is an automatic late filing penalty if the accounts are not filed on time, and Companies House also now moves quite quickly to strike off any company with overdue accounts.
- Registered societies are required to submit annual report and accounts to the Financial Conduct Authority (FCA) within seven months of the year-end, as a part of their annual return.

Circulating annual report and accounts to members

Depending on its legal form, a charity may also have a requirement to provide a copy of its annual report and accounts to members.

- If the charity is an unincorporated body or a chartered body any requirements will be set out in its constitution.
- Companies limited by guarantee have a requirement to circulate annual reports and accounts to members, in accordance with section 423 of the Companies Act 2006. Section 424 specifies that this must be done by the end of the period for filing accounts and reports (i.e. nine months after year end, or if earlier, by the date on which it actually files its report and accounts at Companies House. In addition a member has a right to request a copy of the annual report and account, for no charge (s. 431).
- There is no statutory requirement for an association CIO to circulate its accounts to its members but the model constitution prepared by the Charity Commission states that the annual general meeting of the CIO must receive the annual accounts.

Providing annual report and accounts to the public

Sections 171 and 172 of the Charities Act 2011 state that a charity must provide a copy of its annual report and annual accounts to any person who requests them. A reasonable fee can be charged. The Co-operative and Community Benefit Societies Act 2014, section 81 says that a registered society must, at all times display a copy of its latest balance sheet in a conspicuous position at its registered office. Section 90 of that Act says that a registered society must give a copy of its latest annual return (which will include its annual report and accounts), free of charge, to any member or person interested in the society's funds who asks for it.

Legal requirements for stationery

Many of the regulatory requirements set out above are connected to the need for transparency – it is important that people can find out key facts about charities, such as who is responsible for their management and what their financial performance is. Other means of transparency are the legal requirements for stationery and display of names. When people are dealing with a charity, it is important that they know who they are dealing with, how to contact the charity, and the nature of the organisation. There are legal obligations for charities; companies and in regard to business names.

Charitable law obligations – England and Wales

Section 39 of the Charities Act 2011 states that charities that are registered with the Charity Commission must state that they are a 'registered charity', on:

- notices, advertisements or other documents issued by or on behalf of the charity which solicit money or property for the charity's benefit;
- bills of exchange, promissory notes, endorsements, cheques and orders for money or goods purporting to be signed on the charity's behalf; and
- bills, invoices, receipts and letters of credit.

Charities registered in Scotland

There are also disclosure obligations under Scottish charity law and these must be observed by cross-border charities listed on the Register of Charities in Scotland. The documents that the disclosure must be made on are letters, e-mails, adverts, notices and official publications, items soliciting money or property, invoices, receipts accounts, campaign and educational documentation, and documents relating to land transactions and contracts. The disclosure must include the registration number; the registered name and an indication of the charity's charitable status if the word 'charity' or 'charitable' does not appear in its name.

The requirements under Scottish Charity law are, therefore, potentially broader than those under English and Welsh law. A charity registered across both legislations will need to meet both – so it will need to say that it is registered in England and Wales (but not necessarily to give its registration number) and that it is registered in Scotland (and to give its registration number). Scottish charity law also explicitly covers e-mails.

Use of other names

The use of other names is governed by the Business Names Act 1985. The term 'business name' applies if a body is operating under any name other than its true name (i.e. the name on its certificate of incorporation or governing document). In such a case the true name must be stated on all business letters, orders for goods or services, invoices, receipts and written demands for payments of debts. Any person who fails to comply with this requirement is liable to a criminal fine. The Business Names Act will therefore be relevant if a charity uses another name, or shortens its name or uses its initials only. In all of these cases there is a legal requirement to state the full name of the charity.

Company law requirements

In addition to the charity law obligations there are requirements under company law. These are set out in the Companies (Trading Disclosures) Regulations 2008 SI 2008/495) and the Companies (Trading Disclosures) (Amendment) Regulations 2009 (SI 2009/218). Companies must:

- clearly show in legible characters the name on the company's certificate of incorporation on all:
  - business letters;
  - e-mails and a company's website;
  - notices and official publications;
  - bills of exchange, promissory notes, endorsements, cheques, orders for money or goods; and
  - bills of parcels, invoices, receipts, letters of credit.
- Show the address of the registered office, the place of registration (England and Wales), and the registered company number on all business letters, order forms, e-mails, and a company's website.
- Show their 'limited' status on all business letters and order forms. For most companies this is done by having 'limited' or 'ltd' in the name. However, charitable companies can be granted permission to omit 'limited' from their name, and most do. In these cases, additional words must be used and the usual form is to say 'A charitable company limited by guarantee'.

If other form of stationery, such as complement slips, are used to form a contract or to place an order they are likely to be subject to the above rules and need to show the full name, company registration details etc.

CASE EXAMPLE

Seats for Schools has begun to use the name Buddy Seats. It cannot change its name as there is already a company registered under that name (although Buddy Seats has confirmed it has no issue with Seats for Schools using it as a trading name). So the letterheads and website all say Buddy Seats at the top, along with the logo. At the bottom of the letterhead and on its website, it also states that 'Buddy Seats is the trading name of Seats for Schools, a charitable company limited by guarantee, Registered in England and Wales, Company number: 1234567'.

Governance

Overview of corporate governance

Definition

The term corporate governance is widely used, but there is not always clarity about its definition. It can also seem hard to define because it is a term that is used across all the sectors – the commercial sector, the public sector and the voluntary sector.

- Does the term mean different things in different sectors?
- Is good corporate governance different for a charity and a commercial organisation?

The simplest way to think of governance is to remember that it refers to the ways in which an organisation is governed. The most common definition of governance comes from the Cadbury Commission Report in 1992:

> Corporate governance is the system by which companies are directed and controlled. Boards of directors are responsible for the governance of their companies.

The UK Corporate Governance Code states:

> The purpose of corporate governance is to facilitate effective, entrepreneurial and prudent management that can deliver the long term success of the company ... Corporate governance is about what the Board of a company does, and how it sets the values of the company, and it is to be distinguished from the day to day operational management of a company by full-time executives.

Although both these definitions were drafted for commercial companies, as broad definitions they also fit charities. One of the key differences between charities and commercial organisations is the theory behind corporate governance, and the emphasis within it. In the commercial environment, corporate governance is almost always defined in terms of the agency theory, and the principal–agent relationship between shareholders and directors (see below). The main issue is, therefore, often about the relationship between the board and the shareholders.

Accountability is just as important in charitable organisations, but there is not the same relationship as there is with shareholders.

One definition of corporate governance that refers specifically to voluntary organisations is:

> The systems and processes concerned with the overall direction, effectiveness, supervision and accountability of an organisation.
>
> (*The Governance of Voluntary Organisations*, Cornforth 2003)

The four aspects of this definition are very important.

- *Direction*: providing leadership, setting strategy and being clear about what the organisation is aiming to achieve and how it is going to do it.
- *Effectiveness*: making good use of financial and other resources to achieve the desired outcomes.
- *Supervision*: establishing and overseeing controls and risk management, and monitoring performance to make sure that the organisation is on track to achieve its goals, making adjustments where necessary and learning from mistakes.
- *Accountability*: reporting to those who have an interest in what the organisation is doing and how it is doing it.

Why is governance important?

Returning to these four aspects of governance listed above is a good way of seeing why corporate governance is important. A board that is providing leadership and setting strategy; making good use of resources; controlling and monitoring what is being done on its behalf; and reporting back on all of this will be a more effective board. It will make better decisions; manage its resources and people well; and be as transparent as it can be in its work. All of this is likely to lead to a more effective organisation.

History of corporate governance in the UK

When we consider the history of corporate governance in the UK the impression is often given that the concept of governance has been principally led by the commercial sector. However, it should be noted that developments in the charity sector have occurred alongside developments in the commercial sector. Both the Cadbury Report and *On Trust* were published in 1992. Having said that, many charities seek to look to the principles and models developed in the commercial sector and seek to adopt them, sometimes without adaptation. It must be remembered that the needs of charitable and commercial organisations are different.

Cadbury Report

One of the best-known scandals in corporate governance emerged after the death of Robert Maxwell in 1990 and the subsequent revelation that resources had been diverted from the Mirror Group's pension fund to pay for a series of risky acquisitions. As a result of this, the Committee on the Financial Aspects of Corporate Governance was set up, chaired by Sir Adrian Cadbury. During that time, issues also came to light with Bank of Credit and Commerce International and Polly Peck.

The committee published its report, known as the Cadbury report, in 1992. This made a number of recommendations about the role of directors and established the principles of 'openness, integrity and accountability'. Some of the themes that it reported on are just as relevant today: the relationship between the chairman and chief executive, the role of non-executive directors and reporting on internal controls. A key recommendation of the report was to encourage listed companies to comply with the accompanying Code of Best Practice or, if not, explain why they had not done so – known as the 'comply or explain' concept. This Code became the Combined Code in 1998 and the UK Corporate Governance Code in 2010. The Code is designed for listed companies but it is also considered as the primary corporate governance code, and the foremost statement of best practice. Its principles are often upheld across all sectors.

The Code has developed over the years, and there have been a number of reports that have contributed to it. In 1995, the Greenbury Report made recommendations on directors' remuneration. In 1999, the Turnbull guidance provided directors with guidance on internal controls, following on from the work of the Hampel Committee. The Combined Code was updated in 2003 to incorporate recommendations from the Higgs Report on the role of non-executive directors and the Smith Report on the role of the audit committee. The Code now follows a less prescriptive format than previously, and is principle based. It is reviewed and updated regularly. The latest edition was published in September 2014.

On Trust

At the same time as the Cadbury Committee was meeting, there was a piece of work ongoing in the voluntary sector. In 1992, NCVO published the results of this work *On Trust*. The importance of this report gets forgotten about today, but it is interesting to review its recommendations to see how relevant they still are. They encapsulated, for the first time, themes that would become common in charity governance. The recommendations included:

- the need for clarity in the main roles and responsibilities of trustees, including the role of the chair, treasurer and secretary;
- the need for advice, support and training for trustees covering a range of topics, and recommendations on how that training be approached;
- that general information packs should be provided for trustees;

- that charities should have a policy on the composition, recruitment and appointment of their trustees;
- that attention be given to induction for trustees; and
- that funders should establish a mechanism for monitoring the governance of organisations that they fund.

The Nolan Report

The commercial sector was not the only sector which suffered scandals in the 1990s. Following the 'Cash for Questions' affair in the Houses of Parliament, the Committee on Standards in Public Life was formed in October 1994, under the chairmanship of Lord Nolan. Just as the Cadbury Report had proposed three principles, the Nolan report listed seven principles. These are: Selflessness, Integrity, Objectivity, Accountability, Openness, Honesty, and Leadership.

Although drafted for public sector bodies, these seven principles are often used within the voluntary sector; particularly in organisations that provide public services such as health or housing.

Recent events

In recent times, there has been a revised focus on the need for good governance. The collapse of the charity Kids Company in August 2015 led many to look again at how charities are managed and governed. The Public Administration and Constitutional Affairs Committee published a report on Kids Company (*The Collapse of Kids Company: Lessons for charity trustees, professional firms, the Charity Commission, and Whitehall*) that highlighted a number of governance failings, amongst other failings. In 2015, there was a public outcry about the fundraising methods of some charities; this raised issues on how trustees govern fundraising activities. The increasing number of inquiries by the Charity Commission has also brought to light a range of governance failures. Finally, in September 2016, the BIS Committee launched a new inquiry into corporate governance. This followed on from Theresa May's pledge to overhaul corporate governance, and the recent governance failings highlighted by the Select Committee's investigations into BHS and Sports Direct. This inquiry will focus on directors' duties, executive remuneration and board composition. Its focus appears to be the commercial sector, but its outcomes could well have implications across all sectors.

Governance codes

Essential codes

You will see from the history of corporate governance in the UK that standards and principles of corporate governance are often set out in Codes. There are a number of governance codes, each relating to different sectors. The essential code for charities is *Good Governance: A code for the voluntary and community sector*. This is entirely voluntary; it is up to an organisation if it wants to follow it and to report back on how well it adheres to it (e.g. in its annual report). The voluntary nature of the codes applies across a range of sectors, although it should be noted that it is a regulatory requirement of the HCA that registered providers of social housing adopt a code (they can choose which one to adopt) and then report back on how well they adhere to it in their annual report each year.

Other codes that are good examples and are used regularly are:

- National Housing Federation Code of Governance;
- International Framework: Good Governance in the Public Sector (published by CIPFA and the International Federation of Accountants);
- Corporate governance in central government departments (published by HM Treasury and Cabinet Office); and
- The NHS Foundation Trust Code of Governance (published by Monitor).

Good Governance: A code for the voluntary and community sector was originally published in June 2005. It was developed by the Charity Commission; the National Council for Voluntary Organisations (NCVO); the Association of Chief Executives of Voluntary Organisations (ACEVO); Charity Trustee Networks and ICSA. In many ways, this original code followed the format of the Combined Code (as it was named at the time) and this meant that it could be quite onerous for smaller voluntary organisations to commit to. The code was reviewed in 2009, and a revised edition, with re-fashioned principles, was published in October 2010; a version designed for smaller organisations without staff was published in November 2011. It is now much simpler than its original form and much less prescriptive. The revised principles state that a good board will provide good leadership by:

- understanding their role;
- ensuring delivery of the organisational purpose;
- being effective as individuals and a team;
- exercising control;
- behaving with integrity; and
- being open and accountable.

A revised version of the Code was launched for consultation in November 2016, to run until February 2017. This followed a major overhaul and the draft Code takes on a completely different format to the current Code. The intention is that the Code will act as a tool for continuous improvement, rather than just setting out minimum standards, and the draft code therefore contains some stretching objectives. It is structured around the principles of leadership; integrity; decision making, risk and control; diversity; board effectiveness and being open and accountable. It also, for the first time, includes a recommendation that charities use their annual report to say how they apply the code and to give an explanation of any aspects which they do differently.

Theories of governance

The two principal theories that corporate governance thinking is based on in the commercial sector are the agency theory and the stakeholder theory. Both of these are outlined below, but neither seem entirely applicable to the charity sector. So I have also outlined some alternative theories that can be applied, and the concept of behavioural governance, which, whilst not strictly a theory, is of broad importance across all sectors.

Agency theory

Agency theory has been around in a number of forms for a long time. It is concerned with the relationship between the managers of a company, and the owners (i.e. the shareholders). In some ways, it has been developing as a theory since the eighteenth century, but its most recent formulation has been by Jensen and Meckling in 1976. Back in the eighteenth century, the philosopher Adam Smith was one of the first to raise concerns about whether employed managers would watch over other people's assets with the same vigilance as if they were their own. Since that time, the theory has developed. It argues that there are potential sources of conflict that may result from a separation of ownership and control. In the modern commercial company the shareholders (the owners) give their power to employed managers who exercise control on their behalf. It is an underlying assumption of the theory that there is a goal divergence between the owners (the principals) and the managers (the agents). The theory states that, as a result of this divergence, action needs to be taken to make sure that managers pursue the collective interest rather than pursue their own self-interest. The agency theory perspective has a number of implications for corporate governance. The first is that it is seen that a key role of the board is to monitor managers on behalf of shareholders. Another is the importance that is placed on controlling matters such as director and manager remuneration on behalf of the shareholders in a commercial company.

Stakeholder theory

Stakeholder theory takes the view that the purpose of an organisation is to satisfy the needs of a wider group of stakeholders than the owners/shareholders (e.g. employees, investors, customers and government etc.). The board should, therefore, consider the needs of all these stakeholders, and not just the owners. Stakeholder theory is, therefore, very concerned with the wider social responsibility of an organisation and so may seem to be closer to the principles of accountability that are of key importance for a charity. However, in a charity the interests that need to be considered are those of the beneficiaries and applying the principles of stakeholder theory to a charity could lead to 'mission drift' and divergence from its objects.

The 'fit' with charities

So, neither agency theory nor stakeholder theory seem to 'fit' with charitable organisations. The difficulties with stakeholder theory are outlined above and there are a number of issues with agency theory. A charity does not have shareholders as owners in the same way as there are in commercial companies. A charitable company has members, but they do have an investment in the company in the same way as shareholders do. In addition, in a charitable company the trustees do not have a legal obligation to act in their interests in the same way that applies in a commercial company. The other issue with agency theory is that the principle that managers will tend to act in their own self interest does not seem as applicable. Managers in a charity are often not driven by the same financial rewards as in the commercial sector; they will still have financial incentives, it is true, but often if there is a goal divergence it is over the managers and the members having a difference in view on how best to meet the needs of the beneficiaries.

Stewardship theory

Stewardship theory is a theory that managers, left on their own, will act as responsible stewards of the assets they control. Stewardship theory assumes that the behaviours of the management are aligned with the interests of the principals. Stewardship theory therefore favours governance mechanisms that support and empower the organisation's management and disfavours those that monitor and control it. According to stewardship theory, 'the more crucial factor influencing organisational performance is the design of the organisational structure so that managers can take effective action'. The key issue is therefore how to empower management rather than making the board act on behalf of the 'owners'.

Policy governance

Policy governance is another theory and model of governance that is applicable to charities. It gives a set of principles that are designed to empower boards to fulfil their obligation of accountability for the organisations they govern. It begins with the premise that the board exists to be accountable for the work that its organisation undertakes. Therefore, just as the commercial board exists to speak for the shareholders, the charity board exists to represent and to speak for the interests of the 'owners' in a broader sense. The beneficiaries are perceived to be the 'owners' of a charity.

The theory argues that the board's primary relationships should be outside the organisation. It states that boards have developed their relationships largely inside the organisation (i.e. with staff); it argues that this is the wrong focus. Policy governance goes on to outline mechanisms that are designed to enable the board to focus on the larger issues and to truly lead its organisation. Policy governance separates issues of organisational purpose (which it describes as 'ends') from all other organisational issues ('means'), placing primary importance on ends. It is designed to move the board away from being concerned with 'approving' to focusing on policy making.

Behavioural governance

Behavioural governance is not a theory as such; rather it is a new approach to governance that has led to a shift in the way corporate governance has been considered in recent years. The approach was developed in response to the financial crisis of 2008/2009 and the search for reasons why the governance of banks did not prevent the errors that were made. On the face of it, banks that appeared to meet the standards of good governance clearly had some fundamental flaws in their decision making and the way that they worked. Whilst the concept of behavioural governance was developed in the commercial sector, it is also applicable to the charity sector. In 2009, ICSA issued a report on boardroom behaviour which stated that an 'emerging view is that the system of governance for companies is not inherently "broken", but rather that its effectiveness has been undermined by a failure to observe appropriate boardroom behaviours'. The report argued that appropriate boardroom behaviour is an essential component of best practice corporate governance; and that there is an absence of consideration of, and guidance on, appropriate boardroom behaviours in current corporate governance models and systems.

The report states that best practice in boardroom behaviour is characterised by:

- a clear understanding of the role of the board;
- the appropriate deployment of knowledge, skills, experience and judgment;
- independent thinking;
- the questioning of assumptions and established views; and
- a supportive decision-making environment.

This has led to a rethink in the way organisations approach corporate governance. Less emphasis is now placed on structures and processes and instead work is being done on how the characteristics set out above can be delivered. In recent years, it has been more common for organisations to give consideration to the personality of the directors; the balance of relationships; and group dynamics.

Meetings

Charities are governed by boards; a group of people coming together to take decisions. This means that the concept of collective decision making is very important for them. Trustees act collectively and exercise their powers as a group. Not all collective decision making happens in meetings, but much of it does.

For a charity, the key types of meetings are:

- *General meetings:* meetings of the members of the charity. These should only be concerned with matters that are the members' business and not those matters that are the responsibility of the trustees. They often have limited application, being concerned with the reporting of the annual report and accounts, the amendment of the constitution and (often) the appointment of trustees. General meetings correspond with the need for accountability. They are the way the board reports back to its members. Not all charities are required to hold general meetings, as not all charities have members.

- *Board meetings:* meetings of the board. Board meetings correspond with the need for direction – it is for the board to set the strategy for the charity, and to take key decisions regarding it. So there will often be constitutional requirements regarding how these meetings are held.
- *Committee meetings:* meetings of smaller groups of board members and/or other volunteers, often with delegated powers from the board. Committee meetings correspond with the need for supervision. The trustees retain responsibility for any decisions taken on their behalf, so they need to ensure that there is clarity and control about how these committees operate, and report-back mechanisms.

Legal requirements

What, legally, constitutes a meeting? This may be stated in the charity's constitution. However, if there is nothing in the constitution, the charity will need to rely on the common law definition of a meeting. This states that a valid meeting normally consists of people who can both see and hear each other (*Byng v London Life Association* (1989)). This common law definition means that a meeting cannot be held by teleconference unless there is a specific provision in its governing document stating that this type of meeting is permitted. Model constitutions now allow meetings to be held electronically; charities that have been established in recent years usually have a broad definition of meetings.

General meetings

In many types of charity, particularly in a company, there are some decisions that can only be taken by its members. For these reasons, the constitution of a charity often contains quite a lot of detailed requirements for such meetings. In addition, if the charity is a company, the Companies Act contains many provisions regarding how such meetings are held, and how decisions are taken by members. In some instances these statutory requirements will override the charitable company's articles (e.g. the rights of proxies).

General meetings are often referred to as AGMs (Annual General Meetings) or EGMs (Extraordinary General Meetings). Historically, there was a legal requirement for a company to hold an AGM. There was a difference between these annual meetings, and other types of EGMs which were held to consider specific business. However, the Companies Act 2006 removed this requirement for private companies (including charitable companies); so the term 'general meetings' is now used for all meetings of the members.

Despite the Companies Act changes, AGMs are often still a requirement under the constitution of charitable companies. They are also often held in other types of charities (e.g. registered societies or chartered bodies). A charitable company registered prior to the implementation of the Companies Act will have had a requirement for AGMs contained within its articles and many have chosen not to remove it. AGMs are an important means of accounting to the membership on the activities of the board. So, if a charitable company has only the trustees of the charity as its members, there is no real need for an AGM – they would be accounting back to themselves. They will only need to hold a general meeting when they need to take a decision in their capacity as members (e.g. amending the constitution). However, when a charitable company has a wider membership, it is advisable to retain the requirement to hold an AGM each year.

The requirements for general meetings will usually be set out in detail in the constitution of the charity. For charitable companies, there are also provisions in the Companies Act that will need to be complied with; these are summarised later in this chapter.

Timing

The timing of a general meeting will usually only be specified in the constitution when it contains a requirement to hold an AGM. Prior to the Companies Act 2006, companies were required to hold an AGM within 18 months of incorporation and to hold all further AGMs annually and in each calendar year; no more than 15 months could elapse between each AGM. This model is still followed in the articles of many charitable companies, and even some other types of charity. Note that if there is a requirement to hold an AGM in each calendar year, this will override the maximum number of months there can be between AGMs. For charitable companies, the annual reports and accounts must be circulated to the members within nine months of the year end. If the annual report and accounts are being presented to the members at the AGM this can also influence the timing of the meeting.

Convening

The constitution will specify who can convene a general meeting. It will usually be the trustees. A constitution may sometimes also empower one trustee or any member to convene a general meeting when there are insufficient trustees in the United Kingdom to form a quorum. This power is useful if the number falls below the number required for a quorum of the board at any time. Sometimes, there may also be a provision allowing a certain percentage of members to convene a meeting. There are provisions for this in the Companies Act, which are set out below.

Notice and agenda

A notice for a general meeting should normally include:

- the time, date and place of meeting;
- the agenda for the meeting, including the exact wording of any resolution;
- information on how to vote by proxy; and
- the secretary's or chair's signature and the date.

The agenda will vary, but at an AGM the business will commonly include:

- the receipt of the annual report and annual accounts;
- the election of trustees (if it is within the remit of the members); and
- the appointment of auditors.

While there may sometimes be a general discussion and questions, there is no Any Other Business (AOB) at general meetings. The rules on giving notice to members mean that a resolution cannot be put to the members in a general meeting unless it is sent out with the notice. All of the members need to know what will be considered at a general meeting, and then decide whether to attend or even to vote by proxy (if this is allowable). Therefore, bringing forward matters for voting on at the meeting itself is not giving full notice.

Notice must be sent to all those entitled to receive it. The notice will usually need to be sent to all members, trustees, and auditors. Failure to send the notice of the meeting to all those entitled to receive it can invalidate the meeting (unless, for a company, it is an accidental omission).

For companies, 14 clear days' notice of a general meeting is required (the articles of older companies may require a longer period of time). For other charities, the notice period will normally be specified in the constitution, but it is common for it to be the same as the requirements for charitable companies. The constitution is also likely to specify when the notice is deemed to be served (i.e. how long after despatch it is deemed to have been received). If this is not specified in the constitution, it should be considered to be 48 hours after being posted by first class post. 'Clear days' means that you do not include the day that the notice is deemed to be served or the day of the meeting. This is in addition to the period between a notice being despatched and when it is deemed to be served. Giving notice electronically can shorten the periods when the notice is deemed to be served, depending on the wording of the constitution.

There may be occasions when the charity wants to hold a general meeting without meeting its full notice requirement. In such an instance it is sometimes possible to meet provided there is agreement to shortened notice. For a charity that is not a company, there would generally need to be a mechanism in the constitution stating if this was allowable and how. Even without such a mechanism the signed agreement of everyone who was entitled to get notice of the meeting should suffice.

Voting
Voting at general meetings is usually by a show of hands. However, in many instances, the constitution may permit that a poll can be demanded and if the charity is also a company, there are provisions in the Companies Act that cover this. A poll is conducted by the use of voting papers rather than on a show of hands. Most of the decisions that are taken at a general meeting are dealt with as ordinary resolutions (i.e. a simple majority of members present and voting is required for the matter to be agreed). However, sometimes the constitution may require a higher majority; in company law some matters (such as the amendment of the articles or a change of name) require a higher majority (these are called special resolutions).

Chairman
General meetings are usually chaired by the board chairman who has the authority to run the meeting (e.g. on a vote on a show of hands, a declaration by the chairman that the resolution has or has not been passed, is regarded as conclusive evidence of that fact). The constitution will also usually give the chairman the right to call for a poll vote, or to adjourn the meeting. It is very common for the constitution to give the chairman a casting vote, but note that the Companies Act 2006 abolished the right of a casting vote for the chairman at general meetings for companies established after the Act.

Proxies
A proxy is a person appointed by an individual or corporate member of a charity, to attend, speak and vote on behalf of his appointer at a meeting (including any adjournment thereof) of the members. A member of a company has a statutory right to appoint a proxy (see below). For other types of charity a member can appoint a proxy if the constitution allows. Whether that proxy can be any person or has to be a member will depend on the constitution; but note that in companies there is a statutory right to appoint any person as a proxy.

The rules on proxies may be specified in the constitution together with the form of proxy document, and the deadline by which it must be received. Again, it should be noted that there are provisions in the Companies Act 2006 that relate to these matters. If no deadline is specified, a proxy can be submitted right up to the start of the meeting. Electronic proxies may be specifically permitted by the constitution. In a charitable company they can be used, provided the company and member agree to do so and the company provides an address for electronic lodgement of the proxy. This applies regardless of the charity's articles.

Quorum
The quorum for a general meeting (i.e. the number of members who must be present for the meeting to be valid) will usually be specified in the constitution. If no quorum is specified, at least two members must be present.

Companies Act provisions

Convening

Section 302 of the Companies Act 2006 gives directors (i.e. the trustees) a general power to call a general meeting. The directors may also be required to call the meeting by a requisition lodged under section 303 of the Companies Act 2006. A member, or members, of a company holding between them not less than one-tenth of the voting rights (or in the case of a share company not less than one-tenth of the paid-up capital carrying voting rights) may at any time lodge a requisition requiring the directors to convene a general meeting for the purposes stated in the requisition (s. 303). This percentage is reduced to 5% in some circumstances. On receipt of the requisition (which may consist of several documents in similar form) the directors must, within 21 days, convene the meeting and the meeting must be held not more than 28 days after the date of the notice of the meeting.

Notice

Section 307 of the Companies Act 2006 states that, for a charitable company, the notice for a general meeting must be at least 14 clear days. (The definition of clear days is set out in s. 360.) This section also sets out how a general meeting may be called by shorter notice than required. This can only be done if it is agreed by members who represent not less than 90% of the total voting rights or share capital. These provisions relate to the calling of a meeting at short notice; they do not provide for the giving of notice to be completely dispensed with. A copy of the notice of the meeting should therefore still be given to the members either before or at the start of the meeting.

Section 311 sets out the requirements regarding notice of the meeting. It must include:

- the time and date of the meeting;
- the place of the meeting; and
- the general nature of the business to be dealt with at the meeting.

If a special resolution is to be proposed, the Companies Act requires that the full text is set out. The notice must make it clear that the resolution is to be proposed as a special resolution. Section 213 states that accidental failure to give notice of a meeting will not invalidate the meeting.

Chairman

The Companies Act 2006 removed the chairman's right to a casting vote at general meetings. However, for any company that had a right to a casting vote in its articles prior to 1 October 2007 this will continue to have effect, unless the company itself removes it. (This provision relates to general meetings – this does not affect any provisions regarding casting votes in a board meeting that may be in the articles.)

Voting

Section 284(2) of the Companies Act 2006 states that:

(a) every member present in person has one vote; and
(b) every proxy present who has been duly appointed by a member entitled to vote on the resolution has one vote.

This means that, in a company, a proxy can vote on a show of hands, not just a poll vote. A proxy may hold a number of votes (i.e. they may act as proxy for more than one person). To ensure that all votes can be counted, unless the articles provide for this, it may be better for voting to be conducted via a poll. This is subject to any contrary provision in the articles (s. 284(4)) but there are limitations on reducing a member's voting rights (s. 285).

The constitution usually states who can call for a poll vote. Under section 321 of the Companies Act a provision of a company's articles is void in so far as it would have the effect of excluding the right to demand a poll at a general meeting on any question other than:

(a) the election of the chairman of the meeting; or
(b) the adjournment of the meeting.

A provision of a company's articles is also void insofar as it would have the effect of making ineffective a demand for a poll on any such question which is made by not less than five members having the right to vote on the resolution; or by a member or members representing not less than 10% of the total voting rights or shares.

The Companies Act 2006 states that decisions of members can be taken by either ordinary resolution, requiring a simple majority (s. 281) and as a special resolution, requiring a three-quarters majority of members present and voting (s. 282). A special resolution is required for certain types of decision, including any decision to amend the articles (s. 21). A copy of a special resolution must be filed with Companies House within 15 days of the meeting (s. 30).

Proxies

The Companies Act 2006 gives proxies a number of rights. A proxy is entitled to attend the meeting in a member's place, and vote on his/her behalf (s. 324). This right applies no matter what the articles state. There is also a statutory requirement to include a prominent statement on the right to appoint a proxy on the notice of the meeting (s. 325). Under s. 327 the longest period that can be specified in the articles within which members must give notice of their wish to appoint a proxy is 48 hours prior to the meeting or a poll being demanded (excluding non-working days).

There are a number of charitable companies that were established with a restriction on who can serve as a proxy; often stating in their articles that proxies must be members. The Companies Act 2006 overrides any such restrictions.

A member has a statutory right to appoint any person (not just a member) as a proxy.

Every notice of a meeting of a company must include a statement to the effect that a member entitled to attend and vote is entitled to appoint a proxy. The notice must also state that such proxy need not himself be a member of the company, and should set out any other more extensive rights conferred by the company's articles (s. 325). There is no requirement to circulate proxy forms with notices of meetings. However, it is it is illegal to issue proxy forms by the company to selected members only (s. 326(1)).

Charitable companies also need to be aware that section 333(1) states that:

> Where a company has given an electronic address in a notice calling a meeting, it is deemed to have agreed that any document or information relating to proceedings at the meeting may be sent by electronic means to that address (subject to any conditions or limitations specified in the notice).

This means that if it provides an electronic address, or fax number in a notice convening a general meeting, the company can be deemed to have consented to receiving documents relating to that meeting, such as proxies, using those methods. If you do not want to receive a proxy vote in this way you must ensure that such details are not included on the notice or proxy form, or that you clearly specify this in the notice.

CASE EXAMPLE

Stampton Sports is a charitable company limited by guarantee. Its members and its trustees are comprised of the same group of people. At a board meeting where all the board members were present, the board agreed that the articles should be amended. This required a decision of the same people, but in their capacity as members. Usually, this would be done at a general meeting, which would need 14 clear days' notice. However, the members all signed an agreement to short notice, and agreed to hold the general meeting straight away. The Secretary tabled the notice of the general meeting, which happened immediately after the board meeting. As the short notice had been agreed by all the members, it was a valid meeting and the decision could be taken.

Resolutions of members

General meetings are a means for the board to report back to members; they are also a way for members' decisions to be taken (e.g. to amend the constitution). Meetings are not the only way in which decisions can be taken; they can also be taken by written resolution – effectively agreeing in writing to a resolution put before them. In recent years, decisions by written resolution have become more common. It is now generally accepted that these decision can be taken by e-mail and that an agreement by e-mail meets the requirements of being 'in writing', so it is now much simpler and quicker for organisations to pass resolutions in this way.

Regardless of what type of organisation it is, a charity's constitution will quite often provide for written resolutions as an alternative to voting at a meeting. However, this is more often the case in constitutions that have been written, or redrafted, in recent years. Written resolutions used to be used much less frequently. Also, often provisions for written resolutions have a much higher requirement for a majority (either 90 or 100%) and therefore are of limited application, unless the charity has a very small membership.

No matter what is specified in the articles, charitable companies and trading subsidiaries can now take advantage of the Companies Act 2006 provisions regarding written resolutions (ss 288–300). This allows written resolutions to be passed with a simple majority (or a 75% majority for special resolutions) even if there is no provision in the articles. Note, however, that the majority required is higher than it would be in a general meeting. In a resolution put before a general meeting, it needs to be passed by 50% (or 75% for a special resolution) of those present and/or voting. In a written resolution taken under the powers given by the Companies Act, it needs to be passed by 50% (or 75% for a special resolution) of the *full membership* of the company, not just of those who chose to vote. This can be reduced to the percentages of those voting, but only if the articles specifically allow this.

In a company, the following may not be passed as a written resolution:

(a) a resolution under section 168 of the Companies Act removing a director before the expiration of his period of office; and
(b) a resolution under section 510 of the Companies Act removing an auditor before the expiration of his term of office.

Unanimity rule

There is a common law principle established for companies but that applies to other organisations. This is that members can take decisions unanimously, without the need for a formal meeting or resolution.

CASE LAW

In *Cane v Jones* (1980) it was held that, by unanimous agreement, the members might, without passing a special resolution, alter the articles so that the chairman no longer had a casting vote.

Electronic communications

All communications with members used to be carried out by sending a paper copy through the post. However, there are now other methods of communicating include e-mails and the use of the charity's website. The practice of many charities is changing and these methods of communication are used much more frequently, but care needs to be taken to ensure that they are permitted as a formal means of communication (e.g. giving notice of meetings) both constitutionally and legally. There is also legislation covering electronic communication by companies. The default method of communication to members remains the hard copy, but if a company wants to use electronic communication instead, it does not need to have provision for the use of electronic communications in its articles or to obtain the consent of the members in general meeting unless it wishes to take advantage of the website default procedures (see below). The Companies Act communication provisions override a company's articles in many ways, but they need to be understood because they place restrictions on how these communications can be used. If these provisions of the Companies Act are being relied upon, with the exception of the website default procedures, the intended recipient must have agreed individually to accept communications in this manner. Also, if the member so requests, the company must provide a hard copy form of any document sent by electronic means, within 21 days of receipt of the request, and for no charge.

If the charity is not a company, the method of communication will be as laid down in its constitution. Older constitutions may say that notice of a meeting must be sent via the post. This method must be used, until the constitution can be amended to allow for different means of communication. If the constitution is not explicit, it may be possible to interpret it in such a way that the communications methods can be changed (i.e. adopting a more modern interpretation of 'in writing'). It would be preferable for the constitution to be updated.

If the charity is a company, the Companies Act 2006 introduced a wide range of provisions regarding electronic communications. These built upon the Companies Act 1985 (Electronic Communications) Order 2000 (SI 2000/3373). The Companies Act 2006 allows electronic communications to be used in relation to any document or information required or authorised to be sent or supplied under the Companies Acts (ss 1143–1148 and Schs 4 and 5).

Electronic communications can include texting and e-mail. It also includes posting on a website. The Act allows companies to use their website as their method of communication rather than providing a hard copy. If a company wishes to use its website for formal communication with its members, either its articles must contain a provision allowing it to do this, or its membership must pass a resolution to this effect. The Act allows a company to rely upon deemed consent if it uses its website. There is still an obligation to seek consent, but if no response is received from the member, consent can be deemed to have been given. In other words, the member will need to opt out of the communication method rather than opt in. This means that using its website for electronic communications can be a lot simpler for a company than using e-mail. There are a number of detailed provisions in the Companies Act regarding electronic communications, seeking members' consent and notification. A key point to remember is that the company must notify the members that the document has been placed on the website. Unless the member has also consented to being contacted by electronic means, this information must be provided in hard copy form (e.g. by letter).

If a charity has a large number of members, the provisions under the Companies Act 2006 could provide substantial cost savings. Communications could be used for giving notice of meetings, and sending out the annual report and accounts. However, as it is likely that some members will not consent to e-communication, it will lead to the company having to operate both e-communication and hard copy communication mechanisms.

Board meetings

There is often less detail within constitutions on how board meetings should be run. The constitution will usually state:

- how board meetings are called – who has the power to convene a board meeting;
- the frequency of the meetings – how many board meetings should there be in any one year;
- the chairing of such meetings;
- how much notice must be given; and
- the numbers which will make trustee meetings quorate (it will often state that such matters are to be determined by rules or regulations set by the trustees).

If no notice is specified in the constitution, trustees should always be given reasonable notice. However, what is considered 'reasonable' will depend on the practice and circumstances of the charity. In a small local charity, where meetings are held frequently, reasonable notice may just be a few days. In an international charity, it may be much longer. The notice period can, in fact, be very short if all the directors receive it, and can attend. In this situation, if a director wishes to object to the short notice, they should make their objection known at once (*Browne v La Trinidad* (1888)). A casual meeting of the directors cannot be just converted into a board meeting if one of the directors denies that it is, in fact, a board meeting and if notice has not been sent (*Barron v Potter* (1914)).

Just as members can take decisions by written resolution, so can board members. The constitution of the charity will need to allow for this, and to specify what majority is required. The Companies Act 2006 provisions set out above apply to written resolutions of members, not meetings of trustees. If there is nothing in the constitution, the charity can rely on the common law principle of unanimity (see above re members' decisions) but this requires all trustees to agree. It is quite common for provisions in constitutions for board written resolutions to require a higher level of consent than for voting at meetings (e.g. 75%), as there is no opportunity for debate. If board members take decisions by written resolution, remember that these decisions must be recorded in the same way as board minutes, and should usually be kept with board minutes.

Committees

A board may establish committees, and may delegate some of its work to committees. It will need to agree terms of reference, which will set out the membership of the committees, their functions and powers, and how the meetings of the committees are run. A constitution may sometimes place some regulations on committees. Some charity constitutions specify that there must be a minimum number of trustees on the committee. However, in all other regards, the way in which the meetings of the committees are run will be in the hands of the board in setting its terms of reference.

Types of committees

It is up to a charity board to determine what types of committees it needs, although the need for a particular committee may be set out in its constitution. Research has shown that the number of committees that charities are setting up is reducing, but the most common type of committee is still an audit committee (see *Delivering Effective Governance – Insight from the Boards of larger Charities*, Compass Partnership). Charities often follow the model set by listed companies and have remuneration committees (but usually concerned with staff remuneration instead of board remuneration) and nomination committees. It is also very common to have a finance or operations committee. It is important for a board to understand (a) why it is setting up a committee and (b) its functions. Committees are a means of assisting the board to do its job. The most common reasons for establishing a committee are:

(a) to enable issues to be considered in more depth than is feasible by the board;
(b) to draw on additional expertise and independence, from non-trustees; and
(c) to enable the development of projects and ideas outside the formal setting of the board.

Making meetings effective

So far, we have considered a range of legal and regulatory requirements regarding meetings, but we also need to consider meetings in governance terms and how to make meetings effective. While the legal and regulatory requirements need to be in place, for a board to meet its governance obligations, it needs to work effectively. There are a number of factors which impact on the effectiveness of meetings; these can be grouped into four areas:

- documentation and information;
- focus on board role;

- hygiene factors; and
- behaviour.

We will return to boardroom behaviour in the next section, but will consider the first three of these areas here.

Documentation and information

Trustees need to prepare for a meeting. There should be clarity about the obligations that are placed on a trustee (e.g. that they should set aside the time needed to read the papers for a meeting). It is also sometimes the case that the information is not provided in a way that makes this easy. Typical problems with meetings here are:

- an agenda that is too long;
- little or no clear reasons why an item has been brought to the meeting;
- use of a standard agenda (e.g. a list of reports from officers) with no indication on the agenda itself of what the subject matter really is;
- papers being too long; unclear and with a lack of clarity regarding recommendations;
- insufficient time being given for trustees to read papers; and
- papers being circulated too close to the meeting.

Some of the things that can help are:

- Sometimes board meetings are used as a way of providing information to trustees, rather than focusing on key items that need discussion or decision. If you are using an agenda to pass on information, it can sometimes be a good idea to think about separating these out – perhaps having a board agenda, and a board information pack, with the board information pack being sent out between meetings.
- It is good practice to review the work programme for the year, and consider in advance what you need to agree and when. Devise an annual work programme, to be discussed and agreed by the board.
- Draft the agenda so that each item to be discussed is described, along with the action needed. Be careful of overusing 'matters arising' and 'any other business'. If a matter arising from the last meeting needs to be considered, it should be an agenda item in its own right. 'Any Other Business' should be restricted to urgent or short matters for information only.
- Keeping the agenda short – ideally no more than eight substantive items. This does not necessarily mean shorter meetings – but it should provide more focus on the key issues.
- Have a standard format for board papers and, perhaps, a maximum length.
- Ensure that papers are sent out with sufficient time for them to be read; common practice is at least one week prior to a meeting. Only allow a paper to be distributed any closer to a meeting where there are clear reasons why it could not have been prepared earlier.

Board role

There is a difference between governance and management and boards need to avoid getting bogged down by detail. Effective boards have a clear understanding of their role, and they focus on this. Different boards summarise their key work in different ways, but typically this will include:

- Setting strategy: Determining the strategic direction of the charity; setting the vision, values and mission statement; agreeing the strategic plan and business plan.
- Overseeing the management functions: having an oversight of risk management and internal controls.
- Setting a policy framework for the charity and approving high-level policies.
- Holding staff and committees to account through monitoring performance.

How best to monitor performance is an issue which proves difficult for many charities. When you have delegated decision making, a board must retain an oversight of what decisions are being made on its behalf. It is common practice now for charities to produce regular management accounts which give the trustees an overview of the financial performance. There are a number of different ways to provide other monitoring information. Sometimes, it is just a schedule of performance again plans but other mechanisms are:

- *Key performance indicators*: These are measurable values that demonstrate how effectively a company is achieving key business objectives.
- *Balanced scorecard*: This is structured report, which gives an overview of a small number of data items – usually a mix of financial and non-financial items.

Alongside its standard monitoring mechanisms, a board may also have a system of exception reporting. This is where detailed reasonings are given for any variations to the plan or expected targets which are either unusual or below acceptable performance level.

Hygiene factors

The effectiveness of a meeting can be fundamentally affected by issues such as the meeting time; the length of meeting; the number of breaks in a meeting; and location. Some of the things that you can do to help are:

- Have a timed agenda. Being open about the timings helps everyone to keep to them – and establishes the relative importance of items in advance. If a participant wants more time allocated to an item, they can request this at the start of the meeting.
- If a meeting is being held by teleconference try to focus on one or two key questions for debate. It is very difficult to manage a full agenda during a telephone call. It is probably necessary for the meeting to be conducted in a more

formal way than usual (e.g. members should identify themselves each time they speak). If a meeting is being held with some people in the room, and some participating on the phone, the chairman should ensure that those on the phone are formally asked for their comments on each agenda item.

- Think about how long your board members can take part in a meeting without a break; and schedule breaks at fixed times. Try to ensure that the board does not overrun or work through breaks; board members become less effective if they are working on one task for too long; people lose attention. The general convention on effective meetings is that meetings should not run for more than 90 minutes without a break.

Boardroom behaviour

We have discussed the concept of behavioural governance and the impact that boardroom behaviour has on good governance and the effectiveness of a board. How your board works together as a group is vital and improving this is often a key development need for boards. Some of the things that you can do to help to improve behaviour in meetings include:

(a) *Effective chairing*: A chairman should spend their time listening, moving the discussion on, and then summarising. At the end of each agenda item the chairman should ensure that all present are clear about the outcome reached. A good chairman will encourage everyone to have some input. Some people speak of a chairman adopting a FODA approach to each agenda item, trying to ensure that that the discussion progresses in the following order:
   - Facts
   - Opinions
   - Decisions
   - Action.

(b) *Ensuring that participants respect the chairman, and his or her decisions about the conduct of the meeting*. Board members should address the meeting through the chairman.

(c) *Making sure that the meeting does not get bogged down in formalities*. Whilst meetings should be conducted in an orderly way, there is no need for overly formal procedures. It is not necessary for every issue under discussion to be proposed and seconded, or to be put to a formal vote. Sometimes, voting will need to be by show of hands, especially where there is a different of opinion, but in many instances decisions are reached by consensus, with the chairman summarising the agreed position.

(d) *Adopting some meeting protocols*. Sometimes it is helpful to have a written summary of how people should behave in meetings, particularly where there have been issues in the past. This can include not participating in side conversations during the main meeting; limiting use of telephones, tablets and computers; and ensuring that there is no aggressive, or rude behaviour.

(e) *Ensuring that trustees have the opportunity to meet socially, even if this is just during refreshment breaks at the meeting itself.* This helps to address conflicts and gives opportunities for matters to be discussed appropriately outside the meeting.

(f) *Thinking about different styles of board meetings.* Not all meetings need to be held in the same formal way. Sometimes, it can be useful to create opportunities to think aloud and for creative thinking (e.g. brainstorms and small group working).

Thinking about how the board works together a group is fundamentally important. A board that works well together will be more effective; this is one of the key components of good governance. Often, we look at governance in terms of structure and processes but increasingly boards are beginning to look at things differently to get a better understanding of why they work in the way that they do, and what could make them more effective. Two examples of this are:

- *The need for independent thought and constructive challenge.* Often boards recruit in their own image. This can mean that they often develop with groups of members with a high level of consensus. This is often seen as a good way of working, and when people come on to the board with a more challenging style, this can be seen as having a negative effect on the group. However, the work on behavioural governance shows that there is a need for constructive challenge. Note, it is very important that the challenge is constructive; challenge and criticism need to be given in a context of overall support. Losada and Heaphy developed a concept of a 'critical positivity ratio' which set out the exact ratio of positive to negative comments to assist effectiveness. There has been criticism of this concept, but it remains the case that challenge and criticism does need to be balanced with support and praise.
- *The personality types of board members.* There are a number of models around to determine underlying personality types and the way people work in a team (e.g. Belbin team roles). These can be very useful in the context of board working, giving board members an idea of how they, and the other board members that they work with, will typically approach issues. Sometimes carrying out such an exercise is a good way of the board to get to know each other, identifying why they behave in certain ways.

CASE EXAMPLE

Troubadour is a charitable membership organisation. Its members are all singer-songwriters and its objects are the advancement of the arts, culture, heritage or science. It has a board of 12, all elected by the members. Board meetings are very enjoyable and the members get along very well. However, it has great difficulty in taking decisions. In recent years it has been debating some key strategic decisions, without ever being able to reach a conclusion.

At a recent away day the board undertook a Belbin Team Role exercise. It found that, out of 12 members, four were Team Workers and five were Monitor Evaluators. The other three board members took on other roles, but no one was identified as a Completer Finisher. The board came to the conclusion that these roles could be contributing to its difficulties in taking decisions. It has now established a clear decision-making process, whereby matters come to a board meeting for discussion and then a second meeting for decision. The board has also agreed that one board member at each meeting, selected by rota, should take on the task of challenging recommendations and consensus views. The board has begun to be a bit more effective.

Other governance considerations

Board composition

Research shows that the typical size of a charity board is reducing. Twelve to eighteen members is now the norm in larger charities (*Delivering Effective Governance – Insight from the boards of larger charities*, Compass Partnership). Many charities are now reducing their board size as a result of recruitment difficulties. However, research has also shown that smaller boards work more effectively. Boards operate by collective decision making; how they work together as groups is key to their operation. The larger the board, the more difficult this becomes; debate and discussion become more difficult.

Another trend is the fact that more emphasis is being placed on the method of recruitment for board members. Traditional methods for recruiting new trustees have been personal recommendation and word of mouth; but these are not open and transparent methods of recruitment. Charities are also finding that they are not necessarily the most effective ways of finding people with the right skills and experience. Increasingly, charities are beginning to use other means of recruitment such as advertising; notices on websites and the use of trustee brokerage services or banks. Many charities also find that their existing volunteers, donors or members possess suitable skills, but if looking to these groups it is important that the board is still able to recruit from a diverse group.

Performance review

One of the ways that boards assess their effectiveness is by performance reviews or appraisals; these are becoming more common across the sector.

There are potentially two aspects of performance review – a review of the contribution of individual trustees, and a review of the board's performance as a whole. Ideally, a charity should consider undertaking both aspects, but for many charities the focus is on the review of the board as a whole. This section will therefore focus on the collective review process.

Appraisals of individual trustees normally cover such things as attendance and contribution at meetings; relationships with other trustees and senior staff; opportunities to expand on their role; and training needs. It typically falls to the chairman of the board to carry out such reviews, although they may be supported by the secretary, or an external assessor.

Collective board performance reviews vary widely, but they will normally address such questions as to how effective the meetings are; whether the board receives the information that it needs; whether trustees contribute effectively and whether there is effective leadership from the chair.

Board performance reviews and appraisal may be carried out for a number purposes and it can also be done in a number of different ways. A board review may be part of the regular work of the charity, undertaken every year as a regular review of the board as a whole and/or the contribution of individual board members. It can be used as a means of further developing individuals and improving board performance. An increasing number of charities conduct regular board appraisals and reviews in this way. At the other extreme the appraisal may be a specific task, undertaken as a part of an entire review of the governance structure.

Board review can be a difficult process and this is one of the reasons why the whole concept of board review and appraisal can be challenging for many trustees. Given the potential delicacy of the review, it is essential that it is properly planned and executed.

There are a number of methods of board review. The most appropriate in each case will depend on the purpose of the review and, perhaps most importantly, the culture of the board. For example, a board questionnaire would be best suited to a regular review of board function, whereas a detailed examination of the performance of a board laden with strong personalities and complex histories may be better conducted by individual interviews with an independent, external facilitator. A thorough board review exercise may involve a combination of different methods.

Once the purpose of the review has been agreed, the key question for a charity will be whether to conduct the review internally or to draw on the resources of an external facilitator or consultant.

Internally managed board reviews are often led by a sub-group of the trustee board. (Although staff may input into the review, they should not lead it.) The advantages of this approach are that the team will know the issues, the history, the personalities and the desired outcome. It can also save costs and maintain ownership and continuity. However they may also lack objectivity and a fresh approach. Use of an independent contractor can help to ensure that board members are completely honest. They should also have expertise in conducting such reviews and may bring a fresh perspective. They can help to ensure that the necessary time and energy is devoted to the exercise. Whilst an independent consultant may be a more expensive option, it should again be noted that one would not need to be used each year, and such an approach could be combined with lower key methods in other years.

As well as the issue of cost, a key question to ask in this regard may be: would the board tolerate an outsider's intervention and accept the conclusions expressed or would they disregard any unpopular or difficult opinions? Much will also depend on the quality of the independent consultant.

Methods of board appraisal

Questionnaires

Questionnaires may be the first point of any review process. These can provide information on areas of concern for trustees that will later form the focus for discussion. Trustees should be given adequate time to complete the questionnaires and arrangements should be made for trustees to complete them anonymously if necessary.

Group discussions

These stimulate debate as different ideas can be raised and discussed. Group discussions may involve the whole board or small groups. Although some flexibility may be desirable, discussion should be based on an agenda. Such discussions should be conducted separately from regular trustee meetings. Many charities have 'away days' or retreats in order to discuss these issues away from daily distractions.

Individual interviews

These can be a constructive way of identifying the feelings of individual trustees towards the board as a whole and in respect of their own role on the board.

Observation

Sometimes the review will include observation of board or committee meetings by the assessor. This is particularly the case if there is an external review. The meeting will be observed against a number of criteria, such as effectiveness and participation, and then reported back on.

Conclusion and implementation

Whatever the method of review, the process should end with the preparation of a conclusion. This should include a summary of the findings, interpretation of what these findings mean and proposals for moving forward. Whether the review is conducted internally or externally, the conclusion should be in written form and distributed to the whole board. In many cases, those responsible for the review will also give a presentation of their conclusions. The document and presentation then serve as a starting point for the board to discuss the next course of action. Again, it may be best to have this debate at a retreat or away day, as this allows time for options to be discussed fully, free from the distractions of other board business.

The board may decide to implement any proposals in their entirety or to take a more selective approach. Whatever the outcome, an implementation and review plan should be developed in order to ensure that the proposals are carried through and the work is not lost. As with all plans, this should look at actions, identify those responsible for each action and set timescales. Where significant changes are being made, due consideration should be given to the impact on all those involved and reviews built into the plan to monitor the progress of implementation and the efficacy of any new systems.

Skills analysis

Charities need to understand the skills profile of their boards (i.e. what skills, knowledge and experience board members have, and how this matches the needs of the charity). If gaps are identified, a charity can then decide if it needs to address this by recruiting a new board member or if it can be addressed in other ways.

The usual way that a skills analysis is undertaken is for the board to identify the skills that it thinks need to be represented, and then ask the trustees to complete a self-analysis questionnaire. However, this can be very subjective and does not always give the most accurate results. If you are developing such a questionnaire, it important to ensure there is evidence collected for the skills and some way of evaluating the responses. An alternative would be some form of more detailed quiz – where you do not ask the trustee to assess their skill level, but ask more detailed questions about their experiences, and then assess the answers. Another alternative would be an interview, perhaps with an external assessor, or a group discussion, where the trustees discuss each skill as a group and identify any gaps.

It should also be asked whether skill is the key thing you need to assess or should competencies also be considered? It is arguable that, while board members need to know if they have skill gaps in particular areas (e.g. finance) there are ways that these can be addressed. However, there may be some core competencies (e.g. working in a group, strategic decision making or independent thought) that it is just as useful to measure.

There are some core points to consider in setting up a system for skills analysis:

- A fundamental part of undertaking the skills analysis process is identifying the skills that are required by the board. Often, little regard is paid to this. Charities often use template questionnaires for a skills analysis and copy over the skills to be reviewed, rather than identifying the actual skills that their own charities require. In identifying these skills it is useful to be as specific as possible, rather than using generic terms. The more generic the skill described, the less useful the results. In identifying skills it is useful to think of those that are quantifiable; can be measured by self-assessment (if that is the tool you are using); and where examples can be given of how it can have been achieved.
- The charity should also consider the level of skill that it requires. First, does every board member need to have that skill – is it a core competency – or is it

a skill that the board requires, but not from every member? What level of skill or experience is it looking for? If it needs legal skills, does it need a trustee who works as a lawyer or does it need trustees who have had experience of dealing with legal problems and working with solicitors?

- Questionnaires, quizzes or interview results will need to be assessed, and a summary produced identifying any skills gaps. The board, or a sub-group, should then consider this and what action to take. Skills gaps can be addressed by training or recruitment.

Delegation

The board of a charity is responsible for all of its decisions and actions. However, it cannot do everything itself so will need to delegate certain powers to others to act on its behalf. While the board may delegate power, it can never delegate responsibility; the trustees remain liable for any actions or decisions taken. This is why supervision is an important part of corporate governance. Boards need to know and to understand what is being done in their name. To safeguard the trustees' position, delegations should always be clear and documented and should specify:

- who is being given authority;
- what the authority is (i.e. are there boundaries on those decisions (e.g. financial authority limits)); and
- how the trustees will monitor the exercise of delegated powers.

The constitutions of incorporated charities will usually include an express power for the trustees to delegate powers to committees. They may also include something regarding delegation to staff (e.g. a statement that the chief executive is responsible for the day-to-day management of the charity). If the trustees do not have a power of delegation, this may result in their being liable for a breach of trust, so it is important that there is some wording that covers delegation. For unincorporated charities, the position is a bit simpler as section 11(3) of the Trustee Act 2000 states that trustees of unincorporated charities can delegate the implementation of a decision of the trustees.

It is important that boards do delegate – there is a difference between governance and management. Boards that try to hold on to too many of the decisions regarding the charity will often get bogged down in detail. Professor Bob Tricker wrote in his book *Corporate Governance*, 'if management is about running business, governance is about seeing that it is run properly. All businesses need governing as well as managing'. The distinction between governance and management is not always clear and boards will often find themselves involved in matters that are not at a high strategic level. Boards should be clear about what matters are delegated and then try to keep away from considering them other than for monitoring.

Many boards adopt a statement of matters reserved by the board – a list of things that will always require board consideration, and then set in place delegation for other matters. Matters reserved for the board will typically include:

- approval of the vision, values, strategy and objectives;
- approval of business plans, the annual budget and any material changes to them;
- approval of matters of significant risk to the charity;
- approval of the annual report and accounts;
- approval of the matters reserved by the board, the scheme of delegation and committee terms of reference;
- approval of the risk management policy and risk appetite;
- approval of matters that might create significant financial or other risks to the charity; and
- appointment of the chief executive and secretary.

Charity boards typically delegate in a number of different ways including:

- *Delegated authority to chief executive for day-to-day management of the charity* – often contained in the constitution of the charity.
- *Job descriptions* – these will typically give delegated authority, either express or implied.
- *Committee terms of reference* – if a board is delegating power to a committee this should be specified in the terms of reference. Often, delegated power is implied in a statement on the functions of the committee, but this can lead to a lack of clarity. Is the committee advising the board on this matter or does it have authority to take the decision itself? It is best practice for the terms of reference to include a separate section on delegated powers, very clearly specifying each of them or stating that the committee's role is advisory only.
- *Policies and procedures* – the most common example being financial procedures that often will include a statement of the levels of financial authority for staff.
- *Budget and business plan* – sometimes, when the board agrees a budget and business plan each year, this can be seen as a form of delegated authority – giving authority to staff to act within it. However, care needs to be taken in interpreting this as a delegation; it depends on the practice of the charity. A charity could set a budget and business plan, but still require that decisions over a specified financial limit or with significant risks must come back to it. It could also agree a capital expenditure budget, but require board approval of any specific expenditure within it. It is essential that there is clarity about what level of authority a budget and business plan actually gives to staff.
- *Minutes* – there may be a minute giving a general delegation (e.g. delegating the purchase of property within the business plan to the CEO), or specific (a power to the CEO to negotiate and agree the purchase of a specific building, within agreed financial boundaries).

Although delegations can come about in a number of ways, it is good practice for a charity to have one document that brings them all together in a summarised form. This is called a scheme of delegation and there are a number of models available. Typically, charity boards approach delegation in quite a fragmented way. They may take a co-ordinated approach to setting levels of financial authority but they then deal with other types of delegation as they arise. This can lead to inconsistencies and gaps. Legally, a board must take all decisions, unless they delegate them, and this gets forgotten. Often a charity will operate for quite a long time with the CEO and staff taking decisions on a range of matters, as delegation has been assumed over time. Then, when something goes wrong, it is discovered that there is no formal delegation to back up these actions.

Charity boards should spend some time considering delegation and the approach that they want to take. Getting a board to think about the matters that it wants to reserve is a good starting point. Another approach is to get the board to develop a policy framework approach, such as the one recommended by John Carver. With this type of approach, the board essentially deals with delegations by setting the boundaries, and setting limits on what staff can do, rather than listing everything that they can do. While this can seem like a negative approach, it can be very useful in ensuring that there is a consistent and complete approach to delegation.

Accountability

Accountability is one of the core themes of governance for charities. When we looked at the different theories of governance we saw how the principle of accountably to the shareholders, and owners, was a key factor in governance for the commercial sector. For a charity, the principle of accountability is different. Even if the charity has members, its accountability is not just to its members. Its primary accountability is to its beneficiaries, present and future. A charity can also have a wide range of stakeholders – starting with its donors and the public, but also encompassing local authorities, central government, and other charities. It is important for all of these stakeholders that a charity's trustees are both open and accountable, setting out clearly in advance what it is that they are aiming to achieve and reporting back on how they have performed. Some of the issues that a charity needs to consider include:

- Who should the charity be accountable to?
- If a membership charity, how should it relate to its members and how will that square with its accountability to beneficiaries?
- Should accountability just be about the trustees being required to report and justify their action to stakeholders or should stakeholders also be involved in influencing the running of the charity and, in particular, shaping the services that they provide?

The Good Governance Code gives a number of examples of how a charity can demonstrate accountability, including:

- identifying stakeholders and ensuring that there is regular and effective communication with them about the organisation's achievements and work;
- ensuring that stakeholders have the opportunity to hold the board to account and that their views inform the organisation's planning, decision making and strategic reviews;
- having clear and effective complaints procedures; and
- recognising and acting on broader organisational responsibility towards communities, wider society and the environment (in so far as this does not divert the organisation from achieving its objects).

The trustees are responsible for the decision making in a charity; they set the strategy and determine what is to be done. Often a charity will try to engage with its stakeholders and involve them in developing its strategy and direction. However, the final decision must rest with the trustees. There must be clarity about what a stakeholder's involvement actually means. The trustees have a duty to act in the best interests of the charity; in this regard the interests of future beneficiaries must also be taken into account. Any stakeholders that they consult may have more limited aims and the trustees may need to override these to fulfil their wider, legal obligations.

The key component of accountability is how the charity reports on its actions. There are a number of legal requirements for charities; these were explored in Chapter 3. To summarise:

- Key information about a charity, including its annual report and accounts if it has income above £25,000 per year, is available on the Charity Commission Register of Charities.
- Registered charities must complete an annual return, much of which feeds into the Register of Charities.
- Sections 171 and 172 of the Charities Act 2011 state that a charity must provide a copy of its annual report and accounts to any person who requests them.
- Charities with members often have a constitutional requirement to hold annual general meetings and to use these to account for their actions in the previous year.

You can see from this that the annual report and accounts are vital for the accountability of a charity. However, this format and structure is not always the best way of reporting. Some charities go a bit further by:

- providing a summarised annual review, pulling out the key points from the annual report and accounts, and reporting in a more accessible way;
- ensuring that the annual report is drafted in clear, readable way, whilst meeting the legal requirements;

- providing full information about its targets and achievements, perhaps via its website; and
- preparing an annual impact report – reporting on the broader or longer-term effects of its outputs, outcomes and activities. This can be done either as a part of the annual report, or as a separate report.

While a charity should be as open and transparent as possible, there will be limits on this. Charities work in a competitive and commercial environment. Much of their work is now conducted on a contractual basis, rather than via grants and they will need to protect their decision-making processes around this. A charity should find ways of reporting that respects these needs.

CASE EXAMPLE

Troubadour is a charitable membership organisation. Its members are all singer songwriters and its objects are the advancement of the arts, culture, heritage or science. The charity runs a wide range of events, and provides music education programmes. Its board sees itself as very accountable to the charity's membership and they are all elected by the members. Its board meetings were held in public and it published the minutes on its website. The new secretary had concerns that key decisions were not being taken by the board. Very large contracts and key pieces of work were being agreed informally by the chair and vice chairs. On looking into the reasons for this, she had found out that the CEO and chair were reluctant to bring key decisions to the board, as there were serious issues around confidentiality. She arranged for the board to change the way it works. It still invites members to board meetings, but they need to give notice that they wish to attend as an observer, and there is an agreement regarding confidentiality. The board now publishes a summary of its meetings on the website, rather than the minutes. This leaves out, or reports in an anonymised way, matters that need to remain confidential. Since this practice has begun, the board has been able to go back to taking the lead on key decisions. Feedback from members is that they actually find the report more readable than the minutes.

Sources of income (generating resources)

Key sources of income

Most charities rely on funding from a mixture of sources, including voluntary income, such as donations and legacies, and self-generated income. The common sources of income for charities and the means by which they generate those financial resources are explored below. We will also look at the most important legal and governance issues relating to those income sources and the activities charities participate in to access them.

Trading

Can charities trade?

Charities can lawfully trade, both in direct pursuit of their own charitable purposes (often called 'primary purpose trading') and to raise funds, subject to some fundamental parameters:

- They must remain true to and always within their charitable purposes.
- Charitable funds and assets must not be used for private or commercial gain by third parties or trustees or people and organisations connected to trustees.
- Any conditions or restrictions on commercial trading, or investment in commercial companies, set out in their constitutions must be observed.
- Applicable rules and requirements of charity law and the wider law must be followed.

The charity regulators' perspective

The charity regulators expect trustees to exercise appropriate care and be mindful of their duties and responsibilities when addressing any trading activities (including duties with regard to investments). The Charity Commission has issued specific guidance *Trustees, trading and tax – how charities may lawfully trade* [CC35]. This concentrates on when and how the Commission considers charities may lawfully trade to raise funds (rather than addressing trading to carry out the charitable purposes).

The guidance emphasises that the interests of the charity are paramount and sets out some key principles, including the need to comply with key trustees' duties. In particular, the Commission highlights these general duties in the context of trading:

1. The duty to act in the best interests of the charity.
2. The duty to manage the charity's resources responsibly.
3. The duty to act with reasonable skill and care.

The guidance states that to fulfil these duties properly, particular care must be taken about dealing properly with conflicts of interest, implementing appropriate financial controls, managing risks and obtaining the correct professional advice when it is appropriate and/or a legal necessity to do so.

CC35 states that, due to the complexities of charity law and other legal issues, the complex tax law issues and the potential scale of adverse consequences if mistakes are made in any of these areas, trustees should obtain professional advice in relation to any substantial trading activities.

In the context of potential income or corporation tax on the profits raised by trading, the guidance provides basic information and highlights the significance of this area and its potential impact on the appropriate choice of structure for trading to raise funds for a charity. The Commission has itself taken note of the detailed tax guidance relating to the taxation of trading profits earned by charities that is issued by HMRC. It recommends that trustees and others involved in charity trading should read and consider that detailed guidance, which is available on the HMRC website.

Relevant OSCR guidance should be considered in the context of trading by charities on the Scottish Charity Register.

Public benefit dimension

Charities are obliged to operate for the public benefit and must seek to provide benefit that is appropriate to their charitable purposes (as set out in their individual constitutions). The trustees must, therefore, consider the potentially restrictive effect of any fees charged for charitable services or facilities (i.e. fees charged in the context of trading in direct pursuit of the charitable purposes). They need to have a reasonable basis for making charges and for setting the levels of those charges. Wherever possible, the trustees should seek ways to widen access to charitable benefits for people less able to afford fees. Any private benefit arising from a charity's activities should be purely incidental to the public benefit provided (e.g. a necessary and minor by-product of the charitable services or facilities provided by the charity to its beneficiary group or to the public at large). Care should be taken to ensure significant private benefits and commercial benefits do not arise and potential conflicts of interest must be identified and actively managed. Significant failures in such areas could, at worst, amount to a breach of trustees' duties or even put charitable status at risk.

Primary purpose trading and non-primary purpose trading

A charity can trade in direct pursuit of its charitable purposes, for the public benefit. This is 'primary purpose trading'.

Examples – primary purpose trading

- A charitable theatre, with a charitable purpose to educate the public in the performing arts, selling seats for performances.
- An educational charity charging for providing educational materials to teachers and schools.
- A charitable art gallery charging for entry to an art exhibition.
- A charitable care home charging for provision of residential care.

Such trading is acceptable from a charity law perspective, subject to the terms of the individual charity's constitution and the normal charity rules and principles such as risk management, the correct use of charitable assets and the rules on public benefit. The public benefit requirements are especially important with regard to charges that potentially inhibit access to benefits for those less able, or unable, to afford the charges.

Primary purpose trading needs to be distinguished from commercial trading activities intended to generate funds (i.e. fundraising trading). Even though the funds are used for the charitable purposes, this is 'non-primary purpose trading' (it is not activities being done in direct pursuit of the charitable purposes). Such fundraising trading *by the charity itself* must be treated with some caution. If undertaken on a larger scale or to the detriment of the direct charitable activities, it might incur a tax charge and/or potentially prejudice the charity's charitable status. The use of a trading subsidiary to undertake larger-scale or higher-risk trading may be either desirable or necessary.

Income generation trading

Trading with the aim of raising funds for the charity that are then applied to the charity's purposes (i.e. fundraising trading) is non-primary purpose trading. This is because the trading itself does not directly further the charity's charitable purposes.

It is important to recognise that fundraising, and therefore fundraising trading, is not of itself a charitable purpose or a charitable activity (regardless of the fact that the funds generated are ultimately spent on charitable activities). So a charity cannot have 'fundraising' as its charitable purpose.

A small amount of non-primary purpose trading can usually be carried out by the charity itself, provided it is relatively low risk, although the specific circumstances need careful analysis before deciding to take that route – for example, the charity's constitution may include restrictions and even absolute bans on any trading activity.

In considering the level of significance of proposed trading, to help decide if it can and/or should be undertaken by the charity (rather than through a trading subsidiary), the Charity Commission expects trustees to weigh up these factors (see CC35):

- The size of the charity
- The nature of the business
- The expected outgoings
- Turnover projections
- Sensitivities of the profitability of the relevant business to market changes.

In considering any non-primary purpose trading in the charity, the financial risk issues to assess and consider include the risks from a potential imbalance of the costs of the trading against the income actually generated. They also include the potential risk of losing tax exemptions on the charity's other income, triggered by losses incurred on the non-primary purpose trading activity.

Other areas of risk in non-primary purpose trading also need to be identified and managed correctly, including reputational risks and the potential risks of personal liability for the trustees. Those personal liability risks can arise if the trading activity makes a loss and the trustees are considered to have acted in breach of trust. The Charity Commission's guidance (CC35) indicates that the regulator is unlikely to conclude there has been a breach of trust if:

- there was a rational expectation that the trading would be successful;
- it was reasonable for the charity itself to have carried out the trading (rather than carrying it out in a trading subsidiary); and
- the expenditure that gave rise to the losses was within the trustees' powers.

However, the Commission's guidance warns that risk of loss of charity tax exemptions, due to trading losses, applies regardless of whether there was irresponsibility on the part of the trustees with regard to the failed trading activity.

With regard to taxation of the profits generated by the trading, a certain level of fundraising trading can usually be carried out directly by the charity (tax free). This tax-free level is the 'small-scale exemption' under section 46 of the Finance Act 2000. That tax law provision exempts non-primary purpose trading income of a charity from income and corporation tax provided the *turnover* is within the applicable threshold. The turnover threshold has two elements:

- 25% of the charity's total incoming resources in a year (from all sources); and
- subject to a maximum level of £50,000 turnover in a year.

This enables a modest level of lower risk commercial trading to be undertaken directly by a charity for fundraising purposes, without loss of any of the profits to tax.

Examples of small-scale fundraising trading (subject to financial thresholds discussed above)

- Sales of branded goods (e.g. clothing and badges with the charity's name/ logo on them).
- Sales of seasonal items (e.g. Christmas cards).

Larger-scale trading, above the small-scale exemption threshold and higher-risk trading activities, must be dealt with through a trading subsidiary.

Mixed-purpose trading

Some trading is mixed purpose – partly aimed at furthering the charity's purposes and partly at generating funds for the charity.

Example of mixed-purpose trading

A charitable art gallery with charitable purposes to advance the education of the public in the visual arts has a shop within the gallery premises. The shop sells:

(a) educational books on visual arts topics (primary purpose trading); and
(b) branded promotional items such as clothing, pens, mugs, tea towels (non-primary purpose trading).

In such cases it is important to distinguish properly between the two different elements of the trading and deal correctly with each of them, both with regard to charity law issues and also with regard to the taxation issues. Expenses and income must be apportioned on a reasonable basis between the two elements (with the statutory accounting and reporting reflecting that apportionment).

Ancillary trading

Ancillary trading is trading alongside the charitable activities which directly contribute to the successful furtherance of the charitable purposes of the charity. For both charity law and tax purposes, ancillary trading is regarded as part of the charity's primary purpose trading, provided it remains genuinely ancillary to the charity's charitable purpose. There is no specific threshold to determine what trading goes beyond being ancillary; each situation depends on its own facts. However, trading to raise funds for the charity cannot be treated as ancillary to the charitable purposes (because it does not directly contribute to furthering those purposes).

Example of ancillary trading

A charitable theatre with charitable purposes to advance the education of the public in the performing arts operates a bar within the theatre that is open during intervals in performances, for use by people who are attending those performances.

Taxation – trading

In relation to the trading activities of charities, tax and VAT issues are potentially complex and high-risk areas. It is often wrongly assumed that charities have a blanket exemption from VAT (which they do not). It is also sometimes wrongly assumed that because the underlying nature of charities is non-commercial, any surplus funds generated by trading activities (the income from the trading) could never be taxable. In fact, the key issue in relation to direct taxation is whether any exemption from tax applies to the income in the particular situation. If not, a tax charge may arise.

Whether or not a VAT charge arises in relation to any trading activities depends on the usual VAT rules. VAT is a tax on the business supply of goods and services. The nature of the organisation involved (e.g. charity or non-charity) does not determine whether the relevant activities are within the scope of VAT. There is no general exemption from VAT for charities. There are some specific and quite limited exemptions that can be available to some kinds of charities in relation to particular activities, if particular conditions are met. Careful analysis of all trading activities, with suitable professional advice, is essential to ensure tax and VAT issues are understood and dealt with correctly.

Rate relief

Where a charity occupies premises and uses them for its charitable purposes, it is entitled to 80% mandatory rate relief from non-domestic rates and can also be considered for a discretionary additional 20% relief. Primary purpose trading (in pursuit of the charitable purposes) and selling donated goods do not prejudice this. Commercial trading to raise funds might do so (especially if the trading becomes substantial). The relief does not apply to commercial trading by a trading subsidiary. Under section 43(5) of the Local Government Finance Act 1988, the key conditions for the relief are:

- the charity is the ratepayer for the premises (or its trustees, in the case of an unincorporated charity); and
- the property is used 'wholly or mainly' for charitable purposes.

Social enterprise

Increasingly, some charities use the term 'social enterprise' to describe their trading activities. Although the term does not have a strict legal meaning, broadly 'social enterprise' is the carrying out of trading activities for a wider social purpose. The prime objective is to provide social benefit whilst also generating some level of surplus funds to sustain the organisation's activities. Most of those profits will be re-invested in the activities, although some may be transferred over to relevant community purposes. Some social enterprise activities are carried out in a commercial setting, with external investors who receive a certain proportion of the profits from activities. This kind of arrangement is unlikely to be appropriate in a charity.

In practice, there is a very wide spectrum of organisations and activities that might, in some sense, be considered to be engaging in forms of social enterprise. These range from purely philanthropic and charitable organisations to significant commercial organisations and activities, where some of the profits are paid out to the business owners or third-party investors.

Charities engage with social enterprise in a variety of ways. Some use it as the means of carrying out their charitable activities (e.g. providing chargeable services such as window cleaning or garden maintenance in order to develop the work and life skills of the beneficiaries, with a view to re-integrating them into society and helping them gain independent employment). Others use it as a form of fundraising trading or for mixed purposes. A charity engaging in social enterprise is subject to all the usual restraints on trading activities. It must ensure the benefits provided to the wider community by the activities are both appropriate to and within its charitable purposes and within the limits of the charity's constitutional powers.

It is important to analyse the underlying purposes of any activities regarded by the charity as 'social enterprise' to ascertain whether they are primary purpose, non-primary purpose or mixed-trading activities. These must be structured correctly, depending on which type of trading is involved, so they do not pose unacceptable risks to the charity's charitable funds and assets, have unexpected taxation consequences or put charitable status at risk. Use of a trading subsidiary may be desirable or necessary.

Charity shops

Traditional charity shops sell second-hand goods donated to the charity by its supporters. This amounts to the cash conversion of the donor's gift; HMRC will not seek to tax the funds generated. The charity can operate this kind of traditional charity shop activity without prejudicing its charitable status as the activities are not commercial trading activities. The position is more complex when new goods are being bought in for re-sale; that is commercial trading, so there may also be tax and VAT issues.

If the charity wants to operate a scheme to generate Gift Aid through the sale of goods provided by supporters, there are potential legal and tax complications. The activity must be correctly structured and operated very carefully, to avoid potentially significant problems. The supporters are not strictly making a genuine gift of the goods. Rather, they are providing them for the charity to sell as their agent then making a separate donation of the amount raised with Gift Aid.

Professional advice should be taken before embarking on these wider kinds of trading activities in charity shops.

Key issues for trustees in trading matters

Trading is a complex area for charities; the judgements trustees need to make may be finely balanced. The trustees must ensure the charity pursues its charitable purposes and that its activities and the use of its funds and assets are directed to that end. They must make some careful decisions about the types of trading being undertaken and how those can properly be carried out. The analysis should include (a) whether the activities can or should be undertaken directly by the charity itself; or (b) whether a trading subsidiary should or must be used.

The trustees have a duty to ensure the charity operates within its constitutional powers; it is important to check and observe any trading restrictions in the charity's constitution. The trustees have overall responsibility for the correct management of all the charity's trading activities. In discharging this responsibility, they must particularly consider how the activities fit with the charity's current strategy and address risk management, including risk of losses on the trading activity and the risk of loss of tax exemptions because of trading losses, misapplication of charitable funds and potential reputational damage. They are also responsible for compliance with relevant public reporting and accounting obligations, in relation to all types of trading.

Good performance management of trading activities is essential. This should include setting appropriate targets and monitoring performance against those targets, as well as carrying out regular reviews of all trading activities. The trustees should seek to reduce the exposure of the funds generated to tax, so far as lawful and practicable, whilst ensuring solvency and retaining sufficient working capital. This is a particular challenge in managing trading subsidiaries.

Other legal rules that impact on trading

Potentially, a wide range of other legal rules impact on a charity's trading activities. Depending on the mix of business activities and how those are being undertaken, areas of potential relevance include (but are not limited to):

- Advertising regulations
- Competition law
- Consumer protection and consumer safety legislation
- Contract law
- Data protection
- E-commerce regulations/distance selling regulations/direct marketing regulations
- Financial services legislation

- Food and hygiene regulations, alcohol licensing and other public licensing requirements and
- Intellectual property law (trademarks, patents, copyright, domain names etc).

Donations, gifts and fundraising

Donations and other gifts

Donations involve benefaction on the part of the donor – they are freewill contributions to the charity, made without receiving anything in return. Cash-based donations and other genuine gifts of funds, such as legacies given under wills, are part of a charity's voluntary income. Such funds are gifted income, given to the charity by a genuine donor, rather than payments made to it in return for goods or services supplied by the charity to the purchasers of those goods or services.

Legacies are gifts made to a charity under an individual's will. Such a gift only takes effect on the death of the testator (i.e. the person who made the will). The gift may be of a specific item, such as land or shares, or it may be a pecuniary gift (i.e. a sum of money). Pecuniary gifts may be specific sums or the charity may be given some or part of the residue of the estate (i.e. the balance of funds remaining after payment of taxes, the costs of administering the deceased's estate and satisfying any specific monetary and other gifts made to particular beneficiaries by the will). Some donations, including some legacies to charities, will be given for restricted purposes, specified by the donor. Such restrictions must be observed.

Grants of funds to a charity by a funding body are also a form of donation. However, they are typically subject to conditions and often a grant is made for restricted purposes (rather than for the charity's overall charitable purposes). Grants typically come from public sources or from other charities that are using grant-making as a way to directly fulfil their own charitable objects (rather than carrying out charitable activities themselves).

The overall amounts of grant funding now available to the charity sector are significantly less than was once the case, especially in relation to grant funding available from publicly funded sources. While it was once common for charities to receive significant sums of direct public funding through grants (especially charities operating in areas such as healthcare, social welfare and social housing) this is no longer the case. The reductions in public spending, both centrally and at local government level, combined with prolonged and severe economic difficulties in the UK and beyond, have led to drastic reductions in public spending and driven forward major reforms in the delivery of public services and the custody and care of public assets. Consequently, it is now far more common for charities to be involved with the provision of contracted public services (in return for fees) or custodianship of community assets, formerly held in public ownership.

Loan funding

Loan funding is a potential source of temporary income for charities, perhaps arranged as part of the funding package to acquire or refurbish a building. It is important to recognise that loans must be repaid in accordance with the agreed terms (they are not gifts) so a charity that has taken out a loan has to manage its finances sufficiently well to generate enough income to meet those repayments. There are various legal restrictions and obligations relevant to charity borrowings and the granting of security by a charity.

Tax-efficient giving – general

The range of tax exemptions and reliefs available on certain gifts to charities are valuable and can enhance the charity's income. A charity should seek to use them as widely as possible, to:

- encourage giving, by reducing the cost to the donor of making the gift (tax relief is not a *major* motivator for donors but is a consideration for some donors); and
- maximise the value of gifts to the charity from both individuals and businesses.

When considering tax-efficient giving to charities, independent tax and legal advice should be taken by donors, since personal circumstances vary. HMRC provides very helpful general information about tax-efficient giving to charities on its website, both for individuals considering how best to help their chosen charities; and for the charities themselves, seeking to encourage donors to give in the most effective ways and to maximise the value of their donations. HMRC's guidance includes model Gift Aid declarations, as well as guides to the Payroll Giving Scheme and leaving a legacy to a charity in a will.

Tax-efficient giving – individuals

There is potential tax relief for the donor on gifts of land, certain other property and gifts of qualifying shares to charities. Some of these apply to gifts made during the donor's lifetime; others are available on death and apply to the donor's estate in relation to charitable gifts made in the deceased's will. There are strict limits on the level of any benefits that a donor can potentially receive when making tax-efficient gifts to charities. There are also various anti-avoidance measures, intended to prevent abuse of tax relief for charitable giving.

Payroll Giving Scheme – individuals

Individuals who pay income tax under the Pay As You Earn (PAYE) scheme may be able to make tax-efficient gifts to charities by payroll deductions, if their employer has opted to join the Payroll Giving Scheme. The donations are made before calculation and deduction of income tax (resulting in marginal rate tax relief for the donor).

Gift Aid scheme – individuals

Donations made by taxpaying individuals under the Gift Aid scheme enable the recipient charity to reclaim the basic rate of tax paid by the donor on the sum given out of their taxed income. A higher-rate taxpayer can also claim a certain amount of tax relief on part of their additional tax liability. A range of conditions apply where donations are made by individuals under the Gift Aid scheme, including:

- there must be an outright gift (ticket sales to a charity fundraising event will not qualify);
- the gift must be a cash gift (not a gift of assets);
- the donor must be a UK taxpayer, who will pay sufficient direct tax during the relevant tax year to cover all their Gift Aid donations to charities (payments of council tax and indirect taxes, such as VAT, are excluded from this calculation);
- the donor must provide a Gift Aid declaration including all required information (various models are available on the HMRC website); and
- the charity must keep required records both of the donation and any tax reclaimed in respect of it.

In order to benefit from Gift Aid donations, a charity must be registered for the Gift Aid scheme. Guidance is available on HMRC's website (www.hmrc.gov.uk/charities).

Gifts under a will – tax

Generally, a gift to a charity in a will is free of tax and the value of the gift is deducted from the estate for the purposes of calculating the amount of inheritance tax (IHT) payable on the rest of that estate. Under a special additional tax relief, intended to encourage legacy giving to charities, if a death occurs on or after 6 April 2012 and the deceased's will left at least 10% of their estate to one or more charities, the overall IHT rate applicable to the net estate can be reduced to 36% instead of 40%.

Inheritance tax example – charitable legacy

An unmarried person has an estate valued at £1 million and an unused nil-rate band of £325,000. The baseline amount will be £675,000 [£1m – £325,000]. To qualify for the lower rate of IHT of 36% (rather than full rate of 40%), the charitable legacy will need to be at least £67,500. The effect of making that minimum donation on the estate would be:

Estate (before nil-rate band) £1million

Charitable legacy (% of net estate)	0%	4%	10%	15%	20%	25%	30%	35%	40%	45%	50%
	£	£	£	£	£	£	£	£	£	£	£
Left to charity	–	27,000	67,500	101,250	135,000	168,750	202,500	236,500	270,000	303,750	337,500
IHT liability	270,000	259,200	218,700	206,550	194,400	182,250	170,100	157,950	145,800	133,650	121,500
Left to other beneficiaries	730,000	713,800	713,800	692,200	670,600	649,000	627,400	605,800	584,200	562,600	541,000

Tax-efficient giving – companies

Companies can make donations to charities under the Gift Aid scheme, provided the gift meets relevant conditions. This benefits both the donor and the charity. The gift is made from pre-tax profits, so the amount given is deducted from the overall profits when calculating the company's corporation tax liability and the charity receives full gross sum (without having to reclaim tax). The conditions include:

- a requirement that the payment is a genuine gift (it cannot be repayable);
- that the relief is claimed during the accounting period in which the gift is made (unless the donor company is a subsidiary owned by one or more charities, in which case a nine-month time limit applies); and
- any benefits to the donor or any 'connected' persons are within specified limits.

Tax-efficient giving – Scotland

The Scotland Act 2012 enables a Scottish rate of income tax to be set by the Scottish Government, and makes other tax changes relevant to Scotland. This has a number of consequences for tax relief on giving to charities by individuals who are taxpayers in Scotland. The UK Government has recognised the likely administrative burden on charities regarding Gift Aid administration and reclaims, if charities were obliged to operate separate claims for their Scottish donors due to the variation in income tax rates. It has announced that Gift Aid repayments for charities will continue to apply at the UK basic rate, regardless of the tax position of the donor. This will be reviewed if the rates diverge considerably in the future or if it becomes possible to provide Gift Aid relief for charities at the Scotland-specific rate, alongside the different general UK rate, without placing an undue and disproportionate burden on charities. Tax relief for Scottish taxpayer donors on their gifts to charities (under the Gift Aid scheme or otherwise) will now be calculated by reference to Scottish tax rates.

Fundraising – general

Some charities, in particular some grant-making charitable trusts with significant investment income, do not need to actively fundraise from the general public or other sources. However, this is an increasingly rare situation. Most charities undertake some form of fundraising activity to generate income for their charitable activities and to fund their running costs. For some charities, fundraising is their main (or indeed only) source of income.

Fundraising – context for the regulatory regime

A variety of concerns about some fundraising practices used by or on behalf of charities led to a review of the fundraising self-regulatory system, as it then was, carried out by a panel chaired by Sir Stuart Etherington (Chief Executive of NCVO). The review panel's report (Regulating Fundraising for the Future: Trust in charities, confidence in fundraising regulation, September 2015) concluded that the system was not fit for purpose and proposed a new approach for the future, based on a 'three lines of defence model' with key roles for:

- Charity trustees
- A new fundraising regulator
- Existing other relevant regulators, including the Charity Commission, other UK charity regulators and other regulators that have principal oversight roles for charities not required or permitted to be registered on any of the UK charity registers (e.g. the principal regulators for exempt and excepted charities in England and Wales).

Fundraising – the charity regulator's perspective

The Charity Commission recognises the importance of fundraising as a source of income for charities. It also points out that the public expect charities to raise money in a considerate and responsible way and then to use the funds raised effectively. The regulator's fundraising guidance (see below) reminds charities that the public's trust and generosity should not be taken for granted.

The Commission intends its guidance to help charities fundraise effectively, efficiently and legally, complying with the law and good practice in their fundraising. It encourages charity trustees, staff and all relevant volunteers to use its guidance and also suggests that professional fundraisers, businesses and consultants involved in fundraising and charity donors should also do so.

Fundraising – Key Charity Commission guidance

- *Charity Fundraising: A guide to trustee duties* [CC20]
- *The Essential Trustee – What you need to know, what you need to do* [CC3]
- *Charities and Risk Management* [CC26]

The Charity Commission also recognises that concerns relating to fundraising practices, relationships with potential and actual donors and the proper use of funds raised by charities are critical drivers of public confidence and trust. The regulator acknowledges that it is discharging its own regulatory role in a context where the public expectation of charities:

1. Demands greater accountability.
2. Gives less 'benefit of the doubt' to charities and their trustees.
3. Increasingly emphasises higher moral and ethical standards, beyond mere legal compliance.

The independent research into public confidence and trust that the Commission arranges, as well as the Commission's own compliance casework, evidence this significant change of climate in public expectations and perceptions. The regulator also recognises that intense media scrutiny and criticism of the charity sector, especially (though not exclusively) in matters relating to public fundraising, charities' relationships with commercial organisations and debates over charity staff remuneration and benefits, add to the growing public demands in the three areas listed above.

All of this has contributed to a firm expectation on the part of the Charity Commission that charity trustees will set parameters for their charity's strategy and practices in fundraising and will actively ensure those parameters are adhered to by all involved in fundraising for the charity. Adequate oversight as well as appropriate challenge by the trustee board is considered essential.

There is also an equally firm expectation that charities will adhere to good practice in fundraising, particular when fundraising from the public and when engaging in fundraising ventures with third parties, including commercial organisations and fundraising businesses.

Fundraising – Charity Commission's jurisdiction

The Charity Commission's principal role over funds raised by charity fundraising is a protective one for the funds, their safe custody and the correct application for the relevant charitable purposes for which they were raised. It can use some of its intervention powers where necessary to achieve this. However, the Commission takes a risk-based approach, based on seriousness and imminence of risk. It is not likely to intervene unless it perceives that:

- the circumstances fall directly within the Commission's legal and regulatory remit, with no other agency, investigatory or regulatory body having a more direct role; and
- the concerns are of a sufficiently serious nature to justify deployment of the Commission's resources.

The sorts of issues that might lead to such conclusions are:

1. Misuse of a charity's name and/or intellectual property (logo etc) for fraudulent purposes.
2. Dishonest methods being used to deceive the public into giving money.
3. Funds raised either for charitable purposes or in the name of a charity being used, or being at risk of being used, for private gain or illegal or other non-charitable purposes.
4. Funds raised for charitable purposes not being accounted for properly or being at risk of loss or diversion to other purposes.
5. Intervention by the Commission being necessary to protect public trust and confidence.

The Commission does not directly 'police' adherence to fundraising standards or deal with public complaints about fundraising. These areas largely fall to the oversight and actions of trustee boards of individual charities, to the fundraising regulator and, where the behaviour and practices of fundraising professionals is concerned, to the professional membership body of the charity fundraising sector, the Institute of Fundraising.

Fundraising – activities, law and regulation

These particular charity fundraising activities are subject to specific charity law and regulation:

- Public collections
- Door-to-door collections
- Event fundraising
- Online, broadcast and telephone fundraising
- Fundraising involving:
  - children
  - fundraisers paid by the charity (who are not professional fundraisers)
  - gaming activities (e.g. lotteries, raffles etc) and
  - 'professional fundraisers' or 'commercial participators'.

Many other legal rules can impact on fundraising ventures and initiatives. Obvious examples include law and regulations relating to broadcasting, telecommunications and e-commerce, data protection, the protection of children and vulnerable people, consumer protection laws (particularly important for sales catalogues, shops etc), travel bonding, tour operator and package holiday regulations, insurance and health and safety requirements (particularly important when an overseas 'challenge' event is being considered).

Fundraising – areas of risk for charities

Non-compliance risks obviously arise in relation to specific charity law and regulatory requirements relating to charity fundraising and particular kinds of fundraising activities. In addition, key risks arise in relation to:

- the charity's reputation and good standing;
- public perception and public confidence;
- existing charitable funds and assets which could potentially be lost in a failed fundraising venture;
- fraud and other financial criminal abuse; and
- the level of fundraising costs incurred and both donor and public perceptions of those levels.

Fundraising – issues for trustees

The Charity Commission's guidance on fundraising *Charity Fundraising: A guide to trustee duties [CC20]* sets out six core principles for trustees in relation to fundraising:

1. Effective planning – the trustees must agree and monitor the charity's overall approach to fundraising. In doing so the regulator expects trustees to take into account the charity's values and its relationships with its donors and the wider public, as well as risks and income needs and expectations.
2. Supervision of fundraisers – to ensure their activities are being conducted in a way that furthers the charity's best interests. The regulator expects this oversight for staff and volunteers within the charity and also for third party agents and contractors involved in fundraising activities for the charity.
3. Protection of the charity's reputation, funds and other assets – here strong overall management is expected to ensure all funds due to the charity do reach it and that reputational, as well as other risks, are properly managed. The regulator also expects the trustees to ensure anti-fraud measures are adequate and effective.
4. Ensuring compliance with laws and regulations applicable to the kinds of fundraising being undertaken.
5. Identification and adherence to any codes of practice relevant to the fundraising being carried out (especially the relevant parts of the Code of Fundraising Practice).
6. Commitment to openness and accountability – the regulator has an expectation that trustees will lead in creating a culture of transparency in their charity (this should result in actions well beyond mere compliance with the technical rules on public reporting of fundraising).

The regulator expects trustees to take an active leadership role in relation to fundraising and retain effective adequate oversight of all fundraising, including appeals. It also points out that the trustees must ensure all fundraising appeals are in the best interests of the charity and should actively monitor the performance of appeals against relevant targets.

The regulator also expects the trustees to ensure there is proper control over the fundraising activities and the funds raised, urging particular care if third parties are carrying out the fundraising (paid or unpaid).

In addition, relevant Charity Commission guidance stresses the importance of ensuring the funds are spent on the purposes for which they were raised. That is particularly important when the nature of the appeal for funds means that the funds raised are restricted purpose funds.

The Charity Commission's *Charity Fundraising: A guide to trustee duties* (CC20) emphasises that trustees always have overall legal responsibility for all fundraising done by their charity, whether or not they are actively involved in carrying out the fundraising activities themselves. CC20 specifies that:

> Operating effective control over your charity's fundraising is a vital part of your compliance with your legal duties.

The regulator highlights these as the three most important general legal duties of trustees in the context of fundraising:

1. The duty to act in what the trustees honestly believe to be the best interests of their charity.
2. The duty to manage the charity's resources responsibly (which includes protecting and safeguarding the charity's reputation).
3. The duty to act with reasonable care and skill.

The Charity Commission expects trustees to act prudently, balancing the need to resource the charity with income against potential risks arising in relation to fundraising.

> Charity trustees have overall responsibility and accountability for their charity and this includes its fundraising. They have a key role to play in setting their charity's approach to raising funds, making sure that it is followed in practice and reflects their charity's values. Getting this right can be very rewarding, a valuable and visible result of a trustees' commitment to their charity, those that it supports and those that support it.
>
> As the regulator of charities in England and Wales, the commission expects charities that fundraise to do so in a way which protects their charity's reputation and encourages public trust and confidence in their charity. This includes following the law and recognised standards, protecting charities from undue risk, and showing respect for donors, supporters and the public.
>
> (Charity Commission, *Charity Fundraising: A guide to trustee duties* [CC20])

The Commission strongly encourages charities that undertake fundraising to follow relevant codes of good practice and to have an open and accessible complaints process available to deal with any complaints that may arise.

The Commission's fundraising guidance emphasises that the charity is answerable for its fundraising and should have:

> ...effective systems in place so that [its] fundraising is explained clearly and openly, fully complies with accounting and reporting obligations, and is appropriately open to challenge by complainants.

It also reminds trustees that:

> Every registered charity must produce an annual report and accounts that explain where its money comes from and how the charity expended the funds.

Fundraising costs

There is no set minimum amount that a charity should spend on fundraising and likewise no formal maximum amount or percentage that is acceptable for the costs of fundraising. In its fundraising guidance, the Charity Commission recognises that different types of fundraising will involve different sorts of costs and varying levels of costs. The key issue is that the charity's trustees both manage and explain fundraising costs properly.

In doing so, the regulator expects the trustees to:

- be satisfied that the costs are in the charity's best interests;
- be transparent about what fundraising costs were incurred;
- explain those costs clearly (what they are and why they were incurred);
- explain how the funds raised were then spent; and
- articulate why all of this is in the charity's best interests – the charity needs to communicate clearly how it works and why its fundraising costs are necessary.

The Charity Commission expects trustees to distinguish general administrative costs from fundraising costs. It also expects them to have proper systems in place for setting and monitoring fundraising costs. In deciding whether potential cost levels are justifiable, the regulator expects the trustees to weigh the amounts expected to be raised and other benefits to the charity against the projected cost levels, to ensure that balance is proportionate.

Fundraising security

As part of the risk management processes applied to fundraising, charities should consider the risks of fraud and other forms of criminal abuse (e.g. money laundering). Effective control over cash fundraising is an important part of this, as there are potential risks from both opportunist criminals as well as more organised fraud activities. The Charity Commission expects a charity to:

- have systems in place to authorise those who will carry out cash collections for the charity;

- ensure compliance with applicable charity cash collection rules and relevant regulatory requirements (for instance, regulation of collections in public places or door to door cash collections);
- follow good practice in the security of cash collected and in its counting and banking; and
- ensure that after the collection all collectors return to the charity any official charity branded materials issued to them for the collection, such as collecting tins or buckets, collectors' badges and clothing (e.g. tabards or sashes).

The Charity Commission expects charities to operate 'know your donor' systems and to make staff and volunteers aware of the risks associated with suspicious donations (which include reputational, as well as financial, risks). The regulator also expects charity trustees to ensure their charities have effective systems in place to identify and take action where any suspicious donations are received.

The Charity Commission makes information about common types of fundraising fraud available on its website together with useful tools such as a checklist of anti-fraud measures and its checklist on internal financial controls.

In addition, the Commission and a range of other crime prevention and investigative bodies, including the National Crime Agency and the Fraud Advisory Panel have collaborated to create an online facility for guidance and resources to assist charities in deterring and detecting attempted fraud (see www.charitiesagainstfraud.org.uk).

Fundraising appeals

A fundraising appeal can only be made for something that is within the particular charity's charitable purposes. Fundraising appeals need to be well-planned, taking into account the charity's ethos and reputation. The planning process should address financial risks and also reputational risks. In making appeals for funds, charities should always be honest about all aspects of the appeal.

Charities should consider carefully how they present all appeals for funds to the public. In particular, care is needed to:

- protect potentially vulnerable donors;
- protect the charity's reputation and good standing;
- observe good practice standards; and
- ensure compliance with all applicable legal requirements.

It is essential to avoid misleading potential donors or setting unrealistic expectations about how the funds will be used and what can be achieved, for instance with a particular level of donation. An appeal for funds may be for the charity's general charitable purposes or for a specific more limited purpose, within those overall purposes. Where an appeal seeks funds for a specific purpose, gifts made to that appeal are restricted funds and may only be spent on that stated purpose.

Example of an appeal for a specific purpose (restricted purpose)
'Help us build a new hospice at Nempnett Thrubwell in Somerset.'

Appeal literature and communications (printed or electronic) must include all the required statutory disclosures (such as the full legal name of the charity and its registered charity number). The nature of the appeal being made and/or who is involved in making it and/or the medium through which the appeal is made often trigger additional disclosure requirements or the obligation to include additional statements (e.g. in relation to paid fundraisers or donor cancellation rights).

Unauthorised, inappropriate and harmful charity fundraising activities

Unauthorised and inappropriate fundraising activities using the charity's name and logo (e.g. by individuals outside the charity) can carry reputational or even fraud risks. The Charity Commission expects trustees to have systems in place to deal with any unauthorised and inappropriate fundraising, of which they become aware. This would include prompt action attempting to contact the people or organisations involved and might also include providing guidance to ensure relevant legal requirements and good practice standards are met. In very serious situations, the charity might need to take professional advice and consider using available legal powers to restrain potentially harmful unauthorised fundraising.

Any suspected fraudulent or other criminal activities should be reported immediately to the police and other relevant investigative agencies. In such cases the trustees should also consider whether it is appropriate to make a 'serious incident' report to the Charity Commission. This needs to be done by electronic communication to the Commission's specific email address for serious incident reporting.

Failed specific fundraising appeals

Specific fundraising appeals can fail because they raise insufficient funds to achieve the stated purposes of the appeal (this is initial failure). They can also fail because the appeal is too successful and raises more funds than can be spent on the stated purposes of the appeal (this is subsequent failure). Charity law deals with these two possibilities in different ways.

If there is initial failure, with insufficient funds raised, the trustees have a duty to attempt to return the funds to the donors, who have a right to choose repayment of their donations. Provided donors can be identified, contacted and are willing to give permission, it may be possible for the charity to gain their consent for using the funds for other specific purposes or for the charity's general charitable purposes. If a particular donor requires return of the donation made to the appeal, the charity must respect and comply with that choice. Where donors to a failed appeal cannot be individually identified from the charity's records, there are particular procedures that must be followed seeking to find donors and offer them return of their donations. If some funds from unidentified donors still remain after those procedures have been followed, the Charity Commission can make a scheme enabling the funds to be used for similar purposes to those originally intended.

If too much money is raised (without the appeal having indicated how any surplus would be used) so the appeal fails subsequently, donors do not have a right to refund of their donations. However the charity will usually need formal legal authority from the Charity Commission to use the surplus funds for other purposes. The best way to avoid failed specific appeals is to ensure from the outset that an appeal cannot fail, by careful wording of the appeal that allows surplus funds to be used either for a secondary specific purpose or for the charity's general purposes.

Fundraising – declaring charitable status

It is a specific legal requirement for a charity to declare that it is a charity when fundraising if the organisation is a registered charity with annual income above £10,000. It is good practice for other charities to declare their charitable status when fundraising. Additional disclosure rules apply for charities that also operate in Scotland or Northern Ireland.

Code of Fundraising Practice

The Code of Fundraising Practice sets out recognised standards for charity fundraising. The Code is overseen by the fundraising regulator, to maintain independence from the fundraising sector and those engaged in that sector.

The Charity Commission expects charities to comply with the Code standards when carrying out fundraising directly or when authorising and permitting others to do so on their behalf.

Under the Code, all fundraising should adhere to the four overarching principles of being:

1. Legal
2. Open
3. Honest
4. Respectful.

The Code is supported by two rulebooks for fundraisers engaging in particular areas of fundraising activity:

1. The Street Fundraising Rulebook sets out the standards of conduct expected of fundraisers who engage with the public in publicly accessible local areas (including on the street). These require fundraisers to respect the public and the fundraising environment, to safeguard the public (especially those who are vulnerable) and inform the public clearly about matters such as who the fundraiser works for, how that organisation will be paid, what length of commitment is being sought from the donor and the financial nature of the 'ask'.

2. The Door-to-Door Fundraising Rulebook deals with matters such as approaching households respectfully, the times of day during which fundraisers may knock on doors/ring doorbells etc and responsibilities regarding observing 'no-calling zones', no-calling door stickers and the like.

Public collections and other public fundraising

The regulation of public collections for charitable causes is subject to a mix of statutory regulation, local authority local regulations, good practice and the charity sector's fundraising self-regulatory regime. For the purposes of the relevant legal and regulatory regimes, public collections are personal solicitations of money (i.e. immediate cash or comparable donations (such as credit cards or text giving)) or of committed gifts (such as direct debits and standing orders) in any area where the public has free access (e.g. a street). Public collections in such public places, including door-to-door and street collections, require prior permission from a relevant licensing authority, usually a local authority outside London and in much of London from the Metropolitan Police and/or City of London Police. For door-to-door fundraising, with very few exceptions, it is usually necessary for the promoter of the collection to obtain a licence from each local authority responsible for each area in which the collection will be carried out.

There is a scheme of national Exemption Orders. These are mainly used for some of the major national collections, such as the annual Poppy Day appeal for the Royal British Legion. If such an order is granted, the relevant charity does not have to obtain individual local authority consent in every place where the collection will occur. The order provides the necessary legal authority for the whole collection to take place. Such orders can be granted by the Minister for the Cabinet Office, for a collection taking place across the whole or a substantial part of England and/or Wales. For local collections taking place in a smaller area over a short period, the local police have the power to grant an Exemption Order. The granting of Exemption Orders (for national or local collections) is rare.

For the above legal and regulatory purposes, collections include not only door-to-door collections but also collections that involve visits to pubs, offices or factories to appeal for money for a charity or for property that will be sold to raise money for a charity (e.g. clothes) (see the House-to-House Collections Act 1939 and the House-to-House Collections Regulations 1947 and 1963). Where a collection takes place within an event being held in a public place, a license for the event and a licence for the collection are both likely to be needed.

Collectors taking part in collections in public places must be at least 16 years of age, carry a certificate of authority signed by the licensed promoter and wear an official badge (also signed by the promoter). These items must be shown to any member of the public who requests to see them. They must be handed back to the promoter at the end of the collection. Public collections in other places, including private premises to which the public customarily have access (such as churches and other places of worship, supermarkets, rail station concourses or airport lounges) may only take place with the consent of the owners and/or landlords of the relevant premises.

The Charities Act 2006 set out a new regime for the licensing and regulation of public collections but this has never been brought into force, largely due to a range of perceived practical difficulties with the application of the legal provisions.

Local authorities also have the power to make local regulations about charity fundraising in their areas, especially about how street-based fundraising is carried out. An increasing number of authorities have chosen to do so. Such local regulations are in addition to the principal legal requirements.

The charity sector's fundraising self-regulatory regime is of increasing importance to public fundraising, especially in the context of fundraising from individuals, the protection of vulnerable and potential donors, all kinds of fundraising appeals to the public and all types of fundraising in public places or at locations or events to which the public have access. Adherence to the good practice standards set out in the Code of Fundraising Practice is also of increasing importance in all kinds of public fundraising.

Static collection boxes

There are currently no specific regulations governing static collection boxes, although the usual charity disclosure and information requirements (such as the obligation to display the registered charity number) would, of course, apply. The Institute of Fundraising has issued guidance on the management of static collection boxes. This is available on the Institute's website.

Fundraising ventures with third parties and/or paid fundraisers and solicitation statements

Particular issues and legal obligations are likely to arise when charity fundraising involves third parties or any kind of paid fundraisers, especially if those persons are:

- paid fundraisers soliciting donations (including the charity's staff);
- 'commercial participators'; and
- 'professional fundraisers'.

A professional fundraiser is a person who carries on a fundraising business for gain that is wholly or primarily engaged in soliciting or otherwise procuring money or other property for charitable, benevolent or philanthropic purposes. In addition, any other person who, for reward, solicits money or other property for the benefit of a charitable institution is a professional fundraiser.

A commercial participator is someone who carries on a non-fundraising business and, in the course of that business, carries out a promotional venture indicating that contributions will be made to or applied for the benefit of a 'charitable institution'.

A charitable institution is a charity or another institution established for charitable, benevolent or philanthropic purposes. Relevant ventures are advertising or sales campaigns and any other venture undertaken for a promotional purpose.

Any fundraiser being paid for collecting for a charity must declare that they are being paid when they make a solicitation statement to prospective donors. Other information must also be given to the prospective donor in that statement. The obligation applies to anyone being paid to fundraise in door-to-door and street collections and to those being paid for fundraising in a variety of other situations. A paid fundraiser must state:

(a) for which charity or charities they are fundraising (if it is for charitable purposes rather than one or more particular charities that must be stated instead);
(b) the proportions in which each charity will benefit (if they are fundraising for charitable purposes, they must state how the proceeds will be distributed to different charities); and
(c) whether they are an officer or employee or a trustee of the charity or an officer or employee or director of a company connected to the charity.

Note that a trustee could not be remunerated for acting as a fundraiser unless the charity in question had specific authority for that type of payment to be made to that trustee and the conflicts of interest issues had been correctly dealt with.

A professional fundraiser must provide the above information and also state how their remuneration in connection with the particular appeal is to be calculated and the amount of that remuneration. A commercial participator is required to indicate:

- which charity or charities will benefit from the promotional venture;
- if there is more than one charity the proportions in which each will benefit must be stated; and
- the proportion of the proceeds of the goods, services or promotional venture sold that will be given to each charity must also be stated (or the total amount of donation to each charity as a result of the sale of those goods, services or the running of the promotional venture).

Fundraising – commercial participators and professional fundraisers

Fundraising with commercial participators or professional fundraisers is subject to a specific statutory regime (see Part II of the Charities Act 1992 and associated regulations). Commercial participators and professional fundraisers are regulated persons in this context. The statutory provisions:

- make it unlawful to solicit money and property on behalf of a charitable institution unless the relevant requirements have been met;

- require a written agreement between the charity and the regulated person (which must address particular matters);
- oblige the fundraiser to make specific solicitation statements to the public when making the solicitation; and
- impose criminal sanctions for non-compliance on the fundraiser (rather than the charity).

Certain information must always be given in the solicitation statement (see above) but the further information required in it varies, depending on how the solicitation is made, whether the regulated fundraiser is a professional fundraiser or a commercial participator and whether more than one charitable institution is to benefit from the fundraising activities. Recent reforms have enhanced and clarified the detailed requirements. It should be noted that 'solicit' has a very wide meaning in this context. It covers express and implied requests whether they are made:

- by speaking directly to the person or persons to whom the solicitation is addressed;
- by means of a statement published in any newspaper, film or radio or television programme; and
- other means of communicating.

Anyone responsible for receiving money or property solicited on behalf of a charitable institution is subject to the relevant statutory controls, even if that person did not themselves make the solicitation. For example, if a third party is dealing with the receipts from an appeal made directly by the charity, that third party must comply with the regulatory requirements.

Requirements under the Charities (Protection and Social Investment) Act 2016

The Charities (Protection and Social Investment) Act 2016 enhances the legal and regulatory regime with regard to charities' relationships with professional fundraisers and/or commercial participators. It also amends the obligations relating to solicitation statements.

For agreements with professional fundraisers and/or commercial participators, these additional provisions must be included in all new agreements:

1. Details of any voluntary fundraising scheme or standard that the professional fundraiser or commercial participator undertakes to be bound by.
2. Details of how the professional fundraiser or commercial participator will protect vulnerable people and others from unreasonable intrusion on a person's privacy, unreasonably persistent fundraising and undue pressure to donate.

3. Arrangements enabling the charity to monitor compliance with the agreement.

These obligations are brought into legal force from 1 November 2016. It is expected that there will be a period of grace during which charities can negotiate necessary changes to existing agreements.

With regard to public reporting, the 2016 Act requires charities that have accounts subject to compulsory statutory audit to include a variety of information and statements in their annual trustees' reports (see later).

The 2016 Act also provides a reserve power for the relevant government minister to introduce legal force to the new voluntary regime for fundraising regulation (by statutory instrument – see below).

Particular types of fundraising activities and methods

Particular types of fundraising activities and methods can give rise to further legal and regulatory obligations and requirements, in addition to those already described. They include:

- gaming-based fundraising – such as lotteries, bingo, raffles and other gaming activities;
- event fundraising;
- challenge-type fundraising activities;
- broadcast and telephone fundraising;
- online fundraising; and
- fundraising involving children.

Requirements can include the obligation to obtain one or more licences, travel bonding/insurance obligations, child protection obligations, requirements under electronic communications regulations and/or consumer rights and consumer protection legislation.

Charity sector fundraising 'self-regulation'

Some types of fundraising and fundraising relationships are subject to statutory controls and specific regulatory regimes. However, the overall regulation of charity fundraising remains largely dependent on good practice and the so-called 'self-regulatory regime' for charity-sector fundraising.

The Institute of Fundraising is the representative body for the charity fundraising community, including individuals who are professional charity fundraisers and commercial fundraising organisations, in particular fundraising charities. The old Public Fundraising Regulatory Association merged with the Institute in August 2016.

Charity fundraisers (including fundraising consultants) are encouraged (but not required by law) to join the Institute, observe its professional standards and enhance their skills and knowledge through its professional development activities. (See www.institute-of-fundraising.org.uk.)

The Fundraising Regulator was established in 2016 as a direct result of recommendations made in the review report Regulating Fundraising for the Future (September 2015). Its set-up costs have been met voluntarily by a number of the largest charities. Its ongoing running costs will be met by a levy paid voluntarily by charities wishing to opt into this new voluntary regime for regulating charity fundraising activities and standards (a sliding scale of levy fees will apply, determined by financial thresholds).

Despite its name, the regulator is not established by statute (rather it is a 'not-for-profit' non-charitable company limited by guarantee) and its does not have a statutory remit or direct statutory enforcement powers. Instead it operates a regulatory regime for charity fundraising that is based on a voluntary 'opt-in' system, supported by weighty moral pressure on charities that engage in public fundraising to any significant degree. The Charity Commission expects such charities to join the regulator's scheme but does not currently have power to force them to do so. Increasingly, the Commission and other relevant bodies are likely to encourage other charities that have smaller scale public fundraising activities, to join the regulatory scheme.

The principal areas of activity for the Fundraising Regulator are:

1. Setting and promoting standards of fundraising practice. To this end, the Fundraising Regulator is responsible for updating the Code of Fundraising Practice and for monitoring compliance with the Code.
2. Adjudicating complaints received from the public about fundraising practice.
3. Investigating cases where fundraising practice has led to significant public concern.
4. Operating a 'Fundraising Preference Service'; that enables individuals to make choices about the way charities interact with them regarding fundraising (including 'opt-out' options). At the date of preparation of this edition, the full details of the FPS and its practical operation (including interaction with existing schemes such as the Telephone Preference Service) are still awaited.

The Fundraising Regulator is likely to refer appropriate concerns on to other regulators, such as the Charity Commission, for investigation and possible sanctions. The Commission will take a serious view of any charity that incurs criticism from the Fundraising Regulator and may decide to 'name and shame' in some way. The Commission is also very likely to act on any specific concerns regarding individual charities that the regulator may refer to the Commission.

The Fundraising Regulator itself is not expected to impose direct financial penalties on any organisations or individuals that it considers to have acted in breach of its scheme and relevant Codes and rules.

The Code of Fundraising Practice, the Street Fundraising Rulebook and the Door-to-Door Fundraising Rulebook can all be accessed on and downloaded from the Fundraising Regulator's website, which also provides other useful guidance, resources and links (see www.fundraisingregulator.org.uk).

The Charities (Protection and Social Investment) Act 2016 contains a reserve power for the relevant Minister to introduce regulations providing legal 'back-up' to the voluntary regime for regulation of charity fundraising. In particular, this could be used to:

(a) require charities to comply with requirements set out by the Fundraising Regulator (or some other regulator, for example the Charity Commission);
(b) register with such a regulator; and
(c) pay fees to such a regulator.

This is a 'fall-back' in case the revised regime for charity sector self-regulation of fundraising is considered in the future to have failed to address relevant areas of concern about some aspects of charity fundraising practices.

Fundraising – public reporting

Income and fundraising activities and the costs of generating funds must be clearly reported in the annual accounts and annual trustees' report. In relation to fundraising costs, these would include:

- costs of generating voluntary donations;
- costs of fundraising trading (e.g. costs of goods sold and other costs associated with the trading activity); and
- costs of managing investments.

The Charities (Protection and Social Investment) Act 2016 enhances fundraising reporting obligations, for charities large enough to be subject to compulsory audit requirements. The provisions require trustees' reports to:

1. Explain the charity's approach to fundraising.
2. State whether or not the charity uses professional fundraisers or carries out fundraising ventures involving commercial participators.
3. Indicate whether the charity, or anyone fundraising on its behalf, has undertaken to be bound by a voluntary scheme or standard for regulating fundraising and, if so, specifying which scheme(s) or standard(s) and giving information about any non-compliance.
4. State whether or not the charity has monitored fundraising carried out on its behalf and, if so, how that has been done.
5. Record how many complaints the charity, or anyone acting on its behalf, has received about fundraising.

6. Explain what the charity has done to protect vulnerable people and others from unreasonable intrusion on privacy, unreasonably persistent fundraising approaches and undue pressure to donate.

Whilst these obligations are only compulsory for the larger charities, other charities would be well advised to adopt similar disclosure standards as a matter of transparency and in the interests of good practice and public confidence.

Fundraising in Scotland

Fundraising on behalf of charities or other benevolent bodies in Scotland is subject to the requirements of Scottish charity law (see ss 79–83 of the Charities and Trustee Investment (Scotland) Act 2005 and the Charities and Benevolent Fundraising (Scotland) Regulations 2009).

Fundraising for any charity or 'benevolent body' is subject to these requirements, not just fundraising for charities on the Scottish Charity Register (e.g. fundraising in Scotland for an English charity that is not obliged to register on that Register is still subject to these requirements). Benevolent fundraisers, professional fundraisers and commercial participators (as defined in the legislation) are all subject to this regulatory regime.

- *Benevolent fundraiser:* A benevolent fundraiser includes benevolent bodies and companies. It also extends to individuals in either of those who are:
  - in management or control;
  - acting as employees or agents; or
  - in some situations, acting as a volunteer.
- *Professional fundraiser:* For these purposes, a professional fundraiser is a person who carries on a fundraising business or who, in return for a financial reward, seeks money or other property for a benevolent body or for general charitable, benevolent or philanthropic purposes.
- *Commercial participator*: For these purposes, a commercial participator is an organisation carrying on a business, other than a fundraising business, who, in the course of the business, takes part in a promotional venture where some or all of the proceeds are to be given to benevolent bodies or used for charitable, benevolent or philanthropic purposes.

Regulatory obligations include requirements for written agreements between professional fundraisers or commercial participators and the charity they are fundraising for, as well as requirements for certain statements to be made to prospective donors during relevant fundraising activities. These are intended to provide the public with particular information about the intended beneficiary organisations (if more than one organisation is involved, details must be provided about the proportions in which each is to benefit) and the remuneration of and expenses for the fundraiser/participator. Other detailed disclosure requirements vary depending on whether the fundraising solicitation is oral or written.

Additional requirements apply to the records that must be kept, access rights for the relevant charities to those records and the payment of any funds raised to the charities. Breaches of these requirements are criminal offences and penalties apply (fines) – usually to the fundraiser rather than the charity.

There are some useful protections in the regulations for charities, especially in relation to unauthorised fundraising. Initially they can seek to challenge and obtain prohibitions on such activities themselves. If that fails, it is possible to make application to the court (though, in practice, this may be a rather costly and unattractive option).

Specific legislation in Scotland requires local authority permission for public charitable collections. This regulates collections of money from the public in both public places and by means of visits from place to place. OSCR has issued guidance on the regulations (*Benevolent Fundraising – A guide to the Charities and Benevolent Fundraising (Scotland) Regulations 2009*). OSCR guidance on *Trustees Duties, Meeting the Charity Test* and *Public Charitable Collections* should be considered, as appropriate, in the context of all fundraising in Scotland and any fundraising for charities on the Scottish Charity Register.

The Scotland group of the Institute of Fundraising (the representative body for charity fundraisers and fundraising) provides a range of training and resources to support fundraisers in Scotland and their fundraising. It also offers a number of special interest groups for its members (e.g. in relation to corporate fundraising, community fundraising and individual giving) (see www.institute-of-fundraising.org.uk).

In addition to the legislative regime, there is a voluntary self-regulatory regime for charity fundraising in Scotland. Its principal aims are to give the public trust and confidence in the fundraising process and to promote 'good fundraising'. The scheme is operated by SCVO under the title Scottish Fundraising Complaints (fundraisingcomplaints.scot).

Anyone with a concern about charity fundraising is encouraged first to use the individual charity's own complaints system and, if still dissatisfied at the conclusion of that process, to appeal to the charity's trustees (unless the initial complaint is dealt with by the trustees, as is often the case is small charities). If the complaint is still unresolved after this has been done, the complainant can contact the Independent Standards and Adjudication Panel for charity fundraising in Scotland.

A new 'fundraising guarantee' is being developed by Scotland with a focus on values, culture and practices, rather than legal rules and regulation. For charity fundraising in Scotland, the guarantee will operate instead of the Code of Fundraising Practice. At the time of writing, it is expected that the new guarantee will come into operation during 2017.

Fundraising in Northern Ireland

The Charities Act (Northern Ireland) 2008 provides some specific regulation of charity fundraising, particularly in relation to public charitable collections. Supplementary regulations will be made to support these provisions in due course. There is also separate specific legislation regulating house-to-house collections in Northern Ireland (this is expected to be replaced in due course by some of the regulations mentioned above).

The Institute of Fundraising (the representative body for charity fundraisers and fundraising) continues to work with the Charity Commission and other interested parties to develop appropriate guidance and practice standards for fundraising in Northern Ireland. The Code of Fundraising Practice (issued by the Institute of Fundraising) addresses relevant current legal requirements relating to fundraising in Northern Ireland.

Contracting

Legal definition and key elements of a contract

A contract is a binding legal agreement between two or more parties in which each gives and receives from the other something of value. The law requires certain key elements to be present in order for there to be a contract:

- an offer to enter into a contract;
- an acceptance of that offer; and
- consideration passing between the parties (something of value actually given or intended to be given).

The parties must intend to create legal relations between them in order for a valid contract to be made. The contract is made at the point of acceptance; usually the parties will have agreed the actual price (the value of the consideration) before that point.

It is not a general legal requirement for all contracts to be in writing. Many contracts can, as a matter of law, be made orally; in practice many day-to-day routine contracts are not necessarily recorded in writing (e.g. an office supplies order made by phone can create a binding unwritten contract). However, it can be difficult to evidence oral contracts or prove their terms.

The law requires certain types of contract to be in writing (e.g. a contract in relation to the sale of land or hire purchase contracts and certain kinds of insurance contracts) or the key terms to be evidenced in writing (e.g. a written statement of terms relating to an employment contract that is not itself in writing). It is essential that the terms of a contract are clear and can be accurately understood by both parties. It is usually sensible for all contracts of substance and significance, in financial and/or risk terms, to be written contracts.

Contracts – legal capacity

Only a party with relevant legal capacity to do so can enter into a contract (e.g. a charitable company, a charity's trading subsidiary or a CIO). Essentially, therefore, an organisation can only contract in its own right if it has its own independent legal identity, distinct from its trustees or directors and distinct from its members, if it is a membership organisation. In addition, organisations that have potential capacity can only enter into contracts that are within their lawful powers, including their constitutional powers.

Before entering into a contract in the name of the charity, it is therefore vital to check that a particular charity is in a legal form that provides legal capacity and to consider the relevant powers in its constitution and any restrictions on those powers and how they can be used.

Charities that are in a legal form that does not give independent identity and capacity, such as unincorporated trusts or members' associations, cannot contract in their own right. Instead individuals must enter into contracts on their behalf, which brings personal liability risks. Provided the individuals act with proper authority, observing the terms of the charity's constitution, and the charity remains solvent, it is likely to be the case that the charitable funds could be used to indemnify those individuals against any liability arising on the contract. However each situation depends on the particular facts and there is, inevitably, some level of personal risk involved.

Many contract terms are specific, actually set out in the agreement between the parties. However other terms may be implied into a contract to reflect certain minimum standards required by law in areas such as consumer protection in the supply of goods or services. It is common for commercial businesses and some other parties to contracts to include their own standard terms and conditions as part of a contract, in addition to the specific terms of that particular contract. Provided those standard terms and conditions are brought to the other party's attention before the contract is made they are usually effective as part of the overall contract.

The general legal rule is that in the event of any ambiguity or uncertainty in the contract terms, the relevant matter is interpreted against the party who inserted the relevant provision and subsequently seeks to rely on it. There can be exceptions to this general rule in some circumstances. In addition, some terms may be disallowed by law because they are unreasonable, unenforceable or in breach of various protective legislation.

Contracts – constitutional issues

A charity can only lawfully enter into contracts that are within the terms of its charitable purposes and its constitutional powers and any restrictions or limitations set out in its constitution. In addition, the constitution will almost certainly include provisions about delegation of authority by the trustees and about the signature and/or execution of documents and the authorisation of signatories that are important to the process of creating a legally binding contract.

Signature or execution of contracts

Where a contract made by a company or a CIO is in writing it may usually be signed on behalf of the organisation by one or more individuals who have authority to do so. Alternatively, it may be 'executed' on behalf of the organisation, particularly if it is a company or a CIO. Execution is a particular legal process that commits the organisation to the contract by authorised signatories and particular forms of words being used. For companies and CIOs it is also possible for execution of a document to be carried out using the official seal of the organisation (if it has adopted an official seal) countersigned by authorised signatories and using the correct form of words in the execution clause in the relevant document.

The Companies Act 2006 specifies relevant legal rules and procedures for signature and execution by companies and the Charities Act and the CIO regulations specify relevant rules and procedures for CIOs. In addition, the particular organisation's constitution needs to be considered. The constitution is likely to add detail about how and by whom signatories can be authorised and who can act as an authorised signatory in some circumstances or for particular actions (e.g. execution of documents without use of a seal and/or execution under the organisation's seal).

When dealing with contracts on behalf of unincorporated charities, care should always be taken to ensure applicable requirements have been properly observed and that the individual or individuals signing the contract have proper authority to do so. As explained above, contracts made on behalf of such charities are usually being made by the individuals in their personal capacity, so it is also important that they do understand that. Signature or formal execution of contracts on behalf of charities that are not incorporated will, in part, be subject to relevant Charities Act rules and procedures and, in part, by the terms of the particular charity's constitution. The Charities Act provides a useful power for two or more trustees to execute documents in the names of, and on behalf of, all the trustees to give effect to a transaction to which all the trustees are party. There are specific legal provisions regarding the use of electronic signatures (see the Electronic Communications Act 2000 and relevant regulations). Specific legal rules apply to contracts made and/or executed under the laws of Scotland and Northern Ireland.

Contracts – distinction from grant agreements

It is important to distinguish correctly between whether a particular arrangement is a contract (where the charity is buying from, or selling to, another party goods or services in return for payment) or a grant (where funds are given to the charity by a third party in order that the charity can carry out its charitable purposes or a particular activity within those purposes). Both are important legal commitments for a charity but they have many different detailed legal and regulatory consequences for that charity. Sometimes confusion arises because either the charity's people or the officers or other officials of the third party with whom the charity is dealing do not clearly understand the distinction between a contract and an agreement.

Even the charity regulators sometimes appear to confuse grants/grant-funding agreements with agreements to provide services which are, in law, actually contracts for the provision of services by a charity to a third party ('Government departments or their agencies may pay charities to deliver services for them ... ' [i.e. enter into a *contract for provision of* services] ... .'Your charity can deliver services under a *funding agreement* with a public authority ... [sounds like a grant – but the earlier comment indicates this guidance is in fact addressing *contracts for the provision of services*]'.

Confusion can often arise if communications, the document name or title and/or the contents of the document relating to the arrangement muddle terminology and language. This often occurs when a third party seeking to contract with a charity for that charity to provide services includes terms and clauses that at first sight might appear to be grant provisions. It also often occurs when terms and language are used in grant application forms and/or grant agreements that are more appropriate to a contractual arrangement.

Contracting to provide charitable services

Contracting to provide charitable services that directly further the charity's charitable purposes is now quite a common way for charities to carry out their charitable activities, especially in fields such as social housing, healthcare and social welfare. A charity must ensure it only does this within the boundaries of its own charitable purposes. Particular care is needed to observe this legal obligation when working collaboratively with other organisations or acting as a sub-contractor, to provide part of a service under another organisation's contract to provide services to a third party purchaser.

Contracting to provide public services

Increasingly public authorities obtain public services for the community by commissioning external provision of those services by a third party, sometimes through a competitive tendering process. The services in question may be those the public body is required by law to provide for the community or services which it has the discretion to provide. In either case, if the services are 'contracted out' to a third party, the public authority in question is delivering them indirectly, through that third party.

This is why it is particularly common for contracts for charities to provide charitable services to arise in relation to the delivery of public services on behalf of a public authority. The charity has contracted with that authority to provide particular services, under the terms of the contract, either to the general public or to a particular section of the public. If the service in question is within the charity's own charitable purposes it can be potentially be provided by the charity in direct pursuit of its charitable purposes for the public benefit, without inherently putting charitable status at risk. If the service is outside the charity's purposes, the charity itself cannot contract to deliver it but it might be possible for the charity's trading subsidiary to do so.

Examples of charities contracting to provide public services

- Delivery of home nursing care to elderly or disabled people in their homes under a contract with the NHS.
- Provision of temporary housing for the homeless or sheltered housing for those with disabilities and special needs under a contract with a local authority.

Key governance issues for the trustees relate to the charity's charitable purposes and its powers, their own powers and safeguarding the independence of the charity. Key issues for charities overall in relation to contracts for the delivery of public services include:

- ensuring the charity acts within its charitable purposes and the other provisions of its constitution, including its powers;
- maintaining the charity's independence from other organisations, especially government departments and agencies, local authorities and other public bodies;
- managing financial, reputational and other risks, including operational risks during the actual service delivery;
- establishing and maintaining appropriate relationships with the relevant public authority and others involved in the arrangements;
- following proper trustee decision-making processes and ensuring the trustees act within their own powers; and
- adhering to the charity's public benefit obligations and the trustees' legal responsibilities in relation to public benefit.

Trustees must ensure that they continue to fulfil their duties properly at all times, remaining focused on their overriding duty to act in what they honestly believe to be the charity's best interests, in light of its charitable purposes.

It is important to weigh all risks against possible benefits when assessing possible involvement for a charity in public service delivery under contract. Trustees need to recognise that although, in practice, the charity may have an inequality of bargaining power, in negotiating terms, it is by law required to safeguard its charitable funds and assets. The charity must not commit to an arrangement that places undue risk on its financial sustainability. Equally, it must not allow its own resources effectively to underwrite costs that should properly be either included in the overall payments received by the charity for the services provided or borne directly by the public authority.

> Full cost recovery should apply in any case where a public authority is purchasing a service from a charity, unless it is in the charity's interests to forego full cost recovery. Charities are allowed to achieve a surplus .... (i.e. a surplus on contracts to provide services) (Charity Commission guidance *'Charities and Public Service Delivery – An introduction and overview'* [CC37]).

In addition to the charity-specific guidance above issued by the Charity Commission, the government website provides general guidance on tendering for public sector contracts (see www.gov.uk/tendering-for-public-sector-contracts/overview).

Competitive tendering

The legal and governance issues described above are relevant to the issue of charities taking part in competitive tendering for contracts. Charities choosing to bid for contracts on a competitive basis are likely to find themselves in competition with a range of non-charitable organisations. The competitors will often include commercial organisations that are not subject to the legal restraints of charitable status or the integrity standards and ethical norms expected of charities by the charity regulators in the UK and the general public. Charities must stay true to their mission and stay within all applicable legal boundaries. Their trustees must hold firm in fulfilling their legal duties, even if that means a bid cannot be made or does not succeed.

Investments

Investments – applicable law

General charity law applies to a charity's investments, as they are part of its overall resources. Likewise, the usual duties of charity trustees apply when trustees are managing existing investments or considering making investments. In addition, English charity law has specific provisions relevant to the investments of unincorporated charities (in the Trustee Act 2000). Those legal rules affect both the charities themselves and their trustees.

What is an 'investment'?

'Investment' has a very wide meaning in relation to legal rules about the investment of charitable funds. It includes financial investments, made with the intention of growing capital or generating income (or a mix of both those financial objectives). It can also include cash investments, which are a form of financial investment (i.e. cash deposits) and investments made with a view to achieving charitable outcomes, which are 'social impact' or 'programme-related' investments.

Some investments are 'mixed motive' with an expectation of some financial return, alongside beneficial social outcomes that directly further the charitable purposes. Trustees need to be clear about the duality of purposes in such arrangements and be able to justify the use of charitable funds for them, given the expected levels of both financial returns and charitable outcomes on the sum invested. All investments must be in the charity's best interests and within its charitable purposes and its constitutional powers.

Social impact investments

Charities often invest their funds in order to further their charitable purposes, which is known as 'social impact' investment. This might take the form of a loan to another organisation or guaranteeing another organisation's borrowing because that furthers the charity's own charitable purposes. Other mechanisms can include equity investment via a shareholding in a company and various forms of 'outcomes-based finance', where the funds are used to finance activities that deliver social benefits.

The Charity Commission does not consider social impact in direct furtherance of the charity's charitable purposes to be subject to the legal framework for financial investment (see above). However, it does suggest there should be some expectation of financial return, compared to a grant which is a pure charitable gift, with no expectation of any return.

Trustees must ensure social impact investment is made to further the charity's own charitable purposes and that it is both within those purposes and within the charity's powers. Care should be taken to observe any relevant restrictions in the individual charity's constitution. The board should also make the usual risk assessments and monitor performance against the public benefit objectives they have determined for the relevant activities in which the funds have been invested.

Social investments (Charities (Protection and Social Investment) Act 2016)

Some investments are made with mixed motives of generating a social return and also providing some level of financial surplus for the charity (a charitable outcome with an additional financial gain). Charity law permits this, subject to any particular restrictions (e.g. restrictions set out in the individual charity's constitution (its governing document) or any restrictions on the powers of the charity or on the powers of the trustees).

There has tended to be some nervousness amongst both trustees and professional advisers about the extent to which trustees might feel confident in making an investment with these twin motives; there has been some debate about the balance required between charitable outcome and financial return.

Lord Hodgson's review of the Charities Act 2006 concluded that, if a specific statutory power of social investment was available, charities could be encouraged to be bolder and so provide greater public benefit through social investments made with these twin aims. A subsequent Law Commission recommendation ultimately resulted in the social investment provisions of the Charities (Protection and Social Investment) Act 2016.

The Act provides a statutory power for most (but not all) charities to make social investments. The Act states that charities may invest:

With a view to both:

(a) Directly furthering the charity's purposes; and

(b) Achieving a financial return for the charity.

This statutory power is not available to charities that are Royal Charter bodies or statutory charities.

In addition, the power cannot be used to make social investments with permanent endowment funds, unless the restrictions on the particular permanent endowment are such that in making a social investment with it the charity's trustees would not be infringing those restrictions. Specialist professional advice should be taken and considered carefully by trustees before attempting to make use of this exception.

Other potential restrictions on the scope of the statutory social investment power might come from the charity's constitution.

In deciding whether or not to exercise the statutory power of social investment in any particular situation, the 2016 Act imposes specific duties on the trustees to:

1. Consider whether advice should be obtained.
2. Consider any advice that is in fact obtained.
3. Consider whether it is in the charity's best interests to invest:
   (a) In direct furtherance of the charity's charitable purposes; and
   (b) To achieve a financial return.

It should be noted that these duties override the standard investment criteria set out in section 4 of the Trustee Act 2000. However they do not override the trustees' general duty of care that arises from the Trustee Act (for the trustees of unincorporated charities).

The 2016 Act imposes a further statutory duty on trustees to review their charity's social investments from time to time.

The usual private benefit rules and restrictions apply to any proposed social investment (i.e. that any private benefit may only be that which is necessary in the circumstances, reasonable in amount and in the best interests of the charity). The usual legal principles regarding conflicts of interest also apply.

In addressing their statutory and common law duties, as they consider the making or the review of social investments, the trustees must act reasonably and consider relevant factors. They should also consider all relevant Charity Commission and HMRC guidance on investments and related matters.

The trustees should also take care to follow proper decision-making principles and processes and to make careful and clear records of their decisions. The board also need to ensure that its decisions are properly actioned.

Where a charity (charity 1) is taking certain risks on behalf of another charity (charity 2) (e.g. providing a guarantee against the other charity's borrowing risks) it is possible that the 2016 Act's social investment provisions might apply and need to be followed by the trustees of charity 1.

The Charity Commission has issued interim guidance on social investments in the light of the 2016 Act: Social Investment by Charities – The new power introduced by the Charities (Protection and Social Investment) Act 2016: Interim guidance (August 2016).

The Commission is expected to carry out a substantial review exercise on its general investment guidance for charities during 2017. This will take into account relevant provisions of the 2016 Act.

Ethical investment

The 'norm' for investments is that the best appropriate return (financial and/or charitable) must be sought on the funds invested. It is generally recognised that trustees have some scope for departing from that, to allow an ethical stance to inform their investment strategy. However, trustees do not have 'carte blanche' nor may they follow their own personal ethical preferences, as if they were private investors. Personal views and preferences must be 'left at the door' when trustee boards are considering the charity's potential ethical investment stance.

In considering ethical factors in any investment matter the trustees, both collectively and individually, are subject to overriding trustee duties to act in the charity's best interests and ensure it pursues its charitable purposes for the public benefit. Subject to those overriding legal requirements, the trustees can weigh up ethical factors as part of the overall picture, in order to:

- decide whether an investment would directly conflict with the particular charity's charitable purposes; and
- balance the risks of the charity potentially incurring a substantial loss of current and future support, because of one or more particular investments, against the overall risks of potential financial underperformance in relation to the charity's investments.

In line with these principles, an investment strategy can be informed by moral considerations.

However, trustees should not determine a financial investment direction for the charity, based on an ethical stance, if that involves substantial financial disadvantage to the charity. Likewise, they should not make social investment decisions on an ethical basis that significantly harm the charity's potential to deliver charitable public benefit.

Charity investment powers

Charity investment powers broadly come from a mix of the statutory social investment power (see above), the general statutory investment power (the latter is particularly important for unincorporated charities) and constitutional powers. The scope of constitutional investment powers varies from one charity to another.

The Trustee Act 2000 statutory investment powers and related statutory duties of trustees do not apply specifically to charitable companies. A charitable company is capable of investing funds, subject to any special trusts that exist over particular funds and subject to any specific limitations set out in its articles (or memorandum and articles for older companies). The individual company's articles should also be checked in case they impose limitations or specific requirements on the trustees with regard to investment matters.

A CIO's investment powers will largely flow from its own constitution as will the powers of the trustees to deal with investment matters. The general statutory duties of CIO trustees will apply to investment matters.

The Charity Commission model provides a power that effectively imports the Trustee Act investment powers but also imposes the Trustee Act duties for the trustees. The trustees of a CIO using those or comparable provisions will therefore need to familiarise themselves with the relevant legal rules and must observe the requirements and restrictions of those rules.

Unincorporated charities – statutory investment powers

Section 3(1) of the Trustee Act 2000 provides trustees of unincorporated charities, such as unincorporated trusts, with a wide general statutory power of investment:

> ... a trustee may make any kind of investment that he could make if he were absolutely entitled to the assets of the trusts.

In relation to land, the 2000 Act provides a general power to acquire freehold or leasehold land in the UK. This is subject to any restrictions or exclusions in the individual charity's constitution. Note that no equivalent specific statutory powers exist for charitable companies. Nonetheless, they usually have comparable investment powers, unless the articles of the particular charitable company impose restrictions on that charity's capacity to invest.

Investments – Scotland

The Charities and Trustee Investment (Scotland) Act 2005 provides a general statutory investment power for charities. The relevant provisions impose duties on the charity trustees to obtain and consider proper advice about the way in which this investment power should be used and, also, to have regard to:

- the suitability to the charity of the proposed investment; and
- the need for diversification of the charity's investments, as appropriate to the circumstances.

The legislation specifies that 'proper advice' means the advice of a person who is reasonably believed by the trustees to be qualified, through that person's ability and practical experience of financial and other matters relating to the proposed investment. Further restrictions and obligations apply in relation to the use of investment nominees and the delegation of investment management.

6

Stewardship of funds and assets

Stewardship of funds and assets – the key principles

All charitable funds and assets are held by a charity in order to pursue its charitable purposes for the public benefit. This fundamentally affects the stewardship of such funds and assets. Certain funds and assets of a charity may also be subject to additional legal restrictions that further affect how they can be spent or used and may also affect how they can be disposed of.

The trustees have prime responsibility for the care, custody and correct application of a charity's funds and assets. In particular, they must ensure the funds and assets are:

- safeguarded against accidental loss or deliberate misappropriation;
- applied within the charity's purposes; and
- managed and used effectively and efficiently to deliver the greatest possible public benefit, appropriate to the charity's particular charitable purposes.

Funds and assets of charities – key principles

All the funds and assets of a charity must be used within the powers of that particular charity and in furtherance of its charitable purposes. Misuse of charitable funds is likely to be a breach of trust and can lead to personal liabilities for trustees (even if the charity is incorporated).

In this context, 'funds and assets' includes cash, investment funds, income from all sources and hard assets (e.g. land and buildings or movable tangible assets, such as vehicles or computers). It also includes the charity's staff and volunteers and the charity's goodwill, reputation and good standing.

In its guidance Managing Charity Assets and Resources (CC25) the Charity Commission points out that trustees need to consider these key areas:

1. Protection and correct use of financial resources and other assets and resources (including staff and volunteers).
2. Appropriate investment of charitable funds, in the best interests of the charity.
3. Assessment and review of risks in all areas of the charity's activities.
4. Soundness of the internal financial controls in the charity.
5. Appropriate levels of financial reserves, to meet the unexpected, absorb setbacks and take advantage of relevant future opportunities.

6. Compliance with fundraising law requirements and good practice standards in fundraising.

The guidance also highlights the importance of correct stewardship in relation to maintaining suitable insurances, avoiding improper payments to or benefits for trustees and those connected with trustees, managing trading activities correctly, dealing properly with land and buildings (in particular sales and purchases) and managing financial difficulties effectively.

The overriding importance of the charity's purposes

The charity's purposes are of overriding importance in the stewardship of all its resources, both tangible and intangible. Those resources must not be used for any purpose outside of the charity's own purpose (not even some other charitable purpose).

CASE EXAMPLE

Yellow Trust has charitable purposes to relief the needs of the sick and elderly of the village of Yellow in Gloucestershire. It operates a day-care centre in an old manor house in the village. It is becoming unsustainable for the trust to continue as the property is very costly to run, requires substantial repairs and adaptations to cope with the mobility and other special needs of users. Additional regulatory requirements will soon increase annual running costs beyond the trust's income level.

The trustees wish to gift the property and assets to Seniors Care Charity UK which promotes the health of people over 50 who reside in the UK.

Any gift of funds or assets from Yellow Trust to Seniors Care would have to be restricted to ensure those funds or assets could only be used for the beneficiary group applicable under its objects (not to the wider group applicable under Seniors Care Charity's objects).

Impact of the public benefit obligations on stewardship

Charities exist for the public benefit, which has fundamental legal and practical consequences on how their resources can be used. A charity's entire resources and all its activities should be clearly focused on the delivery of appropriate benefits to the relevant beneficiary group. Those benefits should mainly flow directly from the charity's activities, as indirect, secondary, benefits are only partially relevant to fulfilling the public benefit obligation. The trustees must report on their stewardship of the charity's funds and assets in their annual trustees' report, indicating how they have used the charity's resources to further its purposes and deliver public benefit to the relevant beneficiary group. They must also indicate the strategic objectives they have adopted in their management of the charity and explain the strategies chosen to pursue those objectives. The trustees should also explain how all of those relate to the charity's charitable purposes for the public benefit.

Stewardship of restricted funds and endowed funds

Trustees need to exercise additional care in their stewardship of restricted funds and assets or endowed funds and assets, ensuring these are managed and used within the relevant legal restrictions. To do so effectively, they need to understand what restrictions apply to each restricted fund held by the charity and know which assets represent each such fund. It is also important that the annual trustees' report gives the required details of all restricted funds held by the charity, including a summary of the restrictions, the opening and closing balances of each fund, transactions relating to them during the year and details of the assets that represent each fund.

Example of restricted fund narrative in trustees' annual report

James Fund

The James Fund can be used for the maintenance of the grounds and gardens of the Batch Hospice Trust.

People

A charity's people, including its trustees, other volunteers and any staff employed by the charity are amongst its most important resources. Using them well is central to the good stewardship and effective operation of the charity. The same principles described above and below therefore apply to the trustees' stewardship of the charity's people resources. It is important for charities to encourage a shared understanding amongst everyone in the charity of its charitable purposes and the fundamental nature of the organisation as a charity.

The board, senior staff and key volunteers should also share an understanding of:

- how and where those purposes can be carried out;
- what activities the charity can or must do, and in some cases what it cannot do to further the purposes;
- what charitable benefits should arise from those activities; and
- who should gain those benefits – in legal terms, the correct beneficiary group for the charity.

Trustees

Good quality trustees, working effectively together as a board, give the charity the opportunity for strong and effective leadership. Effective trustee recruitment is crucial for effective future stewardship of the charity. Typically, many charities struggle to find enough trustees or to identify people willing to be appointed to the board who have particular skills that the board lacks. Charities often find their trustees struggle to grasp the particular charity's charitable purposes and the consequences of those purposes. Many trustees also struggle to understand either their role or their legal responsibilities. They may also find it hard to distinguish their role as a trustee from any other roles they, or others, have within the charity.

It is also quite common for trustees to be concerned about risks of personal liability, though this is often due to confusion about which risks fall on the charity and which really do fall on the trustees themselves. Some of the solutions to these common issues lie in providing intelligible information and other appropriate support for trustees. The charity should also seek to facilitate periodic training for all its trustees, not merely induction training for new trustees. Some of the worst challenges charities may face in relation to trustees include a board that does not operate well as a team or is at odds with the charity's CEO. It may also have one or two individuals on the board who are pursuing a personal agenda or who fail to make a meaningful contribution to the governance of the charity. Such severe issues must be addressed quickly and thoroughly to avoid serious harm being done to the charity.

Volunteers

Every charity has some volunteers, not least because its trustees will almost certainly be volunteers. Many charities either rely heavily or are entirely dependent on volunteers to carry out their work, delivering the services of the charity to its beneficiaries and dealing with the day-to-day practical administration of the charity.

Trustees need to establish and make good use of a committed and well-motivated group of volunteers, with the right mix of talents and skills to fill the volunteer roles in that charity. This does require application of some of the charity's resources in finding, keeping and equipping that volunteer team. Inevitably, there are some direct and indirect costs involved. An important legal point is to keep the distinction between volunteers and employees clear at all times, to avoid the risk of unexpected legal responsibilities for the charity or unexpected claims against it.

Most charities have quite limited people resources and it is almost inevitable that some people will have more than one volunteer role in their charity. For example, a trustee of a community transport charity is one of its volunteer drivers or the treasurer of a church is also part of the youth leadership team in that church. It is important for volunteers to distinguish between their roles and to stay within the scope of their authority in carrying out the relevant activities of each role. It is also important for the volunteers to know who they are to within the charity, in each of the different roles they have.

Employees

Employees are individuals with whom the charity has created a legal employment relationship. That relationship brings substantial legal rights and responsibilities on both sides. Any charity that employs staff must deal with all employment matters lawfully and responsibly. There are significant potential risks if the charity fails to do so.

The trustees must ensure they are aware of the charity's legal obligations as an employer and that lawful and effective employment policies and procedures are both adopted and followed. They also need to ensure the effective management and deployment of the charity's staff, so they must ensure there is regular review of:

- staff recruitment procedures and staffing levels;
- the skills and experience that the charity needs amongst its staff; and
- the costs, risks and potential liabilities relating to staff (including, for example, pension deficit risks and the costs of future redundancies).

Staffing should be planned and reviewed in the light of the charity's strategic priorities.

A charity must meet its legal obligations regarding staff pensions; the trustees need to factor that into their financial planning and management of the charity. There are particular financial risks associated with pension fund deficits, especially with regard to defined benefit pension schemes. The Charity Commission has issued a helpful guidance note 'Defined Benefit Pension Schemes: Questions and Answers' (available on its website).

Charities need to exercise particular care to identify and consider all financial and other risks when considering acquiring staff in joint ventures or mergers, transfers of activities from other charities or any other forms of restructure.

Helpful general guidance on employee-related matters is available on the government website and the ACAS website. However employment law and related law, such as tax law, is complex and potentially a high-risk area for charities. Charity trustees should take and consider specific professional advice whenever it is appropriate to do so.

Contractors

Charities may also engage independent contractors to provide services to the charity under a contract.

> **Example – Independent contractors providing services**
>
> Contractors engaged to provide consultancy advice and support in specialist areas like IT, marketing or fundraising, or to provide extra resources during the charity's busy periods in the year.

This is a completely different legal relationship to an employment relationship and it carries with it very different legal issues, practical implications and potential risks. The tax and VAT issues involved with the engagement and use of independent contractors are also very different from those relevant to the employment of staff by the charity. To ensure good stewardship, the charity must ensure there is a suitable contract in place with an independent contractor. It is also important to identify and deal with any potential conflicts of interest that arise before making any such appointment and should check for potential conflicts on an ongoing basis. Charities should also monitor and properly manage the contracted services and should ensure that they are, in fact, delivered and are of sufficient quality.

Members

Most charities have a formal legal membership although charities in some legal forms do not. Charitable companies limited by guarantee, CIOs and unincorporated associations have members. Those members may, or may not, be the same people as the trustees. There are important legal consequences of having a formal membership; the detail depends upon the particular legal form of the charity. Having a membership provides opportunities for recruiting volunteers and raising funds, for influencing external decision-makers and for providing a particular kind of 'stakeholder' accountability for the trustees and the charity.

In exercising stewardship in relation to a charity's members, the trustees need to help set and manage the members' expectations about the benefits of being members in the context of the charity's charitable purposes. Members need to understand that the charity exists to serve the community, not the preferences or the personal interests of its own members. There will sometimes be fundamental decisions that, for legal reasons, must be referred to the members for a formal decision (e.g. changing the charity's constitution or a making the decision to close and dissolve the charity). Amongst the most common challenges of having a membership are:

- People within the charity may not recognise that there is a group of people who are formal members and may not understand the distinctive role of the members from the very different role of the charity trustees.
- The charity may have groups of people it calls 'members' who are not, in fact, proper formal members but rather fulfil some other role, perhaps as a fundraising group or as practical volunteers in delivering the charity's activities.
- Members and others in the charity may not know and accept that governance and key decision making is a matter for the board of trustees, not for the members of the charity.
- People may not understand that the role of members in a charity is not at all like the role played by the owners of a business or the members of a private club. It is not 'their' charity: it exists for the public benefit.

When there is a broad shared understanding of the essential charitable nature of the organisation, it is much less likely that any extreme difficulties will arise in relation to the members (such as a small group of activist members trying to set up a breakaway charity or oust the serving board of trustees).

Honorary officers

In addition to the trustees, a charity may also have some honorary officer roles, certainly a chairman of the board of trustees and perhaps a vice-chairman, a treasurer and a secretary (or clerk to the trustee board). These will usually be voluntary roles (and must be voluntary if they are held by a trustee or involve automatic trusteeship for the office holder). To ensure good stewardship it is important to have clarity about the duties and responsibilities of the role of each officer and whether the office holder is a trustee of the charity. The board should approve a written role description for each post; this must be consistent with the charity's constitution and in line with applicable legal rules and requirements. These should be periodically reviewed and updated.

Presidents and patrons

Some charities have an honorary president. This role largely involves being the public face of the charity and acting as its ambassador. Some charities invite people notable in their relevant fields to act as patrons. It is important to clarify what role the charity expects a patron to play. Typically it is to allow the link between the patron and the charity to lend gravitas and credibility to the charity. To ensure good stewardship, it is often sensible to have limited terms of office for presidents and patrons and to review whether the relationship is still appropriate, before renewing the appointment.

Donors, funders and other supporters

Most charities have donors, other kinds of funders and various other kinds of supporters, with obvious potential benefits to the charity. The stewardship challenges involved often relate to attracting the relevant people in the first place and keeping enough of them to provide the resources the charity needs to carry out its activities. Other challenges can include the financial risk of over-reliance on a few major donors or funding sources, unrealistic expectations or even impossible-to-meet demands from some potential donors and funders.

The trustees need to be alive to independence issues, ensuring they retain their clear governance role and make independent decisions solely in the interests of the charity and its charitable purposes. This can be a particular challenge if a major funder has an expectation about how the trustees will exercise their discretion in relation to unrestricted funding provided by a donor or perhaps historic funding arising from a supporter's family trust. Potential conflict of interest issues can sometimes arise in relation to donors, funders or other supporters. These must be identified and adequately addressed by the charity.

It is of paramount importance that a charity not only complies with all legal obligations with regard to fundraising but also adopts appropriate standards of behaviour in its fundraising activities and in its relationships with, and communications to, donors and prospective donors. Compliance with data protection and privacy laws and standards is essential, as are respectful and honest dealings with the public at all times. Particular care is needed with regard to the protection of potentially vulnerable members of the public.

In all its activities relating to donors, funders and the general public, a charity should observe the principles in the Code of Fundraising Practice, as well as specific legal requirements (the Code is available on the Fundraising Regulator's website).

Restrictions on private benefits

Because of the fundamental legal rule that every charitable purpose must be 'for the public benefit', a charity must not use its resources to provide private non-charitable benefits to anyone inside the charity, an individual or organisation connected to anyone inside the charity or to any third parties. This includes commercial, financial and other material non-charitable benefits. The trustees must therefore ensure that any private benefit that may arise from the charity's activities is only that which is necessary or incidental to carrying out those activities (e.g. paying the charity's staff or purchasing office equipment and supplies).

Trustees and connected persons payments and benefits

It is a fundamental trust law principle that a trustee should not profit from his trust. That is why it is rare for lawful and proper transactions to occur between a charity and any of its trustees or individuals and organisation connected with the trustees. The legal principles that prevent such transactions are sometimes called the 'fair dealings' or 'clean hands' obligations.

Trusteeship is essentially a voluntary role, serving the community. In most charities, payments to trustees or material benefits for trustees are strictly banned (under the principles of charity law – the 'no-benefits' principles – supplemented by provisions in the individual charities' constitutions). These legal principles and supporting constitutional restrictions normally extend to individuals and organisations connected to trustees. These rules not only prevent misapplication of charitable funds to non-charitable activities but also limit the risks of potentially harmful conflicts arising between the interests of the charity and those of its trustees or individuals and organisations connected with the trustees. They also help limit the risk of reputational damage to the charity.

'Benefits' in this context has a very wide meaning, including direct and indirect benefits, payment of 'honoraria' and other kinds of financial payments and benefits in kind. Indirect benefits include:

- payment of a trustee for being a director of the charity's trading subsidiary;
- payments by the charity to a business owned by a trustee; and
- funding by the charity of the school fees for the education of a trustee's child at a fee-paying school, which are not based on any charitable need of the child.

Trustees should ensure they are familiar with relevant charity guidance relating to both trustee remuneration and trustee expenses, including:

- CC11 Trustee Expenses and Payments
- CC25 Managing Charity Assets and Resources

They should also ensure they read, understand and follow all relevant provisions in the charity's constitution (unless there is an applicable legal 'override').

Payment of trustees for being trustees/employment of trustees

The basic legal rule is that a trustee must act without remuneration or any other material reward. So trustees cannot be remunerated for their trusteeship. Due to this principle of voluntary trusteeship and to avoid potential conflicts of interest, trustees should not normally be employed by the charity (or by its trading subsidiary). Some charities have limited exceptions in their constitutions; these may enable them to appoint one or more employees to the board, subject to safeguards. However, such exceptions remain relatively rare.

Trustees' expenses

Reimbursement of genuine and reasonable expenses necessarily incurred by trustees in the proper discharge of their duties is not a remuneration of the trustees. Such reimbursement of legitimate expenses can be made subject to the provisions of the particular charity's constitution and appropriate safeguards, including a process for independent verification of the expenses being claimed. A charity that pays expenses to its trustees should ensure it has an appropriate policy and related procedures in place:

> The charity should have a written policy in place which sets out what claims are covered and the procedures for claiming and approving expenses for all staff and trustees
>
> CC25 Managing Charity Assets and Resources, Charity Commission

Trustees should not normally personally fund, then later reclaim as expenses, governance costs for which the charity is responsible (e.g. the cost of room hire for a board's strategic planning away day). Such costs should be dealt with directly by the charity.

Remuneration of trustees for services other than trustee services

The Charities Act permits the possibility of remuneration of trustees (or 'connected persons') for the provision of services to the charity other than services as a trustee (ss 185–188). Strict conditions must be met to use this statutory power and various public disclosure requirements also apply. The issue of conflicts of interest must also be carefully considered and properly addressed. These include:

1. Any restrictions in the charity's constitution must be observed (the Charities Act provisions do not override the constitution).

2. There must be a written agreement between the charity and the trustee or connected person, setting out the maximum permitted level of remuneration and other required details.
3. Less than half the trustees can be capable of benefiting in this way.
4. The trustees must consider relevant Charity Commission guidance before entering into such arrangements (see CC11 *Trustee Expenses and Payments)*.
   For these purposes 'connected persons' include:
   - spouses or civil partners;
   - parents and grandparents;
   - children and grandchildren;
   - brothers and sisters;
   - spouses and civil partners of any of the relations listed above;
   - business partners of any of the relations listed above; and
   - institutions and corporate bodies controlled by trustees or any of the relations listed above.

Directors' interests (companies)

Companies Act controls and requirements relating to directors' interests apply to charitable companies (with modifications for charities) and to the trading subsidiaries of charities. They include:

1. A duty for a director to avoid a conflict of interests.
2. A duty for a director to disclose any direct or indirect interest they have in any proposed transaction or arrangement.
3. An obligation on a director to disclose any direct or indirect interest they have in any existing transaction or arrangement (CA 2006, s. 182).

A breach of 1 or 2 is a breach of duty, giving rise to the personal liabilities of such a breach. A breach of 3 is subject to criminal penalties.

Duty to avoid a conflict of interest

A director must avoid any situation in which they have, or can have, a direct or indirect interest that conflicts, or possibly may conflict, with the interests of their company (CA 2006, s. 175). The board has no general power to disapply this duty in a charitable company (as it potentially could in a commercial company). Any disapplication could only be made under a specific empowering provision of the individual company's articles.

Duty to disclose an interest in a proposed transaction or arrangement

This duty has a very wide application. It arises if a director is in any way, directly or indirectly, interested in a proposed transaction or arrangement with the company (CA 2006, s. 177). The disclosure must:

- be made before the company enters into the transaction or arrangement;
- be made to the other directors (i.e. the board as a whole, disclosure to a committee or sub-committee does not suffice);
- disclose the nature and extent of the interest; and
- be made for indirect as well as direct interests.

If the original declaration either proves to be, or becomes, inaccurate or incomplete, a further declaration must be made. Any change to the nature or extent of the interest, subsequent to the original declaration, also triggers an obligation to make a further declaration.

Obligation to disclose an interest in an existing transaction or arrangement

This obligation arises where a director is in any way, directly or indirectly, interested in any transaction or arrangement that has been entered into by the company. It arises when the director become aware of the interest. The disclosure must:

- disclose the nature and extent of the interest;
- be made as soon as practicable after the director becomes aware of the interest;
- be made in writing (this can include by electronic means, if the company has agreed to that); and
- be made to the other directors (i.e. the board as a whole, disclosure to a committee or sub-committee does not suffice).

Details of the disclosure must be kept with the records of the next board meeting held after that disclosure was made. If the original declaration either proves to be or becomes, inaccurate or incomplete, a further disclosure must be made. There are some limited exceptions to the obligation to disclose, including if the interest could not reasonably be regarded as likely to give rise to a conflict of interest or if the other directors are already aware of the interest. It is advisable to be cautious about relying on any of the exceptions.

Members' benefits/donors' benefits

Members and donors may benefit from the charity's activities as general members of the community, with the relevant beneficiary group for the particular charitable purposes of that charity. However, they should not have preferential access to benefits or be able to access the charity's services on a substantially more favourable basis than other beneficiaries.

Tax rules and HMRC's regulatory practices substantially limit the extent to which members (and donors, who may or may not also be members) can receive benefits, so care should be taken in this regard. In particular, there should be no significant benefit to any donor as that can prejudice the treatment of the donation as being a genuine voluntary gift and can also put any Gift Aid relating to that donation at risk.

The meaning of 'benefits' in this context is wide and extends to goods and services, provided in connection to the donation, by the charity to the donor or to any person connected with the donor.

A person is connected with the donor if that person is:

- the wife or husband or civil partner;
- a relative (e.g. brother, sister), ancestor (e.g. mother) or lineal descendant (e.g. grandson);
- the wife or husband or civil partner of a relative; or
- a company under the control of the donor, or under control of connected persons.

A benefit is 'associated with a donation' if it's received by the donor or a connected person in consequence of the making of the donation.

HMRC publishes guidance for charities and donors which is available on its website.

Information provided to members and donors and ordinary communications with them about the charity and its activities, such as annual reports, magazines and newsletters, are not regarded as 'benefits' in this context. Small-scale physical acknowledgments of generosity on the part of the donor are not benefits. However, HMRC stresses that this must be modest and not be connected to the donor's business or amount to an advertisement for that business.

For tax and Gift Aid purposes, HMRC states that a right of admission to view charity property is not treated as a benefit if:

- it is in return for a donation of at least 10% more than the admission charge for an equivalent right of admission; or
- the admission is for a period of at least a year at the same times as the general public can gain admission.

However this does not apply if the benefit extends:

- beyond a right of admission to view charity property (e.g. a right of admission to a property in order to attend a concert); or
- beyond the donor and members of his or her family.

HMRC encourages charities to set rules for the maximum number of people that a donor may bring into the charity's premises. It suggests that restricting the right of admission to family groups (e.g. a right of admission for the donor and up to two other adults and six children) would satisfy this 'members of the family' test.

HMRC does not expect the charity specifically to check the identity and family relationship of people who seek admission to the charity's premises as a family group.

Conflicts of interest – overview (common law)

The basic common law framework relating to charities and conflicts of interest flows from trust law. The core underlying principle is that the core fiduciary obligation of a charity trustee is the obligation of undivided loyalty to the charity.

Important facets of this are the 'no conflict' rule (a trustee must not put himself in a position where his duty to the charity conflicts with another interest) and the 'no profit' rule (a trustee must not make a profit from his trust).

An important aspect of the 'no conflict' rule is the 'self-dealing' rule (a transaction between a charity and the trustee, even if for full consideration, is liable to be set aside).

All these rules are strict rules. The trustee can be liable for breaches even where (a) a trustee acts honestly and in good faith and (b) it cannot be shown the interests of the charity have been damaged.

These rules are the deep-seated starting point of charity law. Exceptions in particular charities in particular situations, although possible, require explicit legal authority. Exceptions are rare and always narrow. If a charity and its trustees seek to rely on one they must be extremely careful it does indeed apply and that they are acting within its strict legal boundaries.

These are complex and potentially high-risk areas of law and governance. Extreme care should be taken to ensure all actual and even perceived conflicts are identified and correctly dealt with. Trustees should consider taking professional advice as appropriate to a particular situation and with regard to their general obligations and the correct discharge of their duties relating to conflicts issues.

Conflicts – charity trustees and Charity Commission expectations

Trustees have an overriding duty to act in what they honestly believe to be the best interests of the charity at all times, in particular the interests of its charitable purposes. They must not put themselves in a position where their duties as a trustee may conflict with any personal interest (including any other personal loyalty they may have). Therefore trustees must be diligent in identifying and avoiding potentially harmful conflicts of interest.

> We expect individual trustees and trustee bodies to be able to identify any conflicts of interest at an early stage. The law says that each individual trustee must avoid putting themselves in a position where their duty to act only in the best interests of the charity could conflict with any personal interest they may have.
>
> (CC29 Charity Commission)

The Commission defines a conflict of interest as:

> Any situation in which a trustee's personal interests or loyalties could, or could be seen to, prevent the trustee from making a decision only in the best interests of the charity.
>
> (CC29 Charity Commission)

Trustees must not allow their personal interests to interfere with their independent governance of the charity and their proper decision making. Any potential effect on decision making that a personal interest may have must be eliminated, so that the board's decision will be, and will be seen to be, taken independently in the best interests of the charity.

Whilst trustees may have some discretion about how to deal with any possible conflict, they must act in accordance with the charity's constitution in dealing with the issue. Some charity constitutions impose a ban on an interested trustee from any participation in a meeting where one or more items gives rise to a potential or actual conflict.

In addition, the Charity Commission's guidance on conflicts states that for a serious conflict the trustee must remove that conflict by:

- not pursuing the relevant course of action;
- dealing with the matter in a different way, so that no conflict arises; or
- ensuring the conflicted trustee resigns (or, in the case of a candidate for appointment to the board, avoiding making that appointment).

The trustees must never prefer their own interests to those of the charity. These principles extend to indirect, as well as direct, interests.

Potential conflicts can be transactional (relating to particular transactions) or situational conflicts. In either case the conflict may be one of loyalty and/or duty as well as one of any other type of interest.

The Charity Commission strongly recommends following a three-step approach in relation to conflicts:

1. Identify and declare a potential conflict.
2. Avoid that conflict.
3. If it cannot be avoided, ensure it is managed appropriately – this may require the trustee in question to resign in order to remove the conflict and the risk it poses to the charity.

The regulator also expects trustees to use its guidance to help them fulfil their legal duties in the context of conflicts of interest. It also strongly recommends that written records should be kept of all conflicts identified and of how those conflicts were dealt with.

Where trustees fail to act properly on a conflicts matter and subsequently realise that, the Charity Commission expects them to act promptly to put matters right and to ensure the same issue cannot recur or any similar issue arise.

The regulator specifies in its guidance that:

> Where trustee actions or failings [in conflicts issues] present a serious risk to the charity, we are likely to regard this as mismanagement or misconduct and to take remedial action.

> If the Charity Commission finds evidence of potential criminality in the situation, it will refer the matter to the police for investigation. It may also choose to use its own intervention powers as well, if it considers the seriousness of the matter and the public interest to justify doing so.

See CC29 *Conflicts of Interest: A guide for charity trustees* and the associated checklist.

CASE EXAMPLE

Trustee ABC is trustee of Charity 1 (a charitable company) and of Charity 2. Charity 1 is applying for grant funding to Charity 2. This creates a situational conflict of loyalty and duty. The trustees' general charity law duties regarding conflicts apply in relation to both charities. As Charity 1 is a company, the relevant Companies Act directors' duties relating to conflicts of interest apply to the trustee in relation to Charity 1.

Conflicts of interest – appointment of trustees

Potential conflicts of interest should be addressed before any candidate is appointed as a trustee:

> Prospective trustees should be asked about potential conflicts of interest, and these should be declared to those who will decide on the appointment. Where prospective trustees are likely to be subject to serious or frequent conflicts of interest, the trustees should seriously consider whether that trustee should be appointed.
>
> (CC29 Charity Commission)

Declared interests and conflicts of interest – serving trustees

It is good practice to keep a record of the interests trustees have declared (whether or not they give rise to any potential conflicts). This is often kept in the form of a non-statutory register of trustees' interests.

Completion by all serving trustees of an annual refreshing declaration of interests is also advisable.

It is also most important to record all identified conflicts and what actions were taken by the trustees to deal with them.

Conflicts of interest – constitutions

The constitutions of many charities include provisions relevant to conflicts of interest. These should be followed carefully. Note that in many situations the provisions of the constitution cannot override the general legal principles or specific statutory provisions.

The constitutions of CIOs must include provisions on conflicts of interest. Although this is not a statutory requirement for charitable companies, it is common for company articles to address interests and conflicts of interest, especially in companies formed since the implementation of CA 2006 (or companies that have updated their articles since then).

Conflicts of interest – policies and procedures

The Charity Commission strongly recommends that charities adopt their own conflicts of interest policy with associated procedures and to keep a voluntary register of trustees' interests. This is good governance practice and some of the means by which conflicts risks can be addressed.

The regulator also suggests that, in the interests of transparency, trustees consider making both the policy and the register publicly available.

A charity should ensure its conflicts policy and procedures are consistent with legal principles and any applicable specific statutory provisions. It should also ensure they align with the conflicts provisions of the charity's own constitution. If the constitution is out of line with modern legal requirements and expected governance standards relating to conflicts, the trustees should consider amending those provisions (in a membership charity this will require members' formal approval).

Consequences of failure to address conflicts of interest properly

Conflicts may not be properly addressed for various reasons, including:

- failure to identify a conflict issue;
- failure to address the issue or an inadequate attempt to do so;
- inadequate decision-making processes for relevant trustee decisions;
- an inadequate culture within the charity regarding conflicts issues.

Failure to address conflicts issues properly gives rise to a number of potential risks, in particular:

1. Personal liability risks for the trustees, for example because of a breach of their legal duties or because of losses caused to the charity. The trustees may have to recompense the charity for sums it spent even where the charity did not in fact lose out financially. If there is a loss to the charity, the trustees may also be required to recompense it for that loss.
2. Inherent invalidity of a transaction (or that transaction being liable to be set aside if challenged).
3. Invalidity of one or more trustees' decisions (e.g. if the trustees acted in breach of the charity's constitution).
4. Reputational risks for the charity.
5. Potential damage to public trust and confidence in charities in general.

The Charity Commission's guidance on conflicts (CC29) points out that:

> Trustees should be aware of how the situation may appear to someone from the outside of the charity, and make sure that policies and procedures are in place which will allow trustees to demonstrate that such situations have been dealt with properly.

Investments

Managing charity investments (all charities)

The trustee board as a whole is responsible for the management of the charity's investments and the trustees' general common law duty of care applies. In a larger charity, with more substantial investments, the board may establish an investment committee and delegate detailed investment management to that committee. The terms of reference and the scope of the authority of such a committee needs to be authorised by the trustee board. In particular, the extent to which the committee has the authority to make decisions, including decisions about acquisitions and disposals of investments, should be clearly recorded. The board must still deal with the strategic management of the charity's investments, setting and reviewing the overall investment policy for the charity, as well as monitoring performance against that policy. Trustees may decide to use a professional investment manager to advise and assist them, for example if they do not have sufficient expertise amongst the board members. It is essential to decide whether such an adviser is to be appointed:

(a) to provide advice which the board uses to inform its own decisions, in which case relevant board decisions are needed to authorise investment transactions to occur; or

(b) to act as a discretionary investment manager, with delegated authority from the board to make investment decisions on their behalf and authorise transactions (the scope of that delegation must be clear and should be documented).

Investments – trustees' legal duties

The trustees' common law general duty of care applies in relation to investments (for all legal forms of charities). For trustees of CIOs, their specific statutory general duties are also relevant and should be considered in relation to investment matters (see Charities Act 2011, s. 221). For trustees of unincorporated charities, a range of specific statutory duties arise in relation to financial investments (under the Trustee Act 2000). The trustees must:

(a) adopt an investment policy for the charity, with investment objectives;
(b) measure performance of the charity's investments against those objectives;
(c) report in their annual trustees' report on the policy and its objectives and on the performance of the charity's investments against those objectives;

(d) observe their general statutory duty to exercise reasonable skill and care in relation to investment matters;
(e) obtain and consider proper independent investment advice before using their investment powers; and
(f) have regard to the Standard Investment Criteria.

Further details on the legal obligations for trustees of unincorporated charities in relation to these matters are set out below.

Investments – Charity Commission perspective and guidance

The Charity Commission recognises that investment decisions are matters for the trustees, within the constraints and requirements of their legal duties, applicable law and the individual charity's constitution. It has issued guidance which includes comments on both legal requirements and good practice in investment matters. This aims to support trustees 'in confidently making decisions about investments that comply with their duties' (Charities and Investment Matters [CC14]). The regulator reminds trustees that it cannot give investment advice or legal advice to charities in these areas and encourages them to seek specialist professional advice from appropriate sources whenever that is necessary or advisable. The regulator has also issued 'Legal Underpinning – Charities and investment matters' which summarises its understanding of the background law in this area.

Investments – charitable companies

In general, a charitable company is capable of investing funds, subject to any special trusts that exist over particular funds and subject to any specific limitations set out in its articles (or memorandum and articles for older companies). The individual company's articles should also be checked in case they impose limitations or specific requirements on the trustees with regard to investment matters.

The Trustee Act 2000 statutory investment powers and related statutory duties of trustees do not apply specifically to charitable companies. While adopting an investment policy is, therefore, not a statutory requirement for a charitable company, it is certainly good practice and strongly recommended. When making investment decisions and managing investments, including appointing investment managers and monitoring their performance, the trustees of a charitable company are subject to the normal duties of trustees, especially in relation to risk and the proper application of charitable funds. Although the more detailed Trustee Act investment duties do not specifically apply to the trustees of a charitable company, it is clearly wise for such trustees to follow comparable standards and practices in investment matters.

Investment management statutory requirements – unincorporated charities

The trustees of unincorporated charities are subject to the Trustee Act obligations regarding the management of their charity's investments. There must be a written agreement with any investment manager that is appointed to assist with that management. That agreement must oblige the manager to observe the charity's investment policy. If discretionary management powers are being delegated, the agreement must also address the details of the relevant delegation.

There are statutory restrictions that prevent appointments of an investment manager where there could be a conflict of interest and various statutory limitations (e.g. the investment manager cannot normally include provisions in the agreement to reduce that manager's own duty of care). The trustees' statutory duty of care applies to appointments of investment managers and any delegation of discretionary management authority to such managers. The trustees are also obliged by law to review both the suitability and the performance of investment managers, on a regular basis.

Trustees' general statutory duty of care – unincorporated charities

The trustees of unincorporated charities have a general statutory duty of care which requires them to 'exercise such care and skill as is reasonable in the circumstances' (Trustee Act 2000, s. 1(1)). This duty specifically applies when trustees of such charities exercise either the statutory general power of investment or any other power of investment (e.g. a power arising from the individual charity's constitution). What is reasonable skill and care is a question of fact for determination in each case, taking into account all the circumstances. However the Act does state that specific regard must be had to:

- any special knowledge or experience the trustee holds himself out as having; and
- where the trustee acts in the course of a business or profession, any special knowledge or experience it is reasonable to expect of a person acting in the course of that business or profession.

The general statutory duty of care also applies in a number of other situations, listed in Schedule 1 of the Act, including when the trustees:

- have regard to the Standard Investment Criteria (to comply with s. 4 of the 2000 Act);
- take appropriate investment advice (to comply with s. 5 of the 2000 Act); and
- exercise the statutory power to acquire land, or any other powers in relation to land.

Under trust law, failure to comply with the statutory duty of care could render an investment unauthorised and constitute a breach of trust. Trustees should, therefore, take care to comply with these statutory duties.

Investment advice and the Standard Investment Criteria (unincorporated charities)

Before exercising any power of investment (whether the statutory power or some other power, such as a power set out in the charity's constitution) the trustees of an unincorporated charity must obtain and consider proper advice about the way in which that power should be exercised, having regard to the Standard Investment Criteria. The same obligation to take advice applies when the trustees review investments and consider varying them. The advice does not have to be confirmed in writing but it is clearly both good practice and a sensible protection for the trustees that there should be a written record.

The exception to these obligations is that trustees need not take advice if they reasonably conclude 'that in all the circumstances it is unnecessary or inappropriate to do so' (Trustee Act 2000, s. 5(3)). This exception should be used with care, taking into account all the circumstances, such as the size of the charity and the value of the sums under discussion, as well as the level of financial skills and knowledge amongst the trustees. If in any doubt about their competencies, the trustees would be wise to seek advice.

'Proper advice' is defined as the advice of a person who is reasonably believed 'to be qualified to give it by his ability in and practical experience of financial and other matters relating to the proposed investment' (s. 5(4)). The trustees must consider the advice but are not obliged to follow it. However, to ignore the advice without good reason could be a breach of the general statutory duty of care. The Standard Investment Criteria are:

- The suitability to the charity of the type of investment being considered.
- The suitability of the particular investment as one of that type.
- The need for diversification of the charity's investments, as appropriate to the charity's circumstances.

Note that the duty to diversify the charity's investments applies to the exercise of any investment power (including a constitutional power) not just the exercise of the general statutory power of investment.

Investments – reporting requirements (all charities)

Charity reporting standards require charity trustees to include in their annual trustees' report information about the charity's investment policy, its main objectives and the performance of the charity's investments against those objectives. A charity must also report in its annual accounts the sums that it holds in investments, the income received on those investments and the investment fund balances at both the beginning and the end of the financial year. These obligations extend to all kinds of investments aimed at producing a financial return, whatever investment funds or investment assets they may be invested in (e.g. investment land). For social impact investments, intended to further the charity's charitable purposes, the public benefit reporting obligations apply. Appropriate information should, therefore, be included in the annual trustees' report, as well as relevant financial information being included in the annual accounts.

Land

What is 'land'?

'Land' in the context of charity law and regulation is land held by or on trust for a charity. For centuries, charity law has imposed restrictions on trustees' powers to dispose of charity land. Current law restricts disposals and mortgages (see Charities Act, ss 117–129). The main aims behind these statutory controls are to protect charities from imprudent, even reckless or dishonest decisions by trustees, to ensure best price is obtained on disposals and to ensure charities can afford any obligations taken on with regard to mortgages. If the charity is unincorporated, title to land will have to be held in the names of the individual trustees (or some other custodian) as the charity does not have its own legal capacity. Incorporated charities may acquire and hold title in their own right.

Strategic approach to land

Land is a major asset and can be a major liability. For many charities, land is likely to be their biggest cost after staff costs. Trustees should ensure they take a strategic approach to their stewardship of the charity's land. This includes the acquisition and disposal of land. It also includes management of land held for or by the charity and the use of that land (e.g. ensuring the charity maximises the level of charitable activities if the land is held for carrying out the charity's charitable activities).

Acquisition of land

A charity's powers to acquire land may flow from its own constitution or particularly for unincorporated charities, from statute. Decisions about land acquisitions need to be taken by the full board of trustees; they should not be delegated to committees or staff.

Proper use and good management of land

Trustees must ensure all decisions about land and all land transactions involving the charity are dealt with in compliance with the relevant legal requirements and restrictions. In addition to charity law restrictions and requirements, other important legal areas include building, planning and use regulations, accessibility and equalities requirements and environmental, safety and energy performance regulations. In order to make proper use of land, the trustees must be clear about why the charity holds the land:

- to carry out the charitable activities;
- as a financial investment; or
- for a mix of these reasons.

Planned preventative maintenance of property will be more effective and cost efficient in the longer term than a piecemeal reactive approach. Appropriate care and maintenance of land and buildings, as well as risk management, should therefore be dealt with on a strategic basis.

Charities should have appropriate insurance cover in place for occupiers' public liability relating to their property and for buildings and their contents. A realistic valuation should be used for buildings insurance, taking into account likely costs of reinstatement, such as necessary demolition or site clearance. It is wise to review the insurance arrangements periodically and to obtain independent advice as part of such a review.

Suitable professional advice should be taken on the management of the charity's land whenever appropriate (e.g. from a qualified surveyor or other land and buildings management professionals). Where the charity is carrying out a land transaction there is often a legal requirement to obtain particular professional advice.

Special issues – functional permanent endowment/designated land

Functional permanent endowment land is land given to a charity as part of its permanent endowment and in trust for a particular charitable activity. Designated land is defined by the Charities Act as land held by or in trust for a charity where 'the trusts on which it is held stipulate that it is to be used for the purposes, or any particular purposes, of the charity' (see s. 121). It is also known as 'specie land'. The land must be used within the terms of the trusts to which it is subject. It is usually possible for the original land to be disposed of subject to the relevant statutory designated land disposal requirements in Charities Act, but replacement land must be obtained and used for the same charitable activity.

Examples of designated land

- Land and buildings gifted to a charity under a will on trust to be used as an almshouse for elderly people.
- Land and buildings donated to an educational charity on trust to be used as a school.

Note that not all land held and used by a charity will necessarily be designated land in the technical legal sense. A charity may have chosen to acquire land, free of any particular special trusts, in order to use it directly to carry out the charitable activities or for other appropriate purposes, such as the location for the charity's administrative office.

Disposal of land

Most disposals of land do not require prior Charity Commission consent, though there are exceptions (such as disposals to trustees and connected parties).

Generally, a disposal is likely to fall within one of the disposal regimes specified in the Charities Act, which controls the process by which a disposal decision is reached and certain aspects of the formal legal process. Exempt charities are not obliged to follow the full statutory disposal procedures but must include certain statements in the contract, transfer or lease.

A disposal by an unincorporated charity to vest the title in a new trustee, alongside the existing trustees, is not subject to the normal restrictions and requirements on disposal of charity land. Other special types of disposal, where the full statutory obligations do not apply, are listed below. Special statements must be made in the relevant documents and, in the case of short leases, particular advice must be obtained and considered by the trustees before the disposal is made. The relevant types of disposal are:

- A disposal to another charity, at less than best price, within the trusts of the disposing charity (i.e. in order to pursue the disposing charity's charitable purposes).
- A lease to a beneficiary, under the charity's trusts, at less than best price, with the intention the occupation will pursue the charity's charitable purposes.
- A disposal authorised by statute or by a scheme.
- A disposal authorised under the Universities and College Estates Act 1925.
- A lease of seven years or less (not granted wholly or partly in consideration of a fine).

Disposals regulated by section 117 of the Charities Act 2011

Unless the above exceptions apply, section 117 of the Charities Act requirements must be followed for these types of land disposal:

- the conveyance or transfer of land;
- granting a lease of more than seven years; and
- other disposals.

In summary, the requirements for such disposals are:

1. The trustees must first obtain a written report from a qualified surveyor (regulations specify the qualifications required). The report must address a range of specified matters and that person must be instructed by the trustees and acting exclusively for the charity.
2. The proposed disposal must be publicly advertised in the manner recommended by the surveyor (unless the surveyor advises that advertising would not be in the charity's best interests).
3. Before formally deciding to make the disposal, the full trustee board (not a sub-committee) must consider the advice received in the report and be satisfied that the proposed disposal terms are the best that can reasonably be obtained for the charity.

Required statements must be included in the contract and conveyance or transfer or lease. The precise wording varies according to the specific situation.

Disposals of designated land

If the land to be disposed of is designated land, the above procedures are supplemented by a specific public advertisement obligation (Charities Act, s. 121). The public notice must invite representations to be made to the trustees, within a stated time limit (not less than a month from the notice date). If any representations are made, the trustees must consider those before taking a decision about the proposed disposal.

These advertising requirements do not apply if:

- the disposal is made with a view to acquiring replacement property to be used for the same purposes; or
- the disposal is a lease for no longer than two years (and not granted wholly or partly in consideration of a fine); or
- the Charity Commission gives a direction that the requirements will not apply because that is in the charity's best interests.

Disposals to 'connected persons' (Charities Act, ss 117(1) and (2) and 118)

The general requirements that permit disposals under the procedures summarised above do not apply to proposed disposals to 'connected persons'. Such disposals will require Charity Commission consent (unless they fall within the limited exceptions discussed above). For this purpose, connected persons are:

(a) A charity trustee of the charity.
(b) A person who was the donor of the land to the charity.
(c) A child, parent, grandchild, grandparent, brother or sister of such a trustee or donor.
(d) An officer, agent or employee of the charity.
(e) The spouse or civil partner of anyone in (a)–(d) above.
(f) A person carrying on business in partnership with anyone in (a)–(e) above.

Disposals of investment land

Where land held by a charity as an investment is to be disposed of, the applicable legal rules and procedures relating to investments must be observed, in addition to the disposal requirements that apply to the particular proposed disposal. Unincorporated charities are subject to relevant provisions in the Trustee Act 2000.

Controls and risks

The charity's resources must be safeguarded against harm as part of the proper stewardship of those resources. Areas of particular importance in this regard include:

- appropriate risk identification and management;
- suitable insurance cover; and
- protection from misuse, fraud, theft and other forms of misappropriation or abuse.

Strategic planning and management controls

Strategic planning and ensuring there are adequate and effective management controls in place in relation to risk are key aspects of good stewardship of a charity. The ultimate responsibility for these matters rests with the board of trustees. In a larger charity some of the detailed activity may be delegated to the charity's senior management team. However, the trustees must monitor that delegation and retain the strategic overview and key control of risk identification and management in the charity.

Financial reporting to the trustees

Appropriate financial reporting to the board of trustees is a fundamental tool for good stewardship. Accurate financial information facilitates good decision making and the effective operation of the charity. It also helps manage cash flow and ensure solvency.

Management accounts

Good quality, accurate and up-to-date management accounts should be circulated to and considered by all trustees on a regular basis. Typically, management accounts are produced monthly or quarterly, to suit the particular charity's circumstances. The management accounts should enable the trustees to:

- Monitor the charity's performance against budget.
- Identify any key discrepancies in that performance and the reasons for those discrepancies.
- Identify key areas of expenditure and the reasons for that expenditure.
- Understand the actual costs of major activities.
- Ensure the charity's resources are being deployed in accordance with the strategic priorities set by the board and within the terms of the charity's purposes, powers and constitution.

Financial controls

Everyone in the charity should take financial controls seriously and follow the charity's financial control procedures diligently. Delegation of particular financial functions and procedures should be properly authorised, clearly documented and effectively monitored. The financial limits of any delegated authority, for individuals or groups such as committees, need to be understood and followed.

Key risk areas – financial controls

Some of the key risk areas that should be addressed in the charity's financial controls include:

- custody and security of cash;
- custody and security of assets;
- processing, recording and use of incoming funds from all sources;
- public fundraising appeals and public collections;
- other fundraising activities;
- identification and proper use of all restricted funds and the assets that represent such funds;
- banking transactions;
- purchases and payments; and
- payroll and other employee-related transactions and payments, including tax, national insurance, pension contributions and expenses repayments.

Key risk areas

Key risk areas for charities include:

- solvency;
- financial risks in general;
- breaches of trust;
- fraud, theft and other financial crime risks;
- reputational risks;
- accidental loss or damage to charitable assets;
- accidental loss of charitable funds;
- safeguarding risks in relation to children and other vulnerable people;
- major loss of or reduction in vital resources (including volunteers);
- other people-related risks, such as employee-related risks;
- health and safety risks;
- legal risks in relation to significant legal non-compliance; and
- terrorist activities, including misuse of the charity's name and good standing and/or its funds and assets for terrorist purposes.

Risk approach

What is necessary or appropriate as the right risk approach for a specific charity varies from one charity to another and from one risk to another. However, the key elements of a charity's risk approach should usually include addressing these areas:

- adopting a suitable risk management strategy;
- choosing which key risks to avoid and which to accept;
- establishing some form of key risks and controls register;
- deciding how to control the likelihood of the key risks arsing and limiting the potential damage they would cause if they should arise;

- putting those controls in place and monitoring their effectiveness;
- reviewing the policy and controls, as well as their effectiveness periodically; and
- keeping the key risks and controls register under review and up to date.

Risk controls

The main focus of risk controls should be on identifying and managing in an appropriate way the major risks most likely to arise that could do significant harm to the charity, particularly in terms of its operational and financial viability. All charities should undertake some form of risk analysis and put in place appropriate risk monitoring and control arrangements to deal with the management of these most significant risks. The aim is not to remove risk, which is unrealistic in many cases, but to minimise the likelihood of a major risk becoming a reality and doing significant damage to the charity and its activities.

International transactions and activities

Good stewardship requires charities to make every effort to ensure the correct end use of funds sent overseas and to protect assets acquired with charitable funds. Wherever possible it is best to move funds through formal banking systems. If alternative systems are to be used, trustees must consider what additional measures are needed to ensure the security of transfer and to verify correct end use of those funds. Key operational, financial and reputational risk areas for charities that have international activities or undertake international transactions include:

- personal harm to volunteers, staff or beneficiaries, especially in areas of conflict or terrorist activity;
- loss or misappropriation of assets, particularly when they are being moved between different territories or used in an area affected by civil instability or conflict; and
- fraud, theft, bribery and other abuses of charitable funds.

Serious incident reporting to the Charity Commission

When serious incidents are identified or suspected in a charity, the Charity Commission expects the trustees to report those incidents to the regulator. There is no formal legal definition of 'serious incident' for this purpose. The Charity Commission's guidance on serious incident reporting provides some broad examples, such as theft, fraud and other financial crime, or suspected or actual issues or incidents relating to the safeguarding of children and other vulnerable people. Prompt action can reduce the risk of losses to the charity and control the risks of reputational damage. It believes that there is currently significant under-reporting of serious incidents by charities and is seeking to raise trustees' awareness of its serious incident reporting regime.

If an incident is detected or suspected which could be regarded as a serious incident, prompt action should be taken to prevent any further loss or harm to the charity and make all appropriate disclosures and reports to relevant authorities. That may include the police or safeguarding authorities, as well as the charity's insurers, its auditor or independent examiner, the Charity Commission and any other relevant regulators who have oversight of the charity. The trustees may also need to seek professional advice on the relevant matter.

A charity that is also registered in Scotland or Northern Ireland should consider whether a relevant incident or suspected incident should also be reported to OSCR or the Charity Commission for Northern Ireland.

Risk – public reporting

Trustees must report on risk in their annual trustees' report, disclosing the principal risks and uncertainties to which the charity is subject and commenting on how those are dealt with. This should be broader than simply a statement that major risks have been reviewed and systems are in place to deal with them.

APPENDIX 1

Example terms of reference for a committee

X Committee

Terms of Reference

Purpose

The X Committee is established with the purpose of

Membership and proceedings

1. The members of the Committee shall be appointed by the Board and the profile of the committee is formally reviewed every … year.
2. Members shall include:
   a.
   b.
   c.
3. The (name support staff) may be invited to attend all or part of particular meetings.
4. The Secretary shall act as secretary to the committee.
5. The quorum shall be x members.
6. The committee shall meet not less than x times a year.
7. A meeting may be held by telephone or using any televisual or other electronic or virtual means agreed by the members, in which all participants may communicate simultaneously with all other participants.

Function

The Committee is responsible for:

1.
2.
3.

Powers

1. The committee is authorised by the Board to …
2. The committee may establish subcommittees and delegate to them.

3. In all other matters the role of the committee is advisory, unless a specific delegation power is made by the Board.

Reporting

1. The secretary shall circulate minutes of the committee's meetings to all trustees.
2. A report of the committee's deliberations shall be made to the next board meeting. Papers shall be presented to the board as and when required.

APPENDIX 2

Example trustee role description

Role

To ensure, with the other trustees, that the charity acts in accordance with its constitution and to manage its activities in furtherance of the objects set down in that constitution.

Note: The charity is registered as a charity [and a limited company] [in the form of an unincorporated trust].

Every trustee [is also a director of the company and] has legal responsibilities and potential liabilities in [each] [that] capacity. Full details of these are not included in this role description but can be obtained from the charity's office.

Responsibilities

- Setting the strategy and undertaking the strategic management of the charity.
- Ensuring that the charity complies with its [Articles of Association (A)] [trust deed] and all applicable legislation and regulations.
- Ensuring that the charity pursues its objects as defined in the [A] [trust deed].
- Ensuring that the charity applies its resources exclusively in pursuance of its objects.
- Ensuring the financial stability of the charity.
- Ensuring proper accounting records are kept.
- Ensuring the effective and efficient administration of the charity.
- Protecting and managing the property of the charity.
- Ensuring the proper investment of the charity's funds.
- Approving the charity's policies.
- Safeguarding the good name and ethos of the charity.

Duties

Collective

[Example:

- Approving the rolling five-year plan annually and monitoring progress against it.
- Determining/approving the annual budget and monitoring progress against it.
- Preparing and approving the annual report and accounts.
- Appointing the Chief Executive and monitoring his performance.]

Individual

[Example:

- Attending meetings of trustees.
- Playing an active part in trustees' meetings and deliberations.
- Exercising due care and attention and using reasonable skill in dealing with the charity's affairs.
- Using own skills, knowledge and experience to help the trustees reach sound decisions.
- Taking the lead in any trustees' activities where the trustee has special knowledge.
- Avoiding any conflict of interests.
- Sitting on the Finance and General Purpose Committee when required.
- Serving on one or more advisory groups.
- Sitting on recruitment and disciplinary panels (if required).]

Notes

1. The above specimen should be adapted as appropriate to the particular charity's needs and circumstances.

Key Charity Commission Guidance

Charity Commission guidance – public benefit

PB1 Public Benefit: The public benefit requirement
PB2 Public Benefit: Running a charity
PB3 Public Benefit: Reporting

Charity Commission guidance – other

CC3 The Essential Trustee – What you need to know, what you need to do
CC8 Internal Financial Controls for Charities (and the associated self-checklist)
CC9 Speaking Out: Campaigning and political activity by charities
CC12 Managing a Charity's Finances: Planning, Managing Difficulties and Insolvency
CC14 Charities and Investment Matters: A guide for trustees
Social Investment by Charities – The new power introduced by the Charities (Protection and Social Investment) Act 2016 (interim guidance) [there is no CC document number]
CC19 Charities Reserves: Building resilience (financial reserves)
CC20 Charity Fundraising: A guide to trustee duties
CC25 Managing Charity Assets and Resources: An overview for trustees
CC26 Charities and Risk Management
CC27 It's Your Decision: Charity trustees and decision making
CC28 Sales, Leases, Transfers or Mortgages: What trustees need to know about disposing of charity land
CC29 Conflicts of Interest: A guide for charity trustees
CC33 Acquiring Land
CC34 Collaborative Working and Mergers: An introduction
CC35 Trustees, Trading and Tax: How charities may lawfully trade
CC37 Charities and Public Service Delivery: An introduction and overview

Charity Commission guidance can be viewed and downloaded from the Charity Commission's website: www.charitycommission.gov.uk/detailed-guidance/cc-guidance-numerical-index/
The quick link list is usually the quickest route to finding the item(s) you want.

Directory

Advisory, Conciliation and Arbitration Service
ACAS National (Head Office)
Euston Tower
286 Euston Road
London NW1 3JJ
Tel: 08457 474 747
www.acas.org.uk

Association of Charitable Foundations
Acorn House
314–320 Gray's Inn Road
London
WC1X 8DP
Tel: 020 7255 4499
www.acf.org.uk

Association of Chief Executives of Voluntary Organisations
Regent's Wharf
8 All Saints Street
London N1 9RL
Tel: 020 7014 4600 7014 4600
E-mail: info@acevo.org.uk
www.acevo.org.uk

Association of Chief Executives of Scottish Voluntary Organisations
Thorn House
5 Rose Street
Edinburgh EH2 2PR
Tel: 0131 243 2755
E-mail: office@acosvo.org.uk
www.acosvo.org.uk

Bacs Payment Schemes Limited
2 Thomas More Square
London E1W 1YN
Tel: 0870 165 0018
www.bacs.co.uk

Big Lottery Fund
1 Plough Place
London EC4A 1DE
Tel: 0845 4 10 20 30
E-mail:
general.enquiries@biglotteryfund.org.uk
www.biglotteryfund.org.uk

British Standards Institution
BSI British Standards
389 Chiswick High Road
London W4 4AL
Tel: 020 8996 9001
Fax: 020 8996 7001
E-mail: cservices@bsigroup.com
www.bsigroup.co.uk

Business in the Community
Business in the Community
137 Shepherdess Walk
London N1 7RQ
Tel: 020 7566 8650
E-mail: info@bitc.org.uk
www.bitc.org.uk

Care Quality Commission
Care Quality Commission National Correspondence
Citygate
Gallowgate
Newcastle upon Tyne NE1 4PA
Tel: 03000 616 161
E-mail: enquiries@cqc.org.uk
www.cqc.org.uk

Charities Aid Foundation
Head office
25 Kings Hill Avenue
Kings Hill
West Malling
Kent ME19 4TA
Tel: 03000 123 000
E-mail: enquiries@cafonline.org
www.cafonline.org

Charities Evaluation Services
Society Building
8 All Saints Street
London N1 9RL
Tel: 020 7520 3193
E-mail: ces@ncvo.org.uk
www.ces-vol.org.uk

Charity Commission
PO Box 211
Bootle L20 7YX
Tel: 0845 3000 218
www.gov.uk/government/organisations/charity-commission

Charity Commission for Northern Ireland
257 Lough Road
Lurgan
Craigavon BT66 6NQ
Tel: 028 3832 0220
Email: admin@charitycommissionni.org.uk
www.charitycommissionni.org.uk

Charity Finance Group (CFG)
15–18 White Lion Street
London N1 9PG
Tel: 0845 345 3192
E-mail: info@cfg.org.uk
www.cfg.org.uk

Charity Law Association
PO Box 828
Gillingham ME8 1DJ
E-mail: admin@charitylawassociation.org.uk
Tel: 01634 373253
www.charitylawassociation.org.uk

Charity Learning Consortium
Vine House
Selsley Road
North Woodchester
Stroud GL5 5NN
Tel: 08451 707 702
E-mail: info@charitylearning.org
www.charitylearning.org

Charity Retail Association
4th Floor
Resource for London building
356 Holloway Road
London N7 6PA
Tel: 020 7697 4080
www.charityretail.org.uk

Charity Tribunal
The First-tier Tribunal (Charity) Manager
Tribunals Operational Support Centre
PO Box 9300
Leicester LE1 8DJ
Tel: 0300 123 4504

Chartered Institute of Internal Auditors
13 Abbeville Mews
88 Clapham Park Road
London SW4 7BX
Tel: 020 7498 0101
www.iia.org.uk

Companies House
England and Wales
Companies House
Crown Way
Cardiff CF14 3UZ
Tel: 0303 1234 500
E-mail: enquiries@companies-house.gov.uk
www.companieshouse.gov.uk

London Office
Companies House
4 Abbey Orchard Street
Westminster
London SW1P 2HT

Scotland Office
Companies House
4th Floor Edinburgh Quay 2
139 Fountainbridge
Edinburgh EH3 9FF

Northern Ireland Office
Companies House
Second Floor
The Linenhall
32-38 Linenhall Street
Belfast
Northern Ireland
BT2 8BG

Co-Operatives UK
Holyoake House
Hanover Street
Manchester M60 0AS
Tel: 0161 214 1750
E-mail: info@uk.coop
www.uk.coop

Department for Business, Energy and Industrial Strategy (formerly the DTI, BERR and BIS)
1 Victoria Street
London SW1H 0ET
Tel: 020 7215 5000
E-mail: enquiries@bis.gsi.gov.uk
www.bis.gov.uk

Department for Communities in Northern Ireland
www.communities-ni.gov.u/

Department for Education
Tel: 0370 000 2288
www.gov.uk/government/organisations/department-for-education

Directory of Social Change
352 Holloway Road
London N7 6PA
Tel: 08450 77 77 07
www.dsc.org.uk

Equality and Human Rights Commission
Correspondence Unit
Arndale House
Arndale Centre
Manchester M4 3AQ
Tel: 0161 829 8100
www.equalityhumanrights.com

Federation of Small Businesses
Sir Frank Whittle Way
Blackpool Business Park
Blackpool FY4 2FE
Tel: 0808 20 20 888
www.fsb.org.uk

Financial Conduct Authority
25 The North Colonnade
Canary Wharf
London E14 5HS
Tel: 0800 111 6768
www.fsa.org.uk

Financial Reporting Council
8th Floor
125 London Wall
London EC2Y 5AS
Tel: 020 7492 2300
www.frc.org.uk

Fundraising Regulator
2nd Floor
CAN Mezannine Building
49–51 East Road
London N1 6AH
Tel: 0300 999 3407
E-mail: enquiries@
fundraisingregulator.org.uk
www.fundraisingregulator.org.uk

Gambling Commission
Victoria Square House
Victoria Square
Birmingham B2 4BP
Tel: 0121 230 6666
E-mail: info@gamblingcommission.
gov.uk
www.gamblingcommission.gov.uk

Health and Safety Executive
Head Office
Redgrave Court
Merton Road
Bootle
Merseyside
L20 7HS
Tel: 0151 951 4000
www.hse.gov.uk

HM Revenue & Customs
Charities Savings and International 2
HM Revenue and Customs
BX 1BU
Tel: (Charities Helpline)
0300 123 1073
www.hmrc.gov.uk

Homes & Communities Agency
Arpley House
110 Birchwood Boulevard
Birchwood
Warrington WA3 7QH
Tel: 0300 1234 500
E-mail:
mail@homesandcommunities.co.uk
www: homesandcommunities.co.uk

HSE Incident Centre
(RIDDOR reporting)
Contact Centre Address as above
Tel: 0845 300 9923
www.riddor.gov.uk

ICSA: The Governance Institute
Saffron House.
6-10 Kirby Street
London EC1N 8TS
Tel: 020 7580 4741
E-mail: info@icsa.org.uk
www.icsa.org.uk/knowledge/
charity-resources
www.icsa.org.uk

Information Commissioner's Office
Wycliffe House
Water Lane
Wilmslow
Cheshire SK9 5AF
Tel: 01625 545 745
Helpline: 0303 123 1113 (Mon–Fri 9am–5pm)
E-mail: online via website
www.ico.gov.uk

Institute of Fundraising
Charter House
13 - 15 Carteret Street
London SW1H 9DJ
Tel: 020 7840 1000
E-mail: info@institute-of-fundraising.org.uk
www.institute-of-fundraising.org.uk

Investors in People Head Office
UKCES,
Sanctuary Buildings,
20 Great Smith Street
London SW1P 3BT
Tel: 0300 303 3033
E-mail: info@investorsinpeople.co.uk
www.investorsinpeople.co.uk

Land Registry
Land Registry Head Office
Trafalgar House
1 Bedford Park
Croydon
CR0 2AQ
Tel: 0300 006 0411
E-mail: customersupport@landregistry.gov.uk
www.landregistry.gov.uk

National Council for Voluntary Organisations
Society Building
8 All Saints Street
London N1 9RL
Tel: 020 7713 6161
E-mail: ncvo@ncvo.org.uk
www.ncvo.org.uk

National Housing Federation (NHF)
Lion Court
25 Procter Street
London WC1V 6NY
Tel: 020 7067 1010
E-mail: info@housing.org.uk
www.housing.org.uk

Northern Ireland Council for Voluntary Action
61 Duncairn Gardens
Belfast BT15 2GB
Tel: 028 9087 7777
www.nicva.org

Office of the Scottish Charity Regulator
2nd Floor
Quadrant House
9 Riverside Drive
Dundee DD1 4NY
Tel: 01382 220446
E-mail: info@oscr.org.uk
www.oscr.org.uk

Privy Council
Privy Council Office
Room G/04
1 Horse Guards Road
London
SW1A 2HQ
E-mail: enqurires@pco.gov.uk
www.privycouncil.independent.gov.uk

Scottish Council for Voluntary Organisations (SCVO)
Mansfield Traquair Centre
15 Mansfield Place
Edinburgh EH3 6BB
Tel: 0131 474 8000
E-mail: enquiries@scvo.org.uk
www.scvo.org.uk

The Office of the Regulator of Community Interest Companies
Room 3.68
Companies House
Crown Way
Maindy
Cardiff CF14 3UZ
Tel: 029 2034 6228
(24-hr voicemail service)
E-mail: cicregulator@companieshouse.gov.uk

The Pensions Regulator (TPR)
The Pensions Regulator
PO Box 16314
Birmingham
B23 3JP
Tel: 0345 600 1011
www.thepensionsregulator.gov.uk

Wales Council for Voluntary Action (WCVA)
Baltic House
Mount Stuart Square
Cardiff
CF10 5FH
Tel: 0800 2888 329
E-mail: help@wcva.org.uk
www.wcva.org.uk

Index

www.ingramcontent.com/pod-product-compliance
Ingram Content Group UK Ltd.
Pitfield, Milton Keynes, MK11 3LW, UK
UKHW021418110926
15101UKWH00036B/895

9 781860 726958